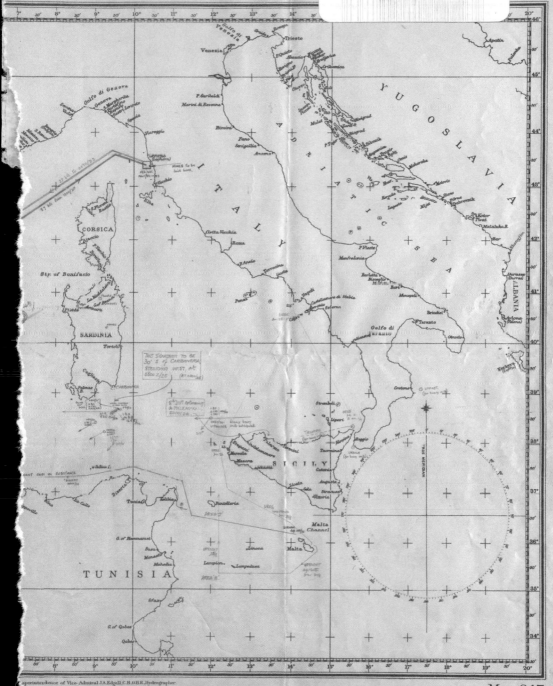

ARK ROYAL

ARK ROYAL

The Life, Death and Rediscovery
of the Legendary Second World War
Aircraft Carrier

MIKE ROSSITER

BANTAM PRESS

LONDON • TORONTO • SYDNEY • AUCKLAND • JOHANNESBURG

TRANSWORLD PUBLISHERS
61–63 Uxbridge Road, London W5 5SA
a division of The Random House Group Ltd

RANDOM HOUSE AUSTRALIA (PTY) LTD
20 Alfred Street, Milsons Point, Sydney,
New South Wales 2061, Australia

RANDOM HOUSE NEW ZEALAND LTD
18 Poland Road, Glenfield, Auckland 10, New Zealand

RANDOM HOUSE SOUTH AFRICA (PTY) LTD
Isle of Houghton, Corner of Boundary and Carse O'Gowrie Roads,
Houghton 2198, South Africa

Published 2006 by Bantam Press
a division of Transworld Publishers

A catalogue record for this book is available from the British Library.
ISBN 9780593055519 (from Jan 07)
ISBN 0593055519

Typeset in 12/16pt Times by
Falcon Oast Graphic Art Ltd.

Printed and bound in Great Britain by
Mackays of Chatham plc, Chatham, Kent

1 3 5 7 9 10 8 6 4 2

Papers used by Transworld Publishers are natural, recyclable products
made from wood grown in sustainable forests. The manufacturing processes
conform to the environmental regulations of the country of origin.

Contents

Picture Acknowledgements   vi

Maps   viii

Acknowledgements   x

Preface   xii

1   The Search Begins   1

2   Building the *Ark*   18

3   'Where is the *Ark Royal*?'   39

4   The Norwegian Campaign   64

5   Death to the French   88

6   The *Odin Finder*   107

7   The Mediterranean War Begins   128

8   Showing the Flag   158

9   Operation Tiger   173

10   The *Bismarck* Incident   197

11   The *Rig Supporter*   224

12   Target *Ark*   241

13   The Journey Back   264

14   The *Ark* Lives On   287

Index   295

Picture Acknowledgements

End papers: Map of the Mediterranean Western Portion. Reports of Proceedings of Force 'H', 1941: The National Archive ADM 199/657

All photos are courtesy the author where not otherwise credited

IWM = Imperial War Museum, London

First Section
Engine room, installation of boilers and launch [ZCL/A015/000]: Wirral Museum, Birkenhead; Lady Maude Hoare, wife of the First Lord of the Admiralty, launches the *Ark Royal*, 13 April 1937: TopFoto.co.uk

Christmas menu and pudding stirring: courtesy Percy North; page from the *Illustrated London News*, 3 December 1938: Illustrated London News Picture Library; Chief Petty Officer R. A. W. King, champion baker: Fox Photos/Getty Images; officers' mess on board the *Ark Royal*, *Illustrated London News*, 10 August 1940: Illustrated London News Picture Library; Michael Wilding, John Clements and Michael Rennie, stars of *Ships With Wings* directed by Michael Balcon, 1942: BFI Stills

Top left, top right: courtesy Percy North; loading a bomb: IWM A3776; Fulmar landing: IWM A3836; torpedoes on deck, April 1941: IWM A3842; Swordfish on the lift to the hangar: IWM A3770; extra pilots standing by: IWM A3740; planes taking off and landing from the *Ark Royal*, taken from HMS *Sheffield*, May 1941: IWM A4042

Photos courtesy of the subjects

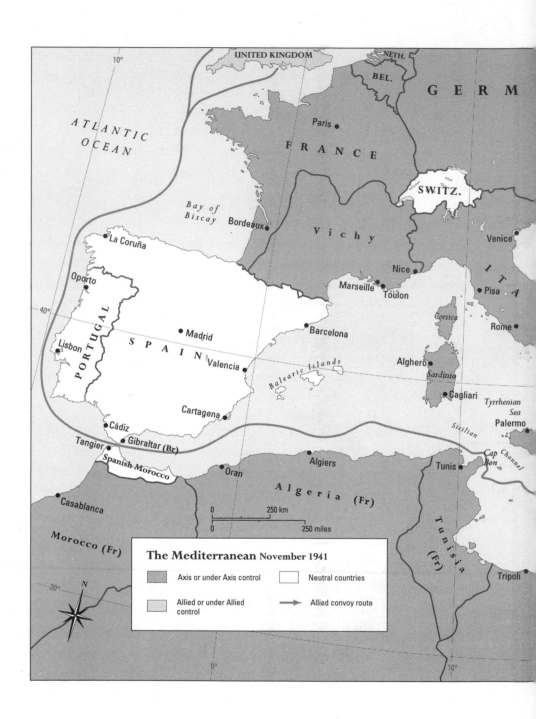

The Mediterranean November 1941

Axis or under Axis control

Allied or under Allied control

Neutral countries

Allied convoy route

Acknowledgements

Throughout the book, I hope I have mentioned everyone who was instrumental in helping me find the wreck of HMS *Ark Royal*, or in finding out more about its past. However, there are a few people whose contribution was vital. The first was Rick Davey, of C&C Technologies Inc., without whose advice and experience the project would probably never have got started. In addition, I have to thank Thomas and Jimmy Chance, the owners of C&C Technologies, who offered the use of their ship *Rig Supporter*, and its highly sophisticated equipment, without any consideration of a return for themselves or their company.

The final key contribution to the search for the *Ark Royal* was provided by Paul Allen, who offered his yacht *Octopus* and everything that was necessary to film the wreck, and to care for and entertain the *Ark Royal* crew members who came aboard. I also have to thank Bonnie Benjamin-Pharris, and Jacqui Sullivan at Vulcan Productions for putting up with me.

I would like to thank all of the former crew members of the *Ark Royal* who gave freely of their time. In particular I must mention John McCrow, whose knowledge of the *Ark Royal* remains remarkably detailed after all these years, and who spent a great deal of time transferring his knowledge on to tapes and letters for my benefit. There was far too much to include all of it in this book, but I hope it will soon see the light of day.

I received a great deal of advice from Professor Andrew Lambert at King's College, whose insight often helped clarify my confusion, and from Adam Harcourt-Webster, a colleague at the BBC, whose knowledge of the history of the Second World War often astounded me. I was greatly encouraged by my agent, Luigi Bonomi, and helped considerably by Simon Thorogood, and others at Transworld.

Finally, I must thank my wife Anne, and my two sons, Alex and Max, for putting up with endless disrupted weekends and holidays while I confronted the unfamiliar prospect of writing a book. Needless to say, any errors that the patient reader might discover are solely my responsibility.

Preface

On a fine September day in 2004 I was on a fantastically well-equipped and luxurious yacht, its dark blue hull and white upper decks gleaming in the Mediterranean sun. As it moved slowly over the calm surface of the sea a pod of about ten pilot whales kept us company. The sound of their breathing as they broke the surface carried for hundreds of metres in the still air. At one point they surfaced barely a dozen metres from the yacht. But no-one on board was paying the slightest attention. Throughout the vessel, people's eyes were intently focused on a variety of screens relaying pictures from a thousand metres below the surface.

Connected by cables to the yacht was an underwater vehicle, or ROV, that was moving along slowly a few metres above the sea floor. It carried an array of powerful lights and cameras, and was making its way towards the wreck of a ship that had lain hidden since 1941, HMS *Ark Royal*, at the time one of the most modern aircraft carriers and perhaps the most famous ship in the world.

At the controls was John Moffat, an eighty-seven-year-old Scotsman still full of mischief and energy. John was once a pilot in the Royal Navy, and he had flown an aircraft called a Swordfish, a single-engined biplane with canvas-covered wings and an open cockpit that was large enough and tough enough to carry a heavy torpedo hundreds of miles across the open sea. In May 1941 John flew one of these aircraft through an intense barrage of shells and bullets directly at the giant German battleship the *Bismarck*, one of the biggest and most powerful ships afloat. The last survivor of that historic mission, John was now staring intently at the image being sent back from the underwater vehicle's cameras as it headed for the flight deck of the *Ark Royal*. John Moffat was attempting to land on her one last time.

I had set out from Gibraltar on the *Octopus* ten days earlier, heading for the spot where I believed the wreck of the *Ark Royal* was located. The captain of the *Octopus* was eager to prove to her owner that all the new equipment that had been fitted on board the yacht was working, and would produce amazing results. A few technical difficulties with the underwater vehicle were still being worked on, but he was certain that the wreck of the *Ark Royal*, a very big ship, would produce some impressive, even awe-inspiring pictures.

That we were going to view the wreck of the *Ark Royal* was something I was fairly certain about, even though when we passed the light at the end of the breakwater at the mouth of the harbour in Gibraltar all I had was a set of images from various surveys of the sea floor, but no clear idea of what I might find once we managed to lower lights and cameras to the spot. Other, more experienced underwater surveyors and wreck hunters, had tried to find the *Ark* and failed, but I was certain that success was within our grasp.

John Moffat joined us on the ship a few days later with some other former crew members. 'Val' Bailey used to be a pilot who flew Fairey Fulmar fighter aircraft from the deck of the *Ark Royal*. He also claimed to be the last person to be rescued from her and was certainly one of the last people actually to see the ship as she went down. Ron Skinner was a petty officer writer and had joined the *Ark* on her very first voyage from Cammell Laird, the shipbuilders. Also on board were Bill Morrison, an able seaman who had joined the *Ark* in 1940 and who worked in the hangar decks and manned the anti-aircraft guns, and John Richardson, a stoker who had worked on the flight deck as well as in the boiler room.

The *Ark Royal* herself had been a remarkable ship, a modern aircraft carrier in a navy that thought, like most navies around the world at the time, that the essential element of sea power was the giant battleship and its supporting fleet. And she had become famous very quickly. As an aircraft carrier and a modern, expensive warship, plenty of newsreels and newspaper stories had focused on her from the time she was launched. Radio documentaries were made about her; a feature film was even shot on board while she was on active service in the Mediterranean. The name *Ark Royal* had quickly assumed a celebrity no other ship possessed during the Second World War.

There have been aircraft carriers called *Ark Royal* for most of the years since the Second World War, and it was this familiarity, this name recognition, that had in part started me on my search for the wreck of the ship that made the name famous. What, after all, was the point of looking for a ship no-one had heard of? What I discovered was the complex history of a ship that mirrored that of the Royal Navy during the war with Germany and Italy before the United States fleet at Pearl Harbor was attacked by the Japanese. It was a period of the war that took the *Ark* from the North Sea to South America, back to the Arctic Circle, then to the Mediterranean, and of course into the Atlantic Ocean.

Running through the *Ark*'s story were tales of ordinary people like the former crew members who had joined us on the *Octopus*, young men, almost boys, who had been snatched up and had lived lives of quite extraordinary danger. They sailed on sunlit seas while bombs whistled through the sky, plummeting directly at their ship. Those that exploded close to the ship were hammer blows against the hull, a frightening reminder that death could be only a few minutes away. Some of them flew flimsy, inadequate aircraft against the modern fighters of the Luftwaffe, sometimes just simply failing to return from a mission or patrol, disappearing into thin air, their fate unknown. Like the Light Brigade of Tennyson's famous poem from another war, they tore 'into the valley of Death' head on against giant battleships, bullets ripping through their canvas-covered wings, shells exploding 50 feet away, tossing their aircraft sideways and filling their nostrils with the stink of high explosive.

Most of the former *Ark Royal* crew who joined us had never met each other before, but when they sat down in the dining room of the *Octopus* they began to remember stories and incidents that like the *Ark Royal* herself hadn't surfaced in over sixty years. The stories were tragic and comic in equal measure. Memories of being under attack from the air, anxious and frightened, but with nobody on the bridge of the *Ark* daring to put their steel helmets on before the captain did. And then, 'within three seconds everybody's tin hat went on'. Memories of raids on convoys, of a single shell hitting an Italian torpedo bomber boring in towards the *Ark Royal*, and the aircraft hitting the sea 200 yards from her. 'You could hear this cheer that went up all over the ship.'

The attack on the *Bismarck* is, of course, the most famous incident in which the *Ark Royal* was involved, the story that was most familiar to the crew of the *Octopus* and the engineers and operators of the ROV. Most of them were from the north of England or Scotland, some of them had in fact served at one time in the Royal Navy, and they were intrigued and fascinated by the prospect of veterans of the *Ark Royal* boarding the *Octopus*.

John Moffat had been down on a sightseeing tour to the underwater vehicle's hangar, which opened out from the side of the hull just above sea level, and he'd shown a great deal of interest in the machine. One of the pilots of the remote vehicle then hit on the idea of letting John land on the *Ark Royal* once again. The ROV was lowered into the water, and the operator in the control room slowly moved it away from the side of the *Octopus*. Then it disappeared, beginning its journey to the sea bed a thousand metres below us.

The ROV pilot sits in what is really a cockpit, a chair with controls for the vehicle on both armrests. In front of him is a screen that shows the picture being captured from the camera on the ROV overlaid with a compass bearing and depth gauge, and below that another screen shows the sonar returns. John sat down in the chair and took the controls. A million dollars' worth of equipment was suddenly in the hands of a Second World War veteran who had never handled an ROV before. But there were no mistakes. John still had a pilot's licence, and he has never stopped flying. His demeanour suddenly changed, and he seemed to be in total control, very focused and clearly understanding the 'feel' of the machine. I was looking at the young man who had flown his aircraft with steely determination through gun- and shellfire towards the *Bismarck*. He glided the ROV smoothly onto the rear of the *Ark*'s flight deck. As a cloud of sediment rose and obscured the camera, everyone who had been watching the feather-light landing on the monitors all around the yacht cheered and clapped.

John was absolutely elated. 'I don't know how I will be able to relate this,' he said, 'I really don't. But I will do my best. Oh Lord,' he added as he got up from the pilot's seat, 'it's hard to be humble.' He walked into the giant equipment hangar where a prototype submarine and an immaculate, super-fast luxury tender were stored, ready to be launched from the rear doors. He shook the *Octopus*'s captain by the hand and said, 'To think I did that after all these years. I'm the first, I'm the first!'

Suddenly, it appeared that the boundaries of time and space had been slightly altered, that the gap between the present and the past had been bridged.

1

THE SEARCH BEGINS

In recent years, many documentaries and films have been made about one of the key naval encounters of the Second World War: the battle in May 1941 between HMS *Hood*, then the flagship of the Royal Navy, and the giant German battleship *Bismarck*. After a brief fight, direct hits from the *Bismarck*'s massive guns caused the *Hood* to explode, killing most of her crew. It was a devastating shock, to the Royal Navy, to Churchill and to the public, at a time when British morale was very fragile.

Almost every ship of the Home Fleet was mobilized in the effort to reverse this defeat, but it was the *Ark Royal* which proved to be the decisive factor in the Royal Navy's hunt to destroy the *Bismarck* and exact revenge for the *Hood*. By sinking the *Bismarck* Britain avoided a humiliating defeat that might have affected the whole course of the war with Germany. For the *Ark Royal*, it meant that not only was she famous in the newspapers and in the newsreels, a fame that had been building since she was launched, but she had now taken a place in history.

The search for the wrecks of the *Bismarck* and the *Hood* have themselves been the subject of many documentaries, and both have now been located on the sea bed. Why, I wondered, had the *Ark* not received the same treatment? Some basic research quickly told me that the *Ark Royal* had herself been sunk in the Mediterranean by a submarine later that same year, in November. The crew had been saved, and an attempt had been made to tow the *Ark* to port in Gibraltar, but after several hours she had capsized and was lost. Photographs taken at the time revealed an impressive ship that towered over the smaller destroyers clustered around her. Although heeling over in the water, she looked undamaged, and I thought immediately that the position of the wreck must be very well known, and that this splendid ship must be lying almost intact at the bottom of the ocean. It surely couldn't be any harder to locate HMS *Ark Royal* than it had been to find the *Bismarck* and the *Hood*.

A film director I greatly respect once said to me that the most important question to ask before shooting a scene, or indeed embarking on a major project, was not how it could be done but why it was being done. In my work as a producer I have made documentaries about other people's fascination with the relics and icons of history. I have spent months in northern Greenland with a group of pilots and mechanics restoring the wreck of a Second World War bomber, and weeks on Coniston Water while the body of Donald Campbell and his boat *Bluebird* were located and recovered from the lake. I think I understand people's interest in hidden objects from the past. When a ship or aeroplane that disappeared is rediscovered or brought back to the public gaze, the past is in some way being brought back to life and another chapter is added to the famous craft's story. Modern life changes quickly and profoundly. It seems to me that people's curiosity when it comes to machines like the B-29 bomber and the jet-propelled *Bluebird* is partly motivated by a realization that they represent a period in the recent past when the world was transforming. The B-29 is an iconic aeroplane because it ushered in the nuclear age; Donald Campbell was the last of the famous record breakers, and *Bluebird* seemed to mark the end of that era when British superiority was a given. Was the *Ark Royal* such a historical symbol, in a way I had yet to understand clearly? Or was there something rather more unbalanced about my interest?

As I did more research on the *Ark*, I learned that there were reasons for her fame other than the action against the *Bismarck*. The *Ark Royal* had fought in most places where the Navy had operated during the first two years of the Second World War. Perhaps most crucially she played a key role in the war in the Mediterranean – one of the bloodiest campaigns the Royal Navy has ever fought and a theatre in which Britain came perilously close to defeat, before the Japanese attack on Pearl Harbor brought the United States into the war. I was excited by the possibility of finding the *Ark Royal*, not only for the chance to see once again this imposing ship, but for the opportunity it would present to tell a different story about the Royal Navy and the early years of the Second World War.

Telling the story was one thing – I knew how to do that; finding the wreck was something else. I had never done anything like it before. Fortunately, a chance for me to find out whether locating the *Ark* was at all possible arose fairly quickly. I had to fly to Aberdeen to meet Hugh McKay, who worked for a Danish company called Kongsberg Simrad, one of the world's leading manufacturers of sonar equipment. The methods originally developed to hunt for submarines in the war had improved enormously in the years since 1945. One of the biggest driving forces had been the oil industry and its exploitation of deposits under the ocean. Equipment made by Kongsberg used sound waves to produce remarkably detailed images of objects just a few metres in size at considerable depths. McKay, a soft-spoken Scot, was one of their salesmen; he had been giving me some advice about Kongsberg's equipment and how I could use it in some projects I was developing. I decided this meeting was a perfect opportunity to raise the question of the *Ark Royal*.

Hugh sat at his desk and stared at me. I could see that I had quickened his interest. As an outsider, I am always fascinated by industries like the underwater exploration business, about which I know little; but to those working inside them the routine tasks can quickly become boring. In my experience, people are always eager to become involved in something out of the ordinary, and a search for the *Ark Royal* was definitely that.

He asked if I knew where the wreck was, and I gave him a position, in latitude and longitude, that I had found on the Internet. Hugh went out of the room and came back with a chart entitled 'Eastern Approaches to the Strait of Gibraltar'. He found the spot and looked at the depth marked on the chart. 'It's in 900 metres of water,' he said. The depth, he went on, was not a problem; it was simply a question of finding a survey ship that was in the area. It was at this point that I began to learn about the complexities of underwater surveying, and the financial implications.

Hugh explained to me that it was normal when hiring a survey vessel to pay for the ship from the time it left its home port to the time it got back. Locating a ship that was already working in the Mediterranean might save on these costs. Then he asked how accurate the position I had given him was. I confessed that I had no idea. Why should it be inaccurate? Hugh pointed out that I needed to be certain. The difference of a minute – one sixtieth of a degree – in a position of latitude or longitude can mean a distance of over a mile. 'Presumably you will want to film the wreck so you will have to locate it first, and fix its position,' he said. 'There's no alternative. You don't want to hire a ship and an underwater vehicle and then find out the position is not quite right. It would be very expensive.'

After our meeting, Hugh drove me to Aberdeen airport. He handed me my bag as I got out of the car, and over the noise of the helicopters that shuttled back and forth to the oil rigs in the North Sea we talked again about the *Ark Royal*. 'I'll make some enquiries, Mike,' he promised. 'It's a grand project, and I'm sure a lot of people will be happy to be involved. I'll speak to you in a week or so. Meanwhile, see what you can find out about the wreck's position. It's *very* important.'

My dream of discovering the wreck of the *Ark* had begun to seem possible, and back in London I immediately started to do what Hugh had suggested. As part of my research for a television series about the history of the Royal Navy, I had been picking the brains of Professor Andrew Lambert, an expert on Nelson and naval history. Shortly after my trip to Aberdeen, at one of our meetings in his King's College office tucked behind Somerset House in the Strand, Andrew gave me a pamphlet that had been published in 1942. Its title was *Ark Royal: The Admiralty Account of Her Achievement*, and it was an illustrated history of the *Ark Royal*. Priced at nine pence, it had, so Andrew told me, sold over a quarter of a million copies. It was a classic of propaganda, so apparently balanced and even-handed in its style and approach that it was hard to believe it had been produced by the government of a country fighting for its existence. Inside the front cover was a stunning photograph of the *Ark* towering above a crowd of workers as she slid down the slipway of the Cammell Laird shipyard at Birkenhead on the south bank of the Mersey. Seeing this photograph – how huge she was! – fuelled my desire to see this great ship now lying at the bottom of the Mediterranean. The pamphlet made no attempt to cover up the ship's loss and made the efforts to save her seem heroic, with descriptions of the captain being rescued in the final moments, and the ship turning over and slowly sinking. Clearly it would not have been produced had the *Ark* not already been a household name. There was little information, however, about where the *Ark* was when she sank.

The maritime charts used by the Navy, the Merchant Marine and many weekend sailors are produced for the government by the UK Hydrographic Office in Taunton. One part of this organization, appropriately called the Wrecks Section, keeps track of all the wrecks that might be a hazard to shipping, and any other significant wrecks they are told about. I enquired if they had any information about the *Ark Royal*, and a few days later I received through the post a piece of paper, known as a 'wreck sheet', for HMS *Ark Royal*. Each wreck has a number, and this is written at the top of the page. Then the sheet gives information about the known position, whether the wreck has a distinctive sonar or radar signature, and goes on to give a brief history. The *Ark Royal* sheet gave several positions, and suggested that a salvage company based in Gibraltar had located the wreck and offered to salvage it – an offer declined by the British government. There were in fact several quite markedly different accounts of the position of the wreck, and all of them at odds with the one I had already found on the Internet.

That position had come from a draft of the *Official History of the War at Sea*, written in 1943, which reminded me that the best place to start some original research into the *Ark Royal* was the National Archives, housed in an elegant oriental-style low-rise building in Kew, on the other side of the railway tracks from the Botanical Gardens. The archives revealed that immediately after the *Ark Royal* was sunk a Board of Inquiry was convened to investigate her loss. At the height of one of the darkest and most dangerous periods of the war, three very senior naval officers, including Admiral of the Fleet Sir Charles Forbes, sailed in a destroyer to Gibraltar to take evidence and produce an initial report. Sixty years later, these documents, bound together in buff-coloured books, were brought to my desk in the reading room. Inside were foolscap sheets with original typewritten minutes, ink annotations and signatures, representing an attempt to form a narrative of the day. But the members of the Board of Inquiry did not arrive in Gibraltar with an entirely open mind. One carbon copy of a letter that was attached at the front of one of the bound documents set an ominous tone to their investigations: 'There is bound to be considerable criticism in the Services, and by the public, when it is known that this modern ship was lost in fine weather after being in tow for several hours, sunk by just one torpedo.'

The effort to make sense of the events started with evidence from Sir James Somerville, the Admiral in Charge of Force H, a flotilla of warships built around the *Ark Royal* and a battleship that was stationed in Gibraltar, and the captain of the *Ark Royal*, L. E. H. Maund. On the day she was sunk the *Ark* had apparently separated from some of the escort vessels to allow aircraft to land and take off. She was following a zigzag course slightly at variance to the rest of Force H, steering an overall course of 286 degrees (think of a compass face as a clock face: 90 degrees would be three o'clock, 180 degrees would be six o'clock, and 270 degrees would be nine o'clock). On one leg of the zigzag, at 1541 hours when her course was 290 degrees, the *Ark* was hit by a torpedo on her starboard side underneath the island – the name for the superstructure that is built to one side of the flight deck on an aircraft carrier. She was steaming at a speed of 19 knots, and the evidence from the captain and the other senior officers was that because communication with the engine room had been cut by the blast, the ship took eleven minutes to slow down and stop. I calculated that this meant the ship had travelled a distance of 3 nautical miles from the point where she was hit by the torpedo, still presumably in the same direction – that is, steaming towards a point slightly to the north of Gibraltar.

I continued to read the evidence to find out what else I could work out from it. Tugs in Gibraltar were quickly ordered to sea to help salvage the *Ark*, and according to the accounts they arrived at around 1800 hours. The pamphlet about the *Ark* that Andrew Lambert had given me claimed that she was towed at 2 knots for almost nine hours. If she was towed at this rate she must have moved another 18 nautical miles to the westward from the position where she came to a halt, and that put her in very close proximity to Gibraltar. I now in effect had three different positions: the one where she was struck by the torpedo, the position where she came to a halt, and the position where the tow was abandoned and she presumably sank. They were separated overall by some 21 nautical miles.

I turned over the pages of the inquiry minutes, stamped SECRET or even MOST SECRET, for any additional evidence that would shed light on the resting place of the wreck. There were a considerable number of attachments to various documents. There was, for example, a dead reckoning track – the record of the ship's course marked on a chart and updated at regular intervals – of the whole of the *Ark Royal*'s voyage through the western Mediterranean on what turned out to be her last operation. Also contained in the files were two drawings, one of them a blueprint of a cross-section of the ship. It showed the ship leaning at an angle of eighteen degrees in the water. The flight deck of the carrier obviously had to be unobstructed, so the funnels, the bridge and masts were located in a structure that rose from the extreme right of the *Ark*'s hull, the island. This meant that the vents from the boilers on the port or left side of the ship had to travel almost horizontally under the flight deck before turning at right angles and going vertically up through the superstructure, on the starboard side. The diagram put before the inquiry clearly showed that with an eighteen-degree list the port boiler vents would fill with water. It was assumed that this was the reason why the port boilers caught fire, and why the electrical supply to the ship, and most importantly to the ship's main pumps, failed.

A second drawing was also based on a blueprint of the hull. This time, however, it was from a sketch by the captain of a motor launch that had picked up the last men to leave the ship, who had seen the ship turn over and sink. It depicted a very large hole in the *Ark*'s side that was almost one third the length of her keel; it looked to my ignorant eyes to be large enough to defeat any damage control efforts that might have been carried out. It was impossible to say whether it was exaggerated or not, but it was accepted as accurate by the Board of Inquiry.

One other piece of evidence intrigued and slightly alarmed me. A chief petty officer testified that only one of the tugs sent out from Gibraltar had managed to secure a tow rope to the bows of the *Ark*; the second tug, after several abortive efforts, had abandoned the task and disappeared into the night, and was not seen again till the following morning. The third had failed to find the *Ark* at all. This sounded a lot more chaotic than the published version suggested, but the Board of Inquiry still recorded the fact that the *Ark* had been towed at 2 knots for up to nine hours.

After two days in the Public Record Office I had a much better idea of the events leading up to the sinking of the *Ark Royal*, but nothing that tallied with the position I had first discovered in the *Official History* of 1943. Moreover, if the account of the Board of Inquiry was true, the *Ark* had sunk very close to Gibraltar indeed. As a further complication, the inquiry added a very bald statement at the end of its evidence saying that the *Ark* sank 22 miles due east from Europa point, the southernmost point of Gibraltar, a statement that did not seem to be backed up by any evidence at all.

I closed the last of the files and reflected on the task that lay before me. I had here minutes and memoranda from one of the blackest periods of British history, when men and women were sent out around the world far away from home to fight and to face incredible danger. The journey these senior Admiralty officers had taken to Gibraltar was itself fraught with the risk of attack from enemy bombers and U-boats. In December 1941 the outcome of the war was uncertain, and thousands of sailors' lives had been lost in the Mediterranean alone. The words they had written were here for me to read over half a century later, but I would never know what these seamen thought or felt about their own lives.

My search had resulted in a great deal more information about the circumstances of the sinking, but had created even more uncertainty with regard to the location of the wreck. The Board of Inquiry had to be the best and most accurate version of events, but discrepancies in the evidence and the bald statement of the *Ark*'s position given at the end didn't seem to tie up. The truth was that the inquiry and everybody involved in the effort to salvage the *Ark* had no real interest in where she had sunk. What was important was *why* she had sunk, and whether it could have been prevented. Did the design of similar ships need modifying, or was the sinking a result of negligence on the part of her commanding officers? These were the only questions to which the Board of Inquiry wanted answers, and in the case of the latter they concluded that there was indeed a guilty man. Captain Maund was charged with negligence at a court martial in January 1942.

A few days later, and true to his word, Hugh McKay telephoned me. He'd been talking to his contacts in the underwater survey industry and he gave me the telephone number of someone called Rick Davey, who he said would like to talk to me. The company Rick worked for, C&C Technologies, had a survey ship in the western Mediterranean. I thanked Hugh, but was mystified by his parting words: 'When you speak to him, Mike, make sure you're sitting down.'

I eagerly phoned Rick the next day to find out what he was offering. The company he represented was conducting an underwater survey for a new gas pipeline to connect Spain and Algeria, and they were using a ship called the *Rig Supporter*. There were no prizes for guessing what the ship was built for. On board the *Rig Supporter* was a unique piece of equipment which had been jointly developed by C&C Technologies and Hugh McKay's employers, Kongsberg Simrad – hence the connection. This marvellous piece of machinery was called an AUV, or Autonomous Underwater Vehicle. In other words, it was a small unmanned submarine. Several similar robots had been built for research purposes, but the one that belonged to C&C was the only one being used in commercial survey work.

There are two ways to survey the sea bed. One of them is to have a sound transmitter and receiver mounted on the hull of a boat. As the boat travels over an area of sea, sound waves pulse towards the sea floor and the echoes that bounce back are processed by computers to create very precise images of objects on the sea bed. However, there is a problem with this method: the image definition deteriorates with depth. To overcome this it's possible to use something called a sidescan sonar. A sound transmitter is lowered to the required depth and towed behind a ship, and because the sonar is closer to the target it can produce a much more accurate picture. But a much larger ship is needed to carry the cable, which can be several miles in length, and the sonar 'fish' needs to be towed at a constant speed and depth. Achieving this can be time-consuming.

The AUV on the *Rig Supporter* carried a combination of sidescan and vertical sonars, but could be set to 'fly' at a fixed depth using its own motors, independently of its support ship, eliminating at a stroke the problems of the more conventional methods of finding out what lies at the bottom of the ocean. It sounded ideal, but then I learned why Hugh had told me to sit down when speaking to Rick Davey: the ship and its AUV were currently on hire for a fee of around $120,000 a day. In a global business like the oil and gas industry such figures are not remarkable, but costs like that are impossible for documentaries, particularly when after spending all that money you still don't have a single picture to transmit. I pointed this out to Rick, but he seemed strangely unconcerned. We agreed to meet.

Rick turned out to be a calm, quietly spoken man with a very laid-back sense of humour, which was lucky, because when we met I was very apprehensive. I knew I would never be able to raise the sort of money he was talking about from the BBC or any other TV company. However efficient the AUV was, a single day seemed inadequate to do what I thought we needed to do, and I realized we could end up having to spend over a quarter of a million pounds just to locate the wreck – more if things didn't go well. Rick still seemed unconcerned, and implied that if the *Rig Supporter* was operating in the Mediterranean, as it was, the company might make the ship available between contracts for a smaller fee, though we didn't discuss how small that might be. As he pointed out, their AUV was the only vehicle of its type in the world working commercially, and Rick thought that locating the *Ark Royal* would be a very good way to show what the AUV could do. In other words, good publicity for the company.

Inevitably we then moved on to the vexed question of just where in the expanse of the Mediterranean we were going to look for the *Ark*. I explained to Rick what I had found in the archives, and we spread out a chart to mark down the various options. My starting point was the spot where the torpedo hit the ship, and this was the most easterly point we marked. The most westerly point was the spot where I calculated the ship must have been towed to if everything that was said in the inquiry was accurate. I mentally discounted this position, because if the ship had been towed as far as this it would have been visible from Gibraltar. There was no evidence that it ever was, but this theoretical position did help me define the furthest western point of the area where the ship might be. I then plotted on the chart the positions mentioned in the information from the Wrecks Section. Using all these points to construct a box gave me a square that measured 16 nautical miles by 20 nautical miles.

Rick went quiet when he saw the results. We were confronted with an area as large as Greater London, and we would be looking for an object just 244 metres long. It was clear that to search an area this large with the AUV would take a long time. But Rick had an alternative plan. 'We need to do a search of this area as cheaply as possible,' he said, 'and then use the AUV to investigate any targets we find.' In short, he wanted to go back to more conventional ship-mounted sonar to search the area. Rick had a survey vessel in mind, one his company was working with, a ship called the *Odin Finder*, which despite its name was owned by a small Italian survey company based in Bologna. I asked how much it would cost; Rick said he thought about $12,000 a day. He did some more calculations and worked out that to cover the area we had plotted on the map, a staggering 320 square nautical miles, it might take as long as three days, with the ship working around the clock. As Rick remarked, in what I was to learn was a typical understatement from him, 'We have quite a large uncertainty factor here.'

My problem now was to find $36,000. This was not going to be easy. As I mentioned, I had been developing a television series about the history of the Royal Navy for the BBC based on the underwater exploration of wrecks of ships from major battles. Some large sea battles, like the First World War battle of Jutland, had left scores of wrecks in the North Sea. They were in relatively shallow water, and although it is never an easy thing to do it was possible for divers to locate and film them. Others, like the wrecks from the battle of Trafalgar, would be almost impossible to find, although I would have tried if someone had suggested a way. Then there were those like the *Bismarck*, in very deep water, and thus extremely difficult to film. The project was still in development stage, but I felt that mounting a search for the *Ark Royal* was worth funding. It involved a fine calculation, it was a significant sum of money, but I knew it was not a very large one in the overall budget of the sort of series I wanted to make. I also knew that success in locating the wreck of the *Ark Royal* would be a boost to getting the series made. Channel 4 had recently broadcast a programme about the *Hood* and the *Bismarck* and had achieved extremely good viewing figures. The quest to find the *Ark Royal* seemed the sort of project that might get similar audiences. As far as using licence-fee money was concerned I thought it justified because the story of the *Ark Royal* was an important part of our recent history. The wreck was part of our heritage, more important perhaps than HMS *Belfast*, which was floating as a museum in the Thames. I felt no qualms on that score.

While I waited for the *Odin Finder* to finish its current contracts, Rick and I refined our plans. The water depth in the box we had drawn on the map varied between 900 and 1,300 metres. At that depth the sonar machine mounted on the hull of the *Odin Finder* would cover a swathe of sea bed about a kilometre wide, so we would have to make a series of journeys at regular intervals across the area of the box to get comprehensive coverage of the sea floor. Sound travels at about 1,500 metres a second in seawater and the sound pulse sent out from the sonar would take one and a half seconds to make its way from the boat to the sea floor and back to the boat again. This meant that the *Odin Finder* would need to travel at 3 knots to get accurate returns. We would be relying on the reflection of just one sound pulse for every square metre of sea bed, or hopefully a wreck, to tell us what we were passing over. Rick assured me that the modern sonar on board the *Odin Finder* could tell a great deal from just a few sample reflections, but I still had my doubts.

Moreover, the maths confirmed that we would need to spend just over three days and nights covering the area where we calculated the *Ark Royal* lay.

We had to wait longer than I anticipated for the *Odin Finder*. That summer there were strong gales in the Mediterranean, too strong for comfortable sailing or efficient surveying. I asked Rick who paid for the time a ship spent in harbour due to bad weather. 'The company hiring the boat,' he said. 'But don't worry, on a small job like yours the chances of a big delay are slim.' This was little comfort, I thought. During this time I was continually reminded of how speculative my quest was, or just how high was our 'level of uncertainty', to quote Rick.

In the meantime I continued my research. I unearthed a series of photos taken from an aeroplane almost immediately after the *Ark Royal* had been hit by the torpedo and before the destroyer *Legion* had joined her to take off the crew. The *Ark* was already listing, and steam was pouring out of the boiler room inlets at the edges of the flight deck. Handwritten down one edge of the photographs was the time and date when they were taken, and the co-ordinates in latitude and longitude. To my horror I realized that on two of the photos separated by just a few minutes in time the position given varied by 8 nautical miles. Moreover, the co-ordinates were outside the box we had drawn on the map. Another reminder, if I needed it, of how inaccurate navigation was before the era of the satellite-based global positioning system. After looking at these photos I had no option but to tell the co-owner of the *Odin Finder*, Elisabetta Faenza, that we needed to enlarge our search area to the east. She agreed, and magnanimously did not increase the fee.

It seemed I had come a long way from my first discussions with Hugh McKay about the possibility of finding one of the major warships of the Second World War. On the face of it I had constructed a search plan, found a vessel to carry out the survey and secured some funding for it from the BBC. However, although I wouldn't admit it to anyone, the uncertainty was making me increasingly anxious, not least about my own judgement in embarking on this project.

2

BUILDING THE *ARK*

On 13 April 1937, there was an atmosphere of celebration in Cammell Laird's shipyard at Birkenhead. Hundreds of dockyard workers in clean suits, collars and ties crowded in the shadow of a ship's hull towering 30 or more metres above the slipway. In smart rows in one part of the crowd were almost a hundred sailors in blue and white uniforms. Immediately in front of the bows a raised platform had been constructed, and on it was a group of men, some in top hats and morning dress, others in uniforms of the Royal Navy. Ships traditionally are launched by women, and true to form the guest of honour on this occasion was Lady Maud Hoare, the wife of Sir Samuel Hoare, First Lord of the Admiralty in Neville Chamberlain's Tory government. And there was cause for celebration. The ship that was going to be launched was not only the result of the first big increase in the Royal Navy's budget since the end of the First

World War, it was the most modern aircraft carrier ever built.

'I name this ship *Ark Royal*,' Lady Hoare announced. 'God bless her and all who sail in her!'

Lady Hoare lifted a bottle of champagne into the air, and as the crowd tensed and got ready to cheer, press men lifted their big cameras to their eyes and newsreel film started rolling. She swung the bottle on its beribboned cord towards the bows of the ship. It bounced off and swung slowly in mid-air. The crowd replaced their hats on their heads and shifted into a more relaxed pose. One of the top-hatted gentlemen on the dais retrieved the bottle and handed it back to Lady Hoare. 'Give it a good throw,' he said to her. The crowd grew expectant again, and drew breath. Once again the bottle bounced off. It was retrieved a second time, and another lady guest, smiling helpfully, leaned forward and told Lady Hoare to throw the bottle against the sharp prow of the ship. The bottle was flung again, and again it failed to break. Finally, on the fourth, rather desperate attempt the bottle smashed open, and the champagne flowed down the bows of the great ship.

At last the cheers roared out, and hundreds of flat caps flew into the air. The ship slowly gathered speed, controlled by the slow unravelling of coils of chains fastened along her length. Then the *Ark Royal*, sending sheets of spray into the air, splashed into the water.

This was a tense moment for the engineers at Cammell Laird. At a certain stage in the launch of any ship, the centre of the hull is not supported either by the water or the slipway. The longer the ship, the greater the strain on the keel, and the *Ark* was very long. For days engineers had calculated the forces that could safely be borne by the hull, and now they would discover if they had got it right. They had, and the ship slid safely out into the Mersey, barely a mile wide at this its narrowest point, and within minutes tugs had secured ropes to the stern of the carrier and were slowly easing her great bulk to the fitting-out basin.

Leonard Sweeney was a sixteen-year-old boy when the *Ark* was launched, and had just joined Cammell Laird as an engineering apprentice. A small, alert figure with a quiet sense of humour, he now lives in a peaceful suburb in Lympstone on the south coast, a world far removed from the smoke and noise of pre-war Birkenhead. The Cammell Laird shipyard stretched for acres along the banks of the Mersey, providing a living for up to twelve thousand people in the yards or the machine shops, as naval architects, electricians, crane drivers, caulkers and any number of other trades. Leonard remembers the yard 'humming with activity. There was this huge engine shop which was three quarters of a mile long. Diesel engines were being built, turbines, propeller shafts, pumps – all sorts of engineering works were going on.' The work often proved fatal to the workers who clambered high onto the scaffolding that rose up the sides of the ship. Indeed, the yard was nicknamed 'the slaughterhouse'. Leonard believes that four people lost their lives while building the *Ark*. It was a hard, noisy, smoke-filled environment. 'There was a blacksmith's shop, and there it was really stinking hot. Dust everywhere. I mean, you could hardly see from one end of the shop to the other because of the fumes.'

A large Victorian pub had been built at the main gates to the yard, and at lunchtime the entire workforce would pour out to slake its thirst. 'The arrangement was that the bartender and bar owners filled as many pint glasses as they could find with beer,' Leonard recalled. 'And these were all laid out on counters and the workmen went in, grabbed a pint of beer, started drinking it and eased their way to the rear of the pub where they paid for it.

Put the money on the table and off they went. So it cleared an awful lot of pints of beer.'

The origins of the *Ark Royal* could be said to date as far back as 1923, when the Admiralty proposed to the government of the day a ten-year programme of shipbuilding to maintain a modern fleet. Along with eight heavy cruisers and other ships, it called for an aircraft carrier and three hundred aircraft. The programme was postponed as a result of the continuing economic crisis in the inter-war period, but the Navy did not let the plans die. Britain needed the Navy, and the Navy knew it would eventually need the ships. By 1930, various committees in the Admiralty working under the direction of the Director of Naval Construction, Sir Arthur Johns, had started to sketch some plans for a new modern aircraft carrier. The most important thing on Johns' mind was to increase the total number of aircraft that could be carried.

The Navy had six carriers in service, all of them dating from the First World War, but because of their limited capacity it was hard for them to operate effectively. These existing carriers stowed their aircraft underneath the flight deck, because the whole length of the deck needed to be kept clear for aircraft landing or taking off. If the aircraft that were landing could be brought to a halt quickly, however, then the forward part of the flight deck could be used to store aircraft, increasing the total number of aircraft that could be operated by the carrier. Arresting wires had been developed in the 1920s but hadn't been put into production, because they tended to damage the aircraft. Now the plans were dusted off to see if they could be improved. Accelerators were also investigated, to see if there was a way to catapult aircraft off the carrier without the need to use the entire flight deck for the aircraft's take-off run.

By 1933, despite the Treaty of Versailles and the creation of the League of Nations, the international situation was becoming unstable. Japan was rearming and was determined to enlarge its sphere of influence in Asia. Hitler had come to power in Germany, and the Italian government under Mussolini was threatening to expand its empire in North Africa. Prompted by these concerns, the British government decided to allocate the money required for the long-delayed naval building programme in the 1934 budget proposals, and construction of the *Ark* was finally allowed to go ahead. Sir Arthur Johns completed the drawings for the new carrier and signed them off in November 1934.

To modern eyes, these original plans seem like works of art, as unique and remarkable as ancient papyri. They are drawn to a scale of one eighth of an inch to a foot on stiff cartridge paper backed with canvas, immaculately rendered and lettered in Indian ink, and gently tinted so that various spaces and machinery can easily be identified. These plans were delivered to Cammell Laird, and the company was invited to tender for the contract to build the ship. By January 1935 estimates were being worked out on foolscap ledgers in the works offices in Birkenhead. Again using pen and ink, the detailed items needed to build a modern aircraft carrier were listed, and the costs: materials, labour and the company mark-up were calculated in the margin. For example, two spare propeller shafts would cost an estimated £6,900, and the labour charge would be £230 plus a 60 per cent mark-up; after a 10 per cent surcharge was added, the grand total was £7,990. Similar sums were done for hundreds of other items and services, right down to the expense of docking at Liverpool for trials in the Mersey.

Eventually these figures were agreed internally, and presented to the Admiralty in a formal tender document in February 1935.

The total cost of the hull alone was going to be £1,496,250, and the main machinery – boilers, turbines, etc. – would cost on top of that another half a million pounds. At a total cost of over three million pounds the *Ark Royal* was not only going to be the most modern carrier, it was going to be the most expensive ship ever ordered by the Navy. The Admiralty accepted these figures quickly enough, though there was some haggling over the cost of special steel, and the contract for the hull and machinery was quickly placed in April 1935. The keel plate was laid on 16 September at an informal ceremony attended by workers, a few officials from the company and twelve-year-old Wendy Johnson, daughter of the managing director of Cammell Laird.

Although contracts had been signed, Sir Arthur Johns wanted to keep his options open about some aspects of the design. It would take time to build the hull, and there were still alternative plans for the flight deck and the ship's main armament to be considered. One thing that had been decided was how the ship was going to be powered. Six boilers would provide steam to three turbines driving three propellers. These propellers, each 16 feet (4.9 metres) in diameter and solid bronze, would turn 230 times a minute and drive the ship at 30 knots, or about 33 miles an hour.

The carrier had to be fast for several reasons. Modern aircraft were faster and heavier, and despite the arrestor wires and catapults on the *Ark*, the ship would still have to steam rapidly into the wind to provide enough windspeed over the flight deck for planes landing or taking off. Furthermore, heading into the wind meant that the carrier would have to separate from the main fleet of ships and steam in a different direction, so speed was again essential to catch up with the fleet once flying operations were finished. The average speed at which the Royal Navy thought its fleet should be able to move was about 20 knots, so the *Ark* was expected to have an edge of another 50 per cent. Finally, speed was necessary for the *Ark* to avoid coming into contact with enemy ships. It was not designed to fight another ship, but to steam rapidly in the opposite direction as soon as the enemy was spotted. At the time the *Ark* was being built her speed compared very favourably with other warships in service, but six years later in 1940 it's unlikely she would have been able to out-run modern German or Italian battleships.

It was obvious that the main weapon of an aircraft carrier was its aircraft, not its guns. Any guns that were placed on the *Ark Royal* were going to be used solely to create an anti-aircraft barrage to protect the ship from attack. The original plans for the *Ark* put these guns low down on the side of the hull, but later Sir Arthur Johns placed them just below the flight deck, in four turrets on either side – sixteen guns altogether – where they had a clear arc of fire. The size of the guns was reduced slightly so that it would be easier for the gun crews to carry the shells. These modified plans were delivered to Cammell Laird in August 1935. As well as these main guns, there were eight machine guns placed at the front and rear of the flight deck on small decks that projected to the side, and four multiple-barrelled guns called 'pom-poms' on the flight deck to the front and rear of the funnel and the island. All of these were part of the anti-aircraft defences. With these modifications to the main gun turrets, the *Ark*'s design was more or less fixed.

There was one major constraint that the designer and the builders had to deal with, however, and that was the limit on tonnage imposed by the various naval treaties that had been signed after the First World War. These arms agreements, the Washington and London Treaties, were due to expire at the end of 1936, and the British government, partly to prevent a naval arms race it could already see developing with Japan and Italy, wanted to impose in any new treaty a limit on aircraft carriers of 22,000 tons.

Sir Arthur Johns and Cammell Laird struggled to fit their new carrier into this self-imposed limit. The amount of armour plating in the hull was reduced, and was confined to a box that enclosed the engine rooms and magazines. This still didn't bring down the weight sufficiently, and the solution eventually arrived at was to use a great deal of welding in the hull as opposed to the more normal method of riveting the plates together. It was estimated that this would save 500 tons of rivet weight in the main hull alone, equal to the weight of the main armament.

Cammell Laird had pioneered welding, and in the 1920s had built the first ship with an all-welded hull, a small coaster; this may have been one of the reasons the company was invited to tender for the *Ark Royal*. But there was a vast difference of scale between a coaster and an aircraft carrier, and Cammell Laird planned to do a lot of experimental work to test out techniques before starting construction. Ultimately about 65 per cent of the ship was welded, including bulkheads, decks, the hull plating and framing above the hangar deck, and the first 100 feet, or 30 metres, of the front of the ship. Skilled welders were not that readily available on the labour market, so the company set up a school to train more than two hundred of them.

After the launch, the *Ark Royal* spent almost another year in the fitting-out dock. Leonard Sweeney remembers the boilers and turbines being hoisted out of the engine shop and into the hull by giant cranes that ran alongside the dock. 'It was a fascinating ship,' he said. 'I think the first thing was, it was a bit awe-inspiring because of the huge flight deck. But the width was the thing. It towered over the engine shop and it looked in some cases a bit unreal. And of course the funnel was on the starboard side, and it was on the edge of the flight deck. But when you looked again it seemed to be slightly outside the edge of the deck. And it had this feeling that it could have fallen off at any minute. So it was a strange-looking ship. There wasn't much symmetry about it. The workforce at Cammell Laird had never seen anything like this before. It was a really innovative ship, and in every corner was something new. You know, hydraulic lifts and everything electrical. And inside were these vast open spaces. It was a big departure from a normal ship. A big departure.'

The most striking part of the ship was indeed the flight deck, which at 800 feet (244 metres) was much longer than the hull, by about 36 metres, with an enormous overhang at the stern of the ship. This helped to reduce turbulence for aircraft landing on the flight deck, but the length of the hull was limited by the size of harbour entrances in Malta and Gibraltar – important harbours for the Navy in the Mediterranean. The sides of the hull rose flush to the flight deck, and at the front of the flight deck there were two accelerators that could catapult aircraft into the air.

The *Ark* towered over everything else in the shipyard because two of the decks below the flight deck were intended to carry – so it was hoped – a total of seventy-two aircraft, which represented a significant increase on existing carriers. This raised the flight deck nearly 20 metres above the water line, and caused some problems to the designers when they considered how to protect the ship against bombs. Protecting the flight deck with heavy armour plate would compromise the stability and weight of the ship, and she had been designed with an emphasis on long range and endurance, with a theoretical ability to travel over 12,000 nautical miles on one load of fuel. So the flight deck was left unprotected, and this vulnerability assumed increasing importance in the minds of those who subsequently commanded the ship.

At a meeting of the Institution of Naval Architects held in 1939, the *Ark Royal* was the subject of a paper given by Sir Stanley Goodall, the new Director of Naval Construction. It was quite clear from his tone that the *Ark* was believed to be a major advance, not only as an aircraft carrier, but in terms of the design of modern ships generally. One of the key aspects of its modernism was the decision to rely almost exclusively on electrical power. Goodall made a lengthy reference to this in his speech. '*Ark Royal* affords a particular example of the steadily increasing use of electricity in warships,' he said. 'Pumps, capstan gear, cranes, winches, gun mountings, steering gear, some engine room auxiliaries, bread baking depend upon electrical power, as well as fans, all lighting, communications and some heating. Two hundred and forty miles of cable and 620 motors are installed in the ship. The control of the whole of the ship, with a few exceptions, is centred in the main control switchboard.' He added, 'Alternative 220 volt supplies are provided to the machines, and low-power batteries are fitted where required so that supplies to essential services may be maintained in the event of damage in action.' Sir Stanley was also proud of the standard of accommodation in the *Ark*. 'A soda fountain, canteen, bookstall and a cinema are provided. Hot and cold running water is fitted to each cabin, and cooled drinking water is supplied to various mess spaces.' In a message to the conference the then Admiral of the Fleet Lord Chatfield gave her an enormous vote of confidence when he said, 'She is a remarkable ship carrying a large number of aircraft of the size and performance we consider essential; fast both for tactical and strategical reasons, well defended against air attack, and a valuable addition to the Fleet.'

Leonard Sweeney said to me, however, that the workers at the Cammell Laird shipyard were never wholly enthusiastic about the *Ark*. When the money was allocated for the *Ark*, the naval estimates also included the funds for a new battleship, HMS *Prince of Wales*. This was the first of what was intended to be a new class of battleship, urgently needed to replace the Navy's capital ships which were now twenty and more years old. The hull of the *Prince of Wales*, a ship that at 35,000 tons was getting on for twice the weight of the *Ark Royal*, was being assembled on the slipway while the *Ark* was in the fitting out basin. 'And here was something which was a real ship,' said Leonard. 'It had ten fourteen-inch guns. Fourteen inches of armour plate on the sides. Five inches of armour plate on the deck. Had two aircraft which were operated by catapult. It was low in the water – in other words, it seemed to be in its element. It was a real fighting ship, and you could picture it hurling itself about in rough weather. So our hearts were really with the *Prince of Wales*. And in retrospect of course we were all, myself included, banking on the wrong ship because the *Ark Royal* was going to be the master.'

The Royal Navy had been starved of funds for over ten years, and the *Ark Royal* was an opportunity to take a great leap forward into a modern world. But one new aircraft carrier could not immediately replace the six that were currently in service, and these ships were going to have to remain with the fleet for some time. Several of them would in fact end up in action with the *Ark Royal*. All of these carriers dated from the First World War. They had been modified to some extent in 1923, but essentially they represented the very first attempts of any navy to get to grips with the invention of flight and utilize it in the fight to control the seas. The Royal Navy had been at the forefront of this revolution.

During the First World War the biggest problem confronting the Royal Navy was how to remove the threat of the German Navy, which had grown under the Kaiser to rival the British Home Fleet. It is difficult now to comprehend the size of the two fleets that opposed each other in 1914. The only major battle between them was in the North Sea, at the battle of Jutland in 1916, and this remains the largest fleet action in all history. The British Home Fleet was composed of thirty-seven battleships and over fifty destroyers, while the German High Seas Fleet was almost the same size, smaller than the British fleet by just six battleships. The battle, despite massive losses in terms of ships and men, was inconclusive, and the German fleet was able to return to port. Admiral David Beatty commanded one part of the Home Fleet, and historians still argue today about whether he or his commanding officer John Jellicoe was responsible for the tactical failures that allowed the German fleet to escape annihilation.

Whatever the truth, Beatty replaced Jellicoe as the First Sea Lord, and he quickly seized on the idea that an attack by torpedo-carrying aircraft on the German fleet while it was in harbour might be the only opportunity to defeat them. Negotiations started with the aircraft manufacturers to develop aircraft to carry out this type of attack. In the meantime, HMS *Furious*, one of three cruisers specially built to shell the German mainland from the Baltic, was converted into a seaplane carrier. This was no great loss for the Home Fleet. The ships carried enormous guns in two turrets fore and aft, but they were lightly built to go fast in the shallow waters of the Baltic, and their hulls were often damaged in rough seas. The forward gun turret of *Furious* was removed, and a hangar for the aircraft and a wooden flight deck was built that projected over the bows of the ship. Aircraft could fly off, carry out their mission and ditch beside the ship, or return to an airbase on land. Seaplanes, mounted on wheeled trolleys, could take off from the flight deck, and on their return would land on the sea and be hoisted back on board. The *Furious* became in effect the Royal Navy's first aircraft carrier, entering service in 1917.

Aviation attracted the wild and adventurous in its early years, and one flight officer on board the *Furious*, Commander Edwin Harris Dunning, thought it ought to be possible to land an aircraft on the flight deck. Aircraft landed at a relatively low speed in those days, and if the ship was steaming into the wind at full power there would be little difference in their relative speeds. Dunning approached the ship in his aircraft and side-slipped so that he was almost stationary above the flight deck. At the last minute deckhands grabbed hold of the plane and he cut the engine, settling onto the deck. Commander Dunning had made history as the first person to land an aircraft onto a moving ship. The difficulty and danger of this feat was demonstrated by Dunning's third landing, when he crashed into the sea and drowned.

He had, however, demonstrated what was possible, and a year later the rear turret on *Furious* was removed and another flight deck was added, so that now wheeled aircraft could land and take off in safety. But the funnel and bridge of the ship were kept in place, which split the flight deck in two. It was obviously preferable to have an uninterrupted flight deck stretching the length of the ship, and two further carriers, the *Argus* and *Eagle*, were ordered, both, like the *Furious* before them, based on the hulls of ships that were already being built in the shipyards. They were completed with flight decks that ran the whole length of the ship.

On 19 July 1918, the newly modernized *Furious* went into action in an operation that would be closely imitated by the *Ark Royal* twenty-two years later. Aircraft carried on the *Furious* launched a bombing attack on German Zeppelin sheds at Tondern, a small town close to the North Sea in what is now part of Denmark. Seven Sopwith Camels carrying two 50lb bombs each managed to destroy two Zeppelins and their shed, and set fire to a second shed. Only four aircraft returned; two others crash-landed and one plane was lost, but the very first attack by aircraft from a carrier at sea was judged to be a success. The Armistice was signed before Beatty's more ambitious plan to attack the German High Seas Fleet could be carried out, but the Navy had clearly grasped with both hands the opportunities presented by aircraft.

HMS *Argus*, with its flush flight deck, was delivered shortly after the war. Having a full-length flight deck had clearly raised some problems in terms of where to put the funnels and the bridge and mast. The designers solved this problem by fitting a retractable chart room that could be raised when the flight deck was not being used, and by taking the funnel exhausts under the flight deck to the rear of the ship. The second carrier, HMS *Eagle*, delivered several years later in 1924, was built with the funnel and superstructure on the starboard, or right side, of the flight deck. Trials using model ships in wind tunnels had shown that placing the funnel in this position caused least turbulence from the hot exhaust gases for aircraft landing at the stern of the ship. This solution is the one that has been adopted by almost every other carrier in the world. A third carrier, HMS *Hermes*, which had been started at the same time as the *Eagle*, was also commissioned into service in 1923. She was a small ship of about 10,000 tons, and no other designs for such a small carrier were ever contemplated.

Finally, the Navy's carrier fleet was substantially reinforced in 1924 when those First World War Cinderellas *Courageous* and *Glorious*, the two sister ships of HMS *Furious*, were themselves converted to carriers, and *Furious* went through a radical rebuild. *Courageous* and *Glorious* had the funnel and the superstructure, now known as the 'island', in the same position as the *Eagle* and *Hermes*. They were much bigger carriers, able to operate four squadrons of aircraft – thirty-two or thirty-six in total. They also had deck lifts, and the lower deck where the planes were stored opened on to a lower flight deck that extended over the front of the ship so that planes could land and take off simultaneously. These carriers had many of the refinements, such as arrestor wires, that were incorporated in the *Ark Royal*, but none was as big or fast or looked so advanced and modern as the *Ark*.

There was, then, a rich experience in the Navy upon which the creators of the *Ark Royal* could draw, but the biggest influence on the newest aircraft carrier in the fleet was a wholly negative one, and that was the total removal from the Navy of the Naval Air Service. In 1918, on 1 April, the Royal Air Force was created, and at a stroke fifty-five thousand officers and men of the Royal Naval Air Service and some two and a half thousand aircraft were taken over by the new service. A protocol was worked out whereby the Navy would operate the ships but the RAF would supply the aircraft, the air crew and the mechanics to operate them. From then on there was constant conflict between the Admiralty and the new Air Ministry which started to affect the quality and numbers of aircraft that became available to the Navy.

This conflict came to a head in 1933 with the appointment of Lord Chatfield as the First Sea Lord. As Admiral in charge of the Mediterranean Fleet, Chatfield had been an enthusiastic proponent of air power. The carriers under his command, *Eagle*, *Furious* and *Glorious*, were totally integrated into the fleet, and they constantly carried out exercises during which carrier aircraft attacked surface vessels. The air crew of the Mediterranean Fleet became a highly experienced élite, and the exercises that were carried out in the late 1920s and early 1930s formed the basis of many future wartime operations. When Chatfield became First Sea Lord, he lobbied hard for an autonomous naval air force arguing that flying had become very sophisticated and maritime operations needed special skills. He drummed up the support of many senior politicians in Parliament, and Winston Churchill wrote to him saying that he 'intended to press continually in the House of Commons for the transfer of control of the Fleet Air Arm to the Admiralty'. Finally, in a last desperate bid to defeat the Air Ministry, Lord Chatfield threatened to resign as First Sea Lord if the Navy was prevented from taking control of its own aircraft. The Fleet Air Arm became once more part of the Navy from the start of 1937.

On the plans for the *Ark Royal* drawn up in 1934, before this change of control took place, there are specific references to Royal Air Force mechanics' spaces, locker rooms and so on – an indication of the extent to which the separate commands would have affected the running of the ship. It is hard to say how damaging this nineteen-year separation was to the Fleet Air Arm and the Navy. The lack of a common experience, of shared custom and practice, even the absence of a common career path, must have had an effect on the character of the Fleet Air Arm. Its effect on the Navy itself was greater. Sixty years later Fleet Air

Arm veterans still talk of the difficulties they experienced on board a ship, even on those carriers that had served under Chatfield in the Mediterranean.

Swordfish pilot John Welham, a chain smoker now in his nineties with the intelligence and energy he had during the war still apparent today, told me, 'Even on the *Eagle* some of the more senior officers were definitely anti-flying. You messed up the ship, you know, so the attitude was not entirely pleasant. Some people were actively unpleasant.' Percival Bailey, or Val as he prefers to be known, was just thirteen years old when he was sent to Dartmouth, the training school for naval officers. Now in his eighties, he retains the wit and easy confidence that took him later in his career to embassy posts in Buenos Aires and Washington. According to Val, the majority of officers in the Navy held similar views to the shipyard workers of Cammell Laird. Battleships were what the Navy was about, battleships meant gunnery, and the gunnery branch dominated the Navy. 'The gunnery world thought that the aeroplane was a waste of money, that this wasn't the job,' he said. 'They didn't want carriers – they take up too much money, they have to turn into the wind and go in another direction, and they are always a bloody nuisance.'

The truth was that the Royal Navy was steeped in tradition, and that played a fundamental role in the way officers in the Navy saw themselves, and indeed in the way the Navy was viewed by the rest of the people in Britain. Val Bailey saw himself as representing something great. 'We had ruled the empire for two hundred years,' he said, 'and the Royal Navy was the world's navy in those days. I presumed everyone else in the world wanted to be a Royal Navy officer so I behaved very kindly to everyone thinking they were very unfortunate to be who they were. I was at the jubilee review, where the Home Fleet assembled, and I remember feeling this tremendous pride in the Navy. The white ensigns stretched for miles.' That emotion appealed to others who weren't necessarily going to become part of the officer class. Vic Walsh, a solid, no-nonsense chap who joined the Navy before the outbreak of war and stayed in it for thirty years, had grown up in Portsmouth. 'As a boy I remember lying in bed on a Sunday morning and hearing the sailors on their way to divisions, and you could hear their boots on the pavement, and their medals clinking. You did feel proud.' So the Navy in which the *Ark* was built to serve was one that was fairly certain of its importance in the world, and could be quite suspicious of aircraft and aircraft carriers.

When the design of the *Ark Royal* was finalized in 1934 it was expected that she would operate in the Far East, where Japanese rearmament and territorial ambitions were seen by the British government as a threat to India and imperial outposts like Singapore and Malaya. Yet almost immediately events in the Mediterranean overturned the calculations of the Admiralty. The Mediterranean Fleet was the Navy's second largest after the Home Fleet, and the maintenance of such a large force was justified on several grounds; it served to defend British interests in the Suez Canal and in the oilfields of Mesopotamia, which were of vital importance for fuelling the Navy. The Mediterranean Fleet could more easily reach Asia and the Indian Ocean if necessary, and could rapidly reinforce the Home Fleet as well.

In 1934, the Italian fascist government under Mussolini attempted to enlarge its North African empire by threatening to invade Abyssinia, or Ethiopia as it is now known, which was on the borders of the Italian colony of Somalia. An incident over a border post had occurred in December 1934, and Italy was in belligerent mood. Italian forces finally invaded in October 1935, which led to the mobilization of the Mediterranean Fleet. The League of Nations met with the intention of imposing sanctions on the Italian regime, and Britain sent the battleships *Hood* and *Rodney* to Gibraltar and *Resolution* and *Despatch* to Alexandria in Egypt.

Italian troopships were constantly passing through the Suez Canal to the exasperation of the admirals in charge of the Mediterranean Fleet, Sir William Fisher and Vice Admiral Andrew Cunningham, who wanted to blockade the canal. They had plans, should war break out, to make a sweep with strong naval forces of cruisers and destroyers up the east coast of Sicily and into the southern entrance of the Straits of Messina to bombard harbours and port installations. Indeed, France and Britain had the forces available to make sure that sanctions against Italy were enforced, but neither government had the political will to do so. Rather than adopt an aggressive policy towards Italy, the threat of war caused a re-evaluation of the Navy's position in the Mediterranean. The fleet's headquarters were in Valletta, Malta, which was only 60 miles from airbases in Sicily, so the Admiralty decided to move the fleet to Alexandria in Egypt. At the height of the international crisis air-raid precautions, including a blackout, were enforced in Valletta. So sanctions, or rather the collective will to enforce them, failed, and the Italians succeeded in their invasion. In May 1936 the Emperor of Ethiopia, Haile Selassie, was evacuated from Djibouti by HMS *Enterprise* and taken to Haifa.

In July of the same year, 1936, fascist forces in Spain under General Franco began their attempt to overthrow the Republican government. By the end of the month there were thirty-six British warships stationed in Spanish ports and in Gibraltar. This time a naval blockade was mounted, to prevent supplies from reaching either side in the civil war, but the German and Italian regimes were determined to see a fascist victory in Spain, and the Italian Navy in particular adopted an extremely aggressive policy at sea. Italian submarines torpedoed civilian ships they suspected of supplying Republican forces, and at times threatened British warships attempting to protect shipping. The Royal Navy also helped evacuate thousands of civilian refugees from the areas affected by the fighting. Val Bailey was serving as a junior officer on the old battleship HMS *Resolution* during the war and is unsure what was most disturbing, the conditions on board the ship or the impact of the conflict on civilians. 'And I was lucky enough, or unlucky enough, to be lent to a destroyer to go in and try to take off some of the Brits in Bilbao. I am seventeen years old and I'm actually seeing women tearing their clothes off to try and get a place in the boat to get away from the Spaniards. [The ship] was at war complement. It was an absolutely stinking ship. The hammocks in those ships absolutely touched each other from one end to the other. The decks were awash because the barbettes on the side weren't waterproof. The stench was not good. And I went down to report sunset to the captain who I had never met, and his cabin was enormous. I remember thinking, I'm not sure that this is absolutely right.'

Thus, when the *Ark Royal* was finally ready to be handed over to the Navy, in the four years that had elapsed between the first drawings being delivered to Cammell Laird and the completion of the carrier the world had been transformed. When the *Ark* was first thought of, the Royal Navy had little control over its aircraft and air crew; now the squadrons that would land on board would be under the control of the Navy for the first time in two decades. Far more crucially, the distant threat of conflict in the Far East had become a much more present threat of war, much closer to home. The Mediterranean was no longer a safe haven for the second largest fleet in the Navy, but a potentially hostile sea. The threat from Germany had also flourished.

Ron Skinner was one of the first crew members to board the *Ark Royal* for her trials in November 1938. A small, quiet man, he speaks forcefully, with a precise command of the English language. He fell in love with the ship at first sight. 'We went up by train from Portsmouth barracks,' he recalled. 'In those days there was a railway siding in the barracks. It took us to Birkenhead, and we marched under the tunnel into Cammell Laird's yard and there was this immense ship overhanging everything. It was quite awe-inspiring. It was absolutely wonderful inside. She was a wonderful and beautiful ship.' Royal Marine gunner Les Asher, now severely deafened as a result of his wartime service, was also part of the first steaming party. 'I got off the train at Gladstone dock and the ship was just being cleaned out. Lady cleaners were sweeping up and crockery was being unpacked in the mess. It was a brand-new ship. When I first saw the ship I was amazed. I thought, by Christopher, this is big. How are we going to find our way around this? But eventually, of course, we did.'

The *Ark Royal* was handed over to her first commanding officer, Captain Arthur Power, on 16 November 1938. Ron Skinner remembers Captain Power, just two months later in January 1939, clearing the lower decks so that he could address the ship's crew. 'I remember to this day; it sent shivers down my spine. He said, "Is there any man here with his hand on his heart who can say that we will not be at war in six months?" He said, "It's my job to get this ship welded together as a fighting ship."'

3

'WHERE IS THE *ARK ROYAL*?'

In conversations with men who served on the *Ark Royal* during the Second World War almost inevitably at some point they will describe their fellow crew members as friendly and helpful, and call the *Ark* 'a lucky ship'. Its 'luck' quickly became part of its legend – and, as we will see, with good cause.

In 1939 there were more famous ships in the Royal Navy than the *Ark*. HMS *Hood*, the largest battleship then afloat, was known around the globe. The *Hood*, the flagship of the Royal Navy, had embarked on a world cruise in 1936, visiting the outposts of the empire, travelling down the west coast of the United States and through the Panama Canal, flying the flag and seeking to impress the world with the undimmed power of Britain's navy. But John McCrow, who joined the ship in 1939 as a newly qualified nineteen-year-old engine room artificer, or ERA, told me he had already heard that the *Ark* was known as the 'Daily

Mirror Ship', because of her frequent mentions in the press. He clearly remembers watching the launch ceremony in newsreels in his local cinema in the small Scottish town of Carnoustie. He never imagined that two years later he would be walking up the *Ark*'s gangplank, the flight deck towering above him. He was particularly impressed by the experience of the crew. 'The Chief ERA had been on board since she was handed over by Cammell Laird, and knew every pipeline, every nut and bolt on the ship. I never met a better chief in the rest of my service.'

The Admiralty knew the value of publicity, but the *Ark Royal*'s fame was not sparked by anything the Navy deliberately did, although in April 1939 a film crew from Movietone News had been shown around the carrier by her captain, Arthur Power. In large part her celebrity arose from Nazi propaganda, which was to have some unintended consequences for the German Navy a little later. That she was a lucky ship, or more to the point had a lucky crew, was something that also quickly became apparent as a result of enemy action.

In 1939, on Good Friday, the Italian Army invaded Albania. The Spanish Civil War ground relentlessly on. But the main threat to peace in Europe was coming from German expansion in central Europe. Both the French and British governments had declared that they would come to the aid of Poland if Hitler moved into Polish territory. Throughout 1939 there was a sense that Europe was poised on the brink of war.

Compared with the Royal Navy the German Navy was still modestly sized, with just two battlecruisers, the *Scharnhorst* and *Gneisenau*, and a further eight cruisers, ships that were roughly the size of HMS *Belfast* (now moored on the Thames), though with larger guns. There were also thirty-one destroyers, but perhaps the most threatening to the Royal Navy was a submarine fleet of fifty-seven U-boats. Two large battleships were being built in shipyards in Kiel, the *Bismarck* and the *Tirpitz*, and when they were ready they were going to be very fast, very well-armed ships, but they were not expected to be in service until the end of 1940. The German Navy had also built three so-called 'pocket battleships', designed to sidestep the various international treaties limiting not only the size of the German fleet as a whole but that of their biggest ships. These three ships, *Graf Spee*, *Admiral Scheer* and the *Deutschland*, were small, fast ships carrying six guns that fired 28cm shells, which could cause an enormous amount of damage but weren't big enough to seriously threaten a large battleship, with its thick armour. The pocket battleships were not designed to confront other warships anyway; their main purpose was to roam the seas attacking merchant ships and poorly protected convoys. They were powered not by steam but by diesel engines, and they could travel great distances before refuelling.

As Hitler's plans to invade Poland matured during the summer of 1939, the German Navy began its preparations for war. On 23 August the pocket battleships, each accompanied by a fast supply ship, set sail, heading for positions in the world's oceans where they could threaten major trade routes. The U-boat fleet also put to sea.

It was always intended that the *Ark*, and the other carriers, would operate as part of the main battle fleet, best described as a combination of warships that could be defeated only by a similar combination of other enemy ships. It was the cornerstone of Britain's naval strategy. Historically, it was the main battle fleet that guaranteed control of the seas, and which secured Britain her resources from overseas trade and the empire. The security of these supply routes was the lifeline that afforded Britain some immunity from the depredations of war on the European land mass. And the key to the main battle fleet was the battleship – the Navy's ultimate weapon. This was not the result of some pur-blind conservatism in Britain's senior service; it was a generally held principle in most other navies.

It was against this backdrop that the Royal Navy eagerly embraced carriers and their aircraft, first and foremost as an aid to the battleships. The Admiralty saw that the carriers could make a vital contribution to the potency of a battle fleet. Aircraft could patrol far in advance of the fleet and locate enemy ships. They could attack the enemy fleet and prevent it from escaping, and once battle between the two fleets was joined they could report on the positions of elements of the enemy fleet, the move-ment of various ships, and, finally, direct the fire from their own battleships' big guns. In short, the carriers' aircraft were expected to control the airspace over the fleet and over a battle so that battleships could be more effective in a grand naval conflict. One thing aircraft were not expected to do was act as a substitute for the main fleet in its task of securing control of the sea. The carrier was there to support the main fleet. The *Ark Royal* would soon change that perception.

Various reports produced by the Admiralty during the 1930s estimated that in order to carry out this support task effectively at the height of a major fleet battle, as many as nine reconnais-sance aircraft would need to be in the air at any one time, with six fighters to defend them. This intensity of aircraft activity would need to be maintained for many hours, if not days. One staff paper produced in 1930 called for a Fleet Air Arm totalling 405 tactical aircraft, at a time when the existing six carriers in the fleet could carry only 250 in all. It had taken almost nine years to find the money to build the *Ark Royal*; it would never be possible for the Navy to find the money for another five similar ships. To overcome this problem of resources, the Navy hoped to build aircraft that could be catapulted from other ships in the fleet, and cruisers and battleships were built with or adapted to have the ability to launch their own aircraft.

By 1939, the Admiral in Charge of Naval Aviation, Rear Admiral Reginald Henderson, a strong advocate of the Fleet Air Arm, had introduced a policy of using more than one carrier in fleet exercises, creating for the first time the possibility of integrated sea and air operations. Despite all the work of various committees and planners, however, in a moment of revealing candour the Director, Naval Air Division admitted in a memorandum dated January 1939 to Admiral Sir Charles Forbes, the Commander in Chief of the Home Fleet, 'We have no practical experience in the operation of modern aircraft with a fleet.' When war started, the *Ark Royal* was going to have to make up the rule book as it went along.

The Home Fleet of the Royal Navy, to which the *Ark Royal* was now attached, sailed to its war stations on 24 August. Under the command of Admiral Sir Charles Forbes, the fleet comprised four battleships, three battlecruisers, two aircraft carriers, the *Ark* and *Furious*, five cruisers and three destroyer flotillas. On 3 September, the day when war with Germany was officially declared, it had just completed a sweep of the seas to the west of Britain and was returning to Scapa Flow, its base in the Orkneys. Ron Skinner was on the *Ark*, and he remembers the announcement of war made by Captain Power over the ship's public address system: 'Do you hear there? This is the captain speaking. I have just received the order to commence hostilities against Germany.' I asked Ron if he had felt any uneasiness now that he was at war and, in a sense, on the front line. Dismissively, he replied, 'We were not surprised in the slightest, or alarmed. It was something we had been expecting.' Val Bailey remembers being more excitable, although he was in a hospital ward in Gibraltar at the time. 'Almost immediately I heard an air-raid siren. I sprang into action, and there I was, this nineteen-year-old moving quite ill people out of their beds to evacuate them to an air-raid shelter. Then a senior doctor came in and told me to mind my own bloody business.'

The war at sea started in deadly earnest within hours of the formal declaration of hostilities, and the advance manoeuvres of the German fleet paid off. A passenger ship, the SS *Athenia*, had sailed from Glasgow on the morning of 3 September bound for Montreal. A German U-boat, *U-30*, sighted the ship when it was 250 miles north-west of Ireland, and despite orders from the German Naval High Command not to sink unarmed vessels without warning the captain of the U-boat, Lieutenant Commander Lemp, fired two torpedoes at the ship. One hundred and twelve passengers, including twenty-eight American citizens, and crew of the *Athenia* were killed – the first casualties of the new war between Germany and Great Britain.

It was immediately obvious that the U-boats that had already taken up their positions around the British Isles were going to present a very serious threat. The Admiralty put into effect a convoy system to defend merchant shipping, but there was still a large number of ships in transit to British ports, and they were perfect targets for the U-boats. In the first week of the war, 65,000 tons of merchant shipping was sunk.

Winston Churchill had been a persistent critic of the Chamberlain government and its policy of appeasement. Now, with war finally breaking out, Chamberlain, in an attempt to silence a powerful and vocal critic, brought Churchill into the War Cabinet, putting him in charge of the Navy as First Lord of the Admiralty. Churchill knew it was absolutely vital to blunt the U-boat menace. German troops were continuing their blitzkrieg in Poland, but the only direct conflict between British and German forces was at sea. If the U-boat campaign against British shipping was successful, it would cause serious damage to British morale and encourage those voices in the Cabinet who believed that the war was an avoidable mistake. There was a severe shortage of escort ships and anti-submarine warships so Churchill moved twelve destroyers from the Mediterranean Fleet to help strengthen the anti-submarine patrols. In addition, three aircraft carriers, *Courageous*, *Hermes* and *Ark Royal*, were mobilized as the nucleus of 'hunter-killer groups' to actively search for and sink the hostile U-boats. The *Ark Royal* with a group of destroyers patrolled the North Western Approaches, where the *Athenia* had been hit, and the other two groups were stationed to the south of Ireland, the Western Approaches. Churchill likened these hunter-killer groups to a cavalry division. It was an extremely risky strategy, and a task for which the carriers had never been intended. In theory, aircraft from the carriers could search large areas of ocean, forcing the submarines to remain submerged, but in practice the carriers themselves were targets. These large, expensive ships had been placed in grave danger.

On 14 September the radio operators on the *Ark Royal* received a dramatic signal for help from a steamship, the SS *Fanad Head*. It said that the ship was being pursued by a surfaced U-boat at a position about two hundred miles away from the *Ark* near Rockall Bank. The *Ark* carried five squadrons of aircraft on board, and usually a squadron was made up of twelve aircraft. There were two squadrons of Skuas, a fighter/dive bomber, and three squadrons of Swordfish, a large, single-engine biplane used as a reconnaissance torpedo bomber. All squadron numbers in the Fleet Air Arm began with 8, followed by a 0 if the squadron was a fighter squadron and 1 if it was a torpedo reconnaissance squadron. A flight of three Skua aircraft from 803 Squadron took off, each armed with a single 100lb bomb and four small 20lb bombs under their wings. Immediately the Skuas had taken off, a flight of six Swordfish aircraft from 810 Squadron followed.

While these aircraft were taking off, another U-boat, which had remained completely undetected by the sonar of the *Ark Royal*'s destroyer escort, was lining up the carrier in its attack periscope. The captain of *U-39*, almost unable to believe his good fortune at having such an enormous target in his sights, fired two torpedoes from his forward torpedo tubes, directly at the sides of the *Ark Royal*. Fortunately, the lookouts on the *Ark* were alert. The wake of the torpedoes was spotted by Signalman Hall, who shouted the alarm. Captain Power on the bridge ordered the helm hard over, turning the bows towards the tracks to present the smallest possible target. The torpedoes missed, one of them exploding harmlessly astern. The destroyers, positioned around the *Ark* so as to screen her from exactly this sort of attack, then located the submarine on their sonar and moved in for the kill, dropping depth charges and forcing the submarine, now badly damaged, to the surface. Forty-nine of her crew were rescued before the submarine sank. The *Ark* had just claimed the first U-boat to be sunk in the war. It was an enormous boost to the morale of everybody on board. But she had been incredibly fortunate to survive this attack. Her reputation as a lucky ship grew from here.

The aircraft that had taken off to find the *Fanad Head* had spread out to search the area, and the first Skua to spot the ship was piloted by Lt Richard Thurston. The U-boat was *U-30*, the same submarine that had torpedoed the *Athenia*. Her commander, Lieutenant Commander Lemp, had fired a shot from his deck gun at the *Fanad Head*, which had come to a stop, but he had allowed its crew to take to the lifeboats and had sent a four-man party to board the cargo ship to salvage food for his submarine, and then to lay demolition charges. Lt Thurston saw the submarine on the surface and in a split second decided to drop his bombs on it; but he was so low that splinters from the explosions hit his plane, setting it on fire. He crashed into the sea. He and his observer, Petty Officer James Simpson, managed to get out of the cockpit, but only Thurston succeeded in reaching the *Fanad Head*. Exhausted, burned and almost overcome by the cold, he was pulled on board by one of the German boarding party.

The submarine, surprised and alarmed by the sudden arrival of the Skua aircraft, had crash-dived, leaving a crew member floating in the sea (he too had swum to the *Fanad Head*). The second Skua to arrive on the scene attempted to bomb what the pilot, Lt Commander Dennis Campbell, believed was the submarine just under the surface. Then he signalled to the ship's crew in the lifeboats that help was near, and returned to the *Ark*. The submarine surfaced again just as the third Skua flew low over the *Fanad Head*. The pilot, Lt Guy Griffiths, reacted instantly and he too dropped his bombs at low altitude. Their explosions ripped his rear fuselage apart, and he crashed into the sea. His observer, Petty Officer George McKay, was trapped in the aircraft as it sank, but Lt Griffiths also made it to the *Fanad Head*, which now had five German seamen from *U-30* on board and the two pilots from the crashed Skuas.

U-30 surfaced once more, and Lt Commander Lemp told the two pilots to jump into the sea with the boarding party, because he was going to torpedo the boat. No sooner had they been dragged aboard the submarine than the first of the six Swordfish aircraft from the *Ark* were spotted. *U-30* dived again, and Lt Commander Lemp fired a torpedo at the *Fanad Head*, which broke in two and sank. One of the pilots, Michael Lawrence, had already dropped his bombs on what he believed was a submerged U-boat shortly after taking off from the *Ark*, so he could only fire his machine gun and drop a smoke float, but the other Swordfish attacked the submarine with their bombs. *U-30* was damaged, but she managed to escape, reaching Iceland a few days later where a severely wounded crew member was put ashore. Then Lt Commander Lemp took his submarine back to port in Germany. The British pilots were taken by the Gestapo and placed in a prisoner-of-war camp.

The *Ark* returned in triumph to Loch Ewe, and the story of the first German U-boat to be sunk in the war was splashed across the front pages of the Sunday papers. Churchill visited the *Ark Royal*, where the crews of all the warships that had taken part in the sinking of the *U-30* were assembled for an inspection by the First Lord of the Admiralty. It was a vindication of the ingenious policy of using carriers to hunt submarines and an extremely important boost to morale.

Churchill returned to London by train the next day, where he was met on the platform by Sir Dudley Pound, the First Sea Lord. What Pound had to tell his political master was extremely serious, and he wanted to be the first to break the news to Churchill. On 17 September the aircraft carrier HMS *Courageous*, one of the three big cruiser conversions, had been patrolling with an escort of destroyers off the south-west coast of England when a U-boat fired two torpedoes at her. They had both hit their target, and one of the Royal Navy's precious carriers and its aircraft had sunk in just fifteen minutes, taking 519 crew to their deaths. The *Ark Royal*, of course, had only narrowly avoided a similar fate. The sinking of *Courageous* spelled the end to the use of carriers against U-boats, and the hunter-killer groups were disbanded.

Before the start of the war, there had been a serious debate at senior level in the Navy about the different types of aircraft needed on a carrier, and how many squadrons of each type should be carried. At the core of this dispute the single most important question was how the fleet could defend itself against air attack. The traditional view was to rely on anti-aircraft fire. This view came under attack from Reginald Henderson, the Rear Admiral Aviation, in 1934, when he raised the question of increasing the numbers of fighter aircraft in the Fleet Air Arm. He had analysed the results of aircraft operations in the First World War and discovered that 95 per cent of aircraft shot down were the victims of aerial combat. Anti-aircraft artillery seemed largely ineffective. The Tactical School in Portsmouth considered the question, and disagreed. Their view was that air interception was too unreliable to be a dependable defence against air attack. It was better, they argued, to rely on massed anti-aircraft batteries.

Many former Fleet Air Arm pilots have suggested to me that the problem was the dominance of the gunnery branch in the Navy, and that the believers in the battleships and their big guns were not prepared to accept that they were vulnerable to air attack. There may be some truth in this, but it is also true to say that aircraft were becoming faster, and without radar the warning time available to launch aircraft against an attacking force of bombers was inadequate. The belief that gunnery was the key to attack from the air was still firmly embedded in December 1939. The Commander in Chief of the Mediterranean Fleet, Admiral Sir Andrew Cunningham (based in Alexandria), felt able to write in a letter to Sir Dudley Pound, who had suggested that the fleet might be easy prey to enemy bombers, 'I hope your new doubts about battleships and aircraft is unduly pessimistic. As far as I know not a single hit has been made on a Navy target and surely our battleships have been constructed and reconstructed to stand up to a bomb or two. The answer is a considerable improvement in the quality and quantity of the ships' anti-aircraft fire.' Before long Admiral Cunningham would be forced to eat his words.

On 24 September, ten days after the *Ark Royal* narrowly avoided two torpedoes, a British submarine, HMS *Spearfish*, was severely damaged by a prolonged depth charge attack by German destroyers in the Kattegat, the stretch of water between Denmark and Sweden. The submarine evaded her pursuers and surfaced, but was so damaged that she had to remain on the surface for the voyage back to port. As she made her way home, she was met first by a group of destroyers and then by the *Ark Royal*, with the battleships *Rodney* and *Nelson*, who escorted the submarine the rest of the way.

The three large ships, which together comprised an important part of the Home Fleet, were shadowed by a group of German Dornier seaplanes slowly circling at a safe distance from anti-aircraft fire. A flight of three Skuas took off from the *Ark* to intercept them, and they succeeded in shooting down one of the reconnaissance aircraft. This again was one for the record books: it was the first German aircraft to be shot down in the war, and once again the *Ark Royal* could claim the credit. However, the small force of valuable capital ships had been spotted and it was reasonable to expect that the Luftwaffe would attempt to mount an attack very shortly.

Despite the fact that the Skuas had been flown off the flight deck to shoot down the reconnaissance seaplanes, Vice Admiral Lioncl Wells, the Vice Admiral Aviation, who was on board the *Ark* at the time, made no attempt to set up an air patrol of fighters to intercept any attacking bomber force. Instead, all aircraft were recalled and struck down into the hangars, where they were drained of fuel to reduce the risk of fire if the ship was hit – further evidence of the deep-seated belief that the correct defence against air attack was anti-aircraft fire.

Within the hour five Heinkel twin-engine bombers approached and were met with a barrage of anti-aircraft fire from the *Ark* and her escort. The *Ark* had been well armed to defend herself against this sort of attack. There were the sixteen 4.5-inch guns that could fire shells set to explode at a predetermined height, there were multiple cannons that fired 20mm shells at any individual aircraft making low approaches, and finally there were the machine guns mounted fore and aft to deter dive bombers. In addition to all this, of course, the destroyers and the battleships were firing their anti-aircraft guns at the approaching planes. The first four bombers took evasive action, but despite the massive ack-ack onslaught the pilot of the fifth Heinkel persisted in his attack until the *Ark* was in his bomb aimer's sights, and he released a large 1,000kg bomb. A bomb of this size would easily have penetrated the *Ark Royal*'s thinly armoured flight deck and caused mayhem inside the hangar decks, killing seamen, destroying planes and starting devastating fires.

Several of the *Ark*'s crew saw the bomb fall. Ron Skinner, who was on the bridge, recalls it well. 'All I can say at that moment is that it looked as big as a bus,' he said. 'It was heading straight for us, and I do not know how it missed.' In a classic manoeuvre, the captain ordered a hard turn to starboard and the ship heeled over. The bomb exploded with incredible force 30 metres off the port bow, producing an enormous plume of water and smoke that rose high in the air. Ron felt the ship lift out of the water, and a tremor travelled along her length. She rolled sideways, and clouds of smoke and soot were blasted out of the funnel. She seemed to hang at this acute angle for a lifetime as water from the blast cascaded onto the flight deck. Inside the ship everything toppled and crashed to the floor – books, papers, crockery, anything that wasn't secured. Then, slowly, the *Ark* righted herself.

It was another incredible near-miss, the second time in less than a fortnight that the *Ark Royal* had escaped catastrophic damage. From now on the crew were convinced that she was a lucky ship. Once again the *Ark* was in the newspapers, this time with the story of the downed German seaplane. But it was Joseph Goebbels, the Reichsminister for Propaganda and National Enlightenment, who was to set the seal on the *Ark Royal*'s celebrity status.

The pilot of the Heinkel bomber whose bomb had narrowly missed the *Ark* reported the possibility that the carrier had been severely damaged. From his point of view, and that of his crew members, it wasn't obvious that the *Ark* had managed to emerge unscathed from the plume of water. Subsequent German reconnaissance flights located two battleships but failed to find an aircraft carrier accompanying them. The propaganda machine of the Nazi government swung into action. The next day at half past five in the evening, Hamburg Radio broadcast in rather broken English: 'We have an important announcement for listeners. Where is the *Ark Royal*? She was hit in a German attack on September 26th at three p.m. Where is the *Ark Royal*? Britons, ask your Admiralty.' The claims escalated. A week later the official newspaper of the Nazi Party in Germany, the *Volkischer Beobachter*, published on its front page an illustration of the *Ark Royal*, her bows rearing out of the sea under the force of a massive explosion on her flight deck. On 26 September this same newspaper had published, under direct orders from Hitler, a story that Churchill had instructed the captain of a British submarine to torpedo the *Athenia*, hoping that it would turn the United States against Germany. The German government had its sights clearly set on Churchill and the Navy.

Churchill was extremely sensitive to the power of propaganda and took all statements made by the Nazi propaganda machine very seriously. He personally assured President Roosevelt that the claims about the *Athenia* were untrue, and told the War Cabinet at its meeting on Sunday, 1 October that the United States naval attaché in London was with the fleet and able to observe for himself that the *Ark Royal* was undamaged, moreover that the British naval attaché in Rome had paid a personal visit to the Chief of the Italian Naval Staff to reassure him that the German claims were false. The cinema newsreels, the equivalent of TV news coverage today, were also encouraged to counter the German propaganda claims.

Remarkably, Hamburg Radio and their English propaganda announcer William Joyce continued to broadcast the question 'Where is the *Ark Royal*?' The claim and counter-claim became the subject of broadcasts and newsreels around the world, and the name of the *Ark Royal* gained an international currency. It was to rebound, with double the force, against the German propagandists.

*

The German pocket battleship *Graf Spee* had sailed from Kiel in August, at the same time as other units of the German fleet had put to sea. With secret orders to be opened in the event of war, the *Graf Spee*'s captain Hans Langsdorff had taken up his station in the South Atlantic.

Captain Langsdorff began his war against British shipping with an attack on a liner that had sailed from the port of Pernambuco to Bahia in Brazil. The ship, the *Clement*, was stopped by the German warship, the crew was allowed to take to the boats, and then the ship was sunk by shellfire from the large 28cm main guns. The *Clement*'s crew were left in their lifeboats to make their way to the coast, but the captain and the chief engineer were taken prisoner aboard the *Graf Spee*. They were treated well, and two days later were handed over to another ship that had been stopped, a Greek freighter. They were bid a fond farewell by Captain Langsdorff and the other officers of the *Graf Spee*. The Greek ship, being neutral, was allowed to continue to its destination, St Vincent.

Captain Langsdorff was a gentleman, and he fought by the gentlemanly rules of warfare of another age. He saw his job as harassing and capturing British trade and shipping, sinking the ships but not killing sailors. He was also, however, a clever tactician, adept at turning his chivalrous instincts to his advantage. News of the *Graf Spee*'s activities in the vicinity carried by released sailors to the nearest port was useful publicity, announcing his presence in an area from which he in fact departed, leaving a false trail for his pursuers. No sooner had the officers from the *Clement* been handed over than the *Graf Spee* headed east, travelling across the South Atlantic at high speed. Within the next ten days Captain Langsdorff sank two further ships and seized two more, then doubled back on his course and headed south to rendezvous with the depot ship *Altmark* to take on fuel and fresh food.

News of the sinking of the *Clement* had reached the Admiralty shortly after it occurred, and the hunt for the raider was started. The *Ark Royal* and the battleship *Renown* were ordered into the South Atlantic. The *Ark* could carry out a search over a wide area, its aircraft able to fly over two hundred miles from the ship in all directions, but the *Graf Spee* was small and fast with a long range, and the depot ship was adept at disguising its identity as it refuelled and provisioned at various ports. Once more the *Ark Royal* found itself detached from the main fleet, searching for a lone commerce raider in the expanse of the South Atlantic – a far cry from its intended purpose of bringing an enemy battle fleet to decisive action.

After sinking a merchant ship named the *Trevanion*, the *Graf Spee* refuelled and provisioned from the *Altmark* almost in the dead centre of the South Atlantic in the last week of October 1939. Three weeks later she reappeared two thousand miles away, this time in the Indian Ocean, and sank the British tanker the *Africa Shell* off the coast of Lourenço Marques in what is now Mozambique. The crew of the tanker were again allowed to escape and make for the shore in the ship's boats. Langsdorff promptly steered a course north, deliberately passing close to a Dutch liner so that the passengers could take photos of the German warship, then headed south and once more steamed into the Atlantic.

The Royal Navy's forces were already stretched very thin. There were several carrier and battleship forces engaged in pursuit of the German raiders. As well as Force K, *Ark Royal* and *Renown*, there was *Glorious* with the battleships *Warspite* and *Malaya*; *Eagle* with two cruisers, *Gloucester* and *Cornwall*; *Hermes* in company with the French battlecruiser *Strasbourg*; *Furious* with the *Repulse*; and *Argus* with the battleship *Queen Elizabeth*. It was remarkable testimony to the extent to which three lone raiders could tie down a large part of the Royal Navy. Apart from HMS *Eagle* in the Indian Ocean and Force K in the South Atlantic all the other task forces were in the North Atlantic. Britain also had a small detachment of four cruisers in the South Atlantic, at Port Stanley in the Falklands, under the command of Commodore Harwood: HMS *Exeter* and HMS *Cumberland* armed with 8-inch guns, and HMS *Ajax* and a New Zealand cruiser *Achilles*, both armed with 6-inch guns. Commodore Harwood believed that sooner or later the *Graf Spee* would need to take on more fuel and stores than could be carried by a single support ship, and it was likely that it would rendezvous with supply ships heading out from Montevideo or Buenos Aires. His cruisers headed north to patrol off these ports.

The *Ark Royal* and *Renown* continued to patrol in the South Atlantic, and on 1 December they headed for Cape Town to refuel. The long periods steaming at sea meant constant hard work, and wear and tear in the engine room. John Asher remembered the drudgery of the boiler rooms:

'The boiler rooms were pressurized, by fans forcing air into them from intakes under the flight deck. Airlocks were essential, for a sudden drop in pressure can cause flames from the oil sprayers to blow back into the boiler room, causing fires and serious burns to the stokers on duty.

'Each boiler has ten oil sprayers in place, and speed is regulated by increasing or decreasing the number of sprayers operating at any time. An oil sprayer has to be frequently changed for cleaning to maintain its efficiency. Changing over oil sprayers requires thick leather gloves as all the metal parts are extremely hot. The sprayer is held in a bench vice and stripped down and all the parts are thoroughly cleaned in paraffin. It's then reassembled and made ready for use. Another stoker will be working, using a long steel poker to chip away the clinker which has built up around the edge of the combustion chamber in the boiler. It is very hard work especially when aircraft are always landing on and off, and a lot of sprayers are in use to keep up speed.

'It seems that as soon as all the combustion chambers and sprayers are cleaned, the job has to start all over again.'

As the *Ark Royal* neared the Simonstown naval base a message was received from the *Doric Star*, a British cargo vessel, saying that she was being shelled by a battleship. She gave a position that was off Walvis Bay, a port in what is now Namibia. It was 1,500 miles away, and it would take the *Ark* and *Renown* three days to reach the spot. Captain Power, of the *Ark*, decided that before he could make the run more fuel was necessary. Even if Force K went to the spot where the *Doric Star* was under attack, the *Graf Spee* would be long gone by the time they arrived. It was no way to hunt down a single ship in the expanse of the southern oceans, especially one with the speed and range of the German commerce raider.

Twenty-four hours later another distress signal was intercepted, this time from the *Tairoa*, which was sunk in a position west of the point where the *Doric Star* had been attacked. The *Graf Spee* was busy and seemed to be heading south-west. The German raider had been at sea now for over three months. Was it now time for the *Graf Spee* to meet up with other German cargo ships that were getting ready to depart from ports in South

America? Vice Admiral Wells, in command of Force K, agreed with Commodore Harwood's reasoning that the most likely place for the *Graf Spee* to head for was the River Plate area between Argentina and Uruguay, with the ports of Buenos Aires and Montevideo to the north and south of the wide bay. So Force K also headed west, but on 6 December the Admiralty ordered the *Ark Royal* and *Renown* to change course and head north.

On 13 December, Commodore Harwood in the *Ajax*, with the cruisers *Exeter* and *Achilles* in formation, saw smoke on the horizon. His forces had been reduced because *Cumberland* had had to return to Port Stanley to refuel. Nevertheless, *Exeter* was sent to investigate and her captain reported, 'I think it is a pocket battleship.' After months at sea, the German battleship had finally been spotted, not by the large number of carrier and battleship task forces that had been scouring the oceans, but by a small force of ships that was significantly weaker than its quarry. Force K, with bombers, torpedo-carrying aircraft and the large guns of the *Renown*, was several days' sailing away and would not be much help to Commodore Harwood.

He decided to split his force in two, so that the captain of the *Graf Spee* would be forced to divide his fire, or ignore one of the British units, which would make it easier for them to get closer and bring the battleship in range of their smaller guns or torpedoes. The *Exeter* had bigger guns than the other two cruisers and was the first to return fire on the *Graf Spee*. Captain Langsdorff concentrated his ship's fire on *Exeter*, and the 28cm shells caused carnage. Two of her gun turrets were hit and put out of action, killing and maiming the gun crew inside. A direct hit on the *Exeter*'s bridge killed or wounded everyone except the captain, and fires broke out on the mess decks. The ship was also hit in the hull, and seawater was flowing in, causing the ship to list by seventeen degrees. *Exeter* had become a place of death and destruction, with fire, smoke and fumes filling the crew spaces, the terrible noise of exploding shells, and the firing of the one remaining turret adding to the chaos. Within an hour she had to stop firing and slow down. In the words of Captain Parry on the *Achilles*, 'My own feelings were that the enemy could do anything he wanted to. He showed no sign of being damaged. His main armament was firing accurately. The *Exeter* was out of it so he had only two small cruisers to prevent him attacking the very valuable River Plate trade.' The casualties on board *Exeter* were sixty-one dead.

With the *Exeter* crippled and no longer a threat, the *Graf Spee* did not then direct her guns against the two smaller cruisers; instead she put up a smoke screen and headed away to the west. Captain Langsdorff had quickly made a tour of his ship and decided to run for port, for the *Graf Spee* had not escaped from the battle as lightly as the British imagined. She had been hit by seventeen shells that had caused damage to the bow and killed thirty-seven German sailors. But among the senior officers on board there was some doubt as to why Langsdorff broke off the attack. Nothing vital to the ship's machinery or armament had been damaged.

Throughout the day the two cruisers *Ajax* and *Achilles* trailed the *Graf Spee*, until she reached the River Plate and anchored off Montevideo harbour. International law stated that any warships belonging to a country at war could stay in a neutral harbour for twenty-four hours without jeopardizing the host country's neutrality. If the ship stayed longer than a day it was liable to be interned, along with its crew. The British naval attaché in Montevideo, Captain Rex Miller, and an intelligence officer from the embassy sailed around the *Graf Spee* in a boat and were perplexed as to why the ship had taken refuge in the harbour. Both they and the Uruguayan authorities believed that the ship was relatively undamaged. There was a large shell hole in the bow, but it was well above the water line, so the British ambassador requested that the Uruguayan government enforce the neutrality regulations against the *Graf Spee* – that is, order it to leave Uruguayan national waters or face internment.

However, Commodore Harwood didn't want to face the *Graf Spee* again without some reinforcements to his battered little flotilla of cruisers, and on 16 December he asked the British Embassy to do what it could to delay the departure of the German battleship. Several methods were used. A British cargo ship was instructed to leave port immediately, thus taking advantage of another convention that stated a warship from a belligerent country must not leave port within twenty-four hours of a departing merchant ship of a country involved in hostilities. The British naval attaché and the intelligence officer visited Harwood on the *Ajax*, still patrolling outside the three-mile limit. The 8-inch-gun cruiser HMS *Cumberland* had now arrived from her station in the Falklands, but this was no guarantee of over-whelming success. *Exeter* had suffered badly at the hands of the *Graf Spee*, and so too could the *Cumberland*.

As soon as the *Exeter* had first sighted the *Graf Spee* she had sent a general signal, and Force K had turned around and headed towards the impending battle. But the *Ark* and *Renown* were almost two thousand miles away at the time, and the former was also low on fuel again. Although *Renown* was better armed and more heavily protected against shellfire than the *Graf Spee*, Admiral Wells did not want to go into battle without good reserves of fuel. He made the decision to refuel at Rio de Janeiro, in Brazil. When the *Renown* and the *Ark Royal* docked at Rio the

British Embassy staff in the city, eager to counter the still prevalent German propaganda about the *Ark* having been sunk by a German bomber, encouraged the local press and newsreel crews to film the ship in dock. But Rio de Janeiro was a thousand miles away, and even if Force K could make 30 knots, it would take them almost thirty-six hours to join the cruisers outside Montevideo. Captain Langsdorff must have realized this. The *Graf Spee* was loading stores quickly and had told the Uruguayan government that it would leave port the following day.

Captain Miller, the British naval attaché, then came up with a plan to throw dust in the eyes of Captain Langsdorff and the German Embassy officials in Montevideo. Fuel for the *Ark Royal* was ordered in the port of Buenos Aires in Argentina, on the other side of the River Plate. Information about this order was quickly and deliberately leaked to the press in the city, where it was immediately passed to the German Embassy in Montevideo. It naturally reached the ears of Captain Langsdorff too. Already uncertain about his course of action, the threatened presence outside the harbour of the *Ark Royal* with her companion the *Renown* tipped the balance. Langsdorff became convinced that there was no possibility of escape. In a signal to Berlin he said, 'Strategic position off Montevideo. Beside the cruisers and destroyers *Ark Royal* and *Renown*. Close blockade at night; escape into open sea and breakthrough to home waters is hopeless ... request decision on whether the ship should be scuttled in spite of insufficient depth in estuary of the Plate or whether internment is preferred.' The reply from Berlin rejected internment.

Langsdorff was correct in his assessment. There was no way out for him. However brave or skilful his crew or however fast

his ship, it was inevitable he would be tailed until an overwhelming force of British ships and aircraft sank his ship and
killed his men. At just after five o'clock in the evening of 17
December, the *Graf Spee* slowly steamed out of Montevideo
harbour and the British cruisers altered course to meet her, no
doubt with some trepidation on the part of the crew. When the
Graf Spee was about six miles out of Montevideo she stopped
her engines. Boats began to ferry the crew to a German freighter
that had followed her out, and then there was a stunning
explosion. In the words of Commodore Harwood, 'She was
ablaze from end to end, flames reaching almost as high as the top
of the control tower. A magnificent and most cheering sight.'

The German crew, in the freighter *Tacoma*, were taken to the
harbour of Buenos Aires in Argentina where they remained
interned for the rest of the war. Three days after the *Graf Spee*
was scuttled, in his room at the Naval Arsenal in Buenos Aires
Captain Langsdorff shot himself. He understood only too well
that his greatest weapon was his ability to disappear in the vast-
ness of the southern oceans, and that once he had been found his
life, and those of his crew, would be measured in days. But it was
German propaganda that had made the *Ark Royal* a famous ship,
and that fame had made it easier for the British Embassy in
Montevideo to spread their web of deceit and misinformation,
and turn the screw on Captain Langsdorff. It was the first time
that ships a thousand miles away had taken part in a battle at sea.

The victory at River Plate was exceptionally welcome news
for Churchill, the Admiralty and for the country as a whole.
There had been a depressing series of losses at sea, caused not
only by the *Graf Spee* but by the new magnetic mines U-boats
were releasing around Britain. The casualties grew, and on 4
December the battleship *Nelson* had been hit and damaged. But

in the three months since the start of the war the *Ark Royal* had constantly been in the newspapers and on the newsreels, and the stories had been of victories over the enemy. Only her crew knew how lucky she had been.

The *Ark Royal* and *Renown*, still hundreds of miles from the River Plate, changed course and sailed east once more, to Dakar on the African coast. After a few days' leave for the crew they put to sea again, this time bound for Portsmouth.

4

THE NORWEGIAN CAMPAIGN

By February 1940, the *Ark Royal* had returned from its lengthy voyages in the South Atlantic and was moored at the dockside in Portsmouth harbour. The almost six months that had elapsed since the start of the war with Germany had, after the initial flurry of false alarms and the panicked rush for air-raid shelters, been peaceful on the mainland. The war was not delivering the airborne destruction and chaos that had been thought inevitable, and in Britain it began to be known as the 'Bore war', or the 'funny war'.

The war at sea, however, was far from boring or funny, as the losses caused by German U-boats and pocket battleships mounted. Britain had already suffered the loss of an aircraft carrier, and a U-boat had penetrated the Home Fleet's harbour at Scapa Flow, sending the battleship *Royal Oak* to the sea bed with hundreds of her crew. There had been some victories though, and the First Lord of the Admiralty Winston Churchill had done everything in his power to make sure that these success stories were brought to the attention of the public, with triumphant headlines in the press and constant references to them in the House of Commons. The *Ark Royal*, which had brought down the first German aircraft and sunk the first U-boat, always featured heavily.

The men who were now coming aboard the *Ark Royal*, taking the place of those who had been promoted or had been transferred to other ships, knew that they were joining a ship that had started to become a legend. Robert Elkington, a signalman who had already been in the Navy for several years, joined the *Ark* from the battleship HMS *Barham*, stationed in the Mediterranean. A tall, thin man now in his eighties, with a slightly sardonic sense of humour, Robert talks slowly, perhaps as a result of the years he spent surfing the radio waves, hunting down transmissions from enemy aircraft and ships hundreds of miles away. On *Barham*, one of the elderly battleships in the Mediterranean Fleet, he listened to and copied down the coded messages of the Spanish and Italian navies, sending the results in sealed envelopes directly to the Admiralty in London. He claimed to be able to tell the nationality of a telegraphist sending Morse code from the minute variations in timing between the long and short signals that Morse comprises. As far as he is concerned, moving from an old battleship like the *Barham* to the *Ark Royal* can be summed up in one word: 'Glamour! It was sheer glamour. She had that aura. As soon as you stepped on board you knew that everybody loved the ship. Fantastic.'

From Portsmouth, the *Ark* sailed to Scapa Flow where its squadron of Skua aircraft were flown off to the naval air station at Hatston to strengthen the defences of the anchorage in the

Flow. Then the *Ark* sailed south to carry out exercises with the Mediterranean Fleet.

The Skua aircraft, which had been on the *Ark* since the beginning of the war, were the most modern in the fleet. They were all metal, low-winged monoplanes with a single radial engine. The pistons were arranged in a circle around the propeller shaft, giving it a stumpy, sawn-off look at the front. The tail fin was upright, and the wings were straight and square at the ends. The Navy thought that all aircraft should carry an observer, to act as navigator, to carry out reconnaissance and to operate a rear defensive gun. As a consequence the cockpit was a lengthy structure with an upright canopy that looked more like a greenhouse than the rounded canopy of a Spitfire. The Skua was meant to be both a dive bomber and a fighter, and the general opinion of it was that it could do neither job very well. This wasn't completely true, as some of the pilots of 801 Squadron based at Hatston would prove, but the most modern fighter carried on the *Ark Royal* was certainly inferior to the best fighters in the RAF and other European air forces of the time.

The Skua had taken years to come into service and the Fleet Air Arm was paying a price for years of neglect caused by lack of funds, and the loss of control of its aircraft to the Royal Air Force. Reading some of the documents concerning the origins of the Skua now available in the National Archives, it becomes quite clear that the process by which the Navy had to acquire its aircraft from the Air Ministry was riven with distrust and incomprehension on the part of both services. The process wasn't helped by the desire on the part of the Navy to have aircraft that could be catapulted from battleships and cruisers, which meant that they had to be light in weight and fitted with floats, as well as be able to fly from aircraft carriers on a wheeled undercarriage. The Air Ministry suggested that the Navy acquire two different types of aircraft, but the Navy was unwilling to accept this for budgetary reasons. When the Air Ministry couldn't find an aircraft manufacturer to accept what was clearly an impossible design brief, the Admiralty admitted defeat and settled for an aircraft that would fly from carriers, have a considerable range and carry a crew of two. It also had to carry a 500lb bomb, as well as be able to shoot down other aircraft. At the time the Admiralty was finalizing this requirement, naval doctrine was that fighter aircraft flying from carriers would only be in combat with other carrier-based aircraft, and that their main purpose was to protect other aircraft that were acting as spotting planes during a naval battle.

So poisonous had the relationship between the Admiralty and the Air Ministry become by this point that the documents in the National Archives suggest that the final specification for the Skua was sent by the Air Ministry to its contacts in the aviation industry without the Admiralty having had an opportunity to approve it. The resulting plane was dogged by problems. When the prototype was tested, it was found that the plane had a dangerous habit of falling into an uncontrollable spin. The Air Ministry informed the Admiralty that they thought the Skua was incapable of doing its job. Blackburns, the manufacturers of the aircraft, solved the problem of the plane's stability by lengthening the fuselage, but in the Navy's eyes the plane was fatally compromised. Two other aircraft had also been placed on order: the Roc, based on the Skua airframe but with a four-gun turret mounted in the rear of the cockpit, and the Fulmar, a fighter that was earmarked to replace the Skua as the main fighter for the fleet. All these aircraft suffered massive delays in production and were extremely late in entering service.

The Admiralty were in utter despair at the state of their aircraft as war approached. One memorandum summed up the situation:

> The Skua was designed four years ago by Blackburns to combine the functions of fighting and dive bombing. This was a mistake, since the functions are incompatible, and dive bombing will not again be combined with fighting. The Roc, a two-seat fighter, and the Fulmar, a two-seat front-gun fighter, are also on order. The Fulmar is unnecessarily large since it was designed as a light bomber and was forced on us because of delays in Skua and Roc.

The Air Ministry then informed the Admiralty that the Roc was also not up to specification, and that they wanted to cancel it. This caused consternation in the Admiralty. Another internal memorandum reveals the hopelessness with which the situation was viewed:

> The position from the point of view of the development of specialized aircraft is serious. No concrete advance has been made since the Nimrod and Osprey [two biplanes designed in the 1920s] started to come into service 7 years ago. If the Skuas fail and the Roc is abandoned there will be no fighter aircraft but Gladiators in the Fleet Air Arm worth mentioning until the Fulmar comes along. This may be delayed and then further deficiencies will arise.

It was out of this mess that the Skua finally entered service. Its reputation preceded it, and as an aircraft it is generally seen to be a failure, though among pilots who actually flew the Skua opinions can be more nuanced. Lt Peter Goodfellow, who eventually became a Fulmar pilot in 808 Squadron on the *Ark*

Royal, flew Skuas as part of his training and doesn't have a good word to say about them. 'The Skua was a terrible aeroplane,' he said. 'You got the feeling that if you got too slow then you were in terrible trouble because the thing would spin and spin violently. It was a pretty desperate aircraft.' On the other hand, Lt George Baldwin, who later became a squadron leader, went on to serve in the Naval Air Fighting Development Unit, and flew over ninety types of aircraft in his flying career, thinks the Skua wasn't at all bad. It was, he claims, a very easy aeroplane to deck-land, with a wonderful view. 'It was quite a modern aeroplane in many ways, but its flying controls were heavy, so to do a roll it was a good hard heave. And it was slightly under-powered. You couldn't do proper aerobatics in a Skua. It was a very good dive bomber; the dive brakes were super. You could do a seventy-degree dive with full control and it dive-bombed very accurately.'

In March 1940, George Baldwin had just finished his pilot training, and he had learned to do deck landings in the Skua on the old carrier HMS *Argus*, which then was stationed in the French port of Toulon. It wouldn't be long, however, before the deficiencies of the Skua were to be a matter of life and death for him and other air crew in the Fleet Air Arm. Britain's war with Germany was soon to become very intense.

On 7 April a German fleet set sail from harbours in northern Germany on Operation Weserübung, a lightning invasion of Denmark and Norway whose audacious aim was the capture of key points along the 1,000-mile length of the Norwegian coastline. To make sure that the invasion was perfectly co-ordinated, the forces of troop-carrying ships and escorting warships staggered their departure over two days. Those task forces heading for Narvik and Trondheim in Norway had the longest journeys to make and were the first to depart. Fourteen troop-carrying destroyers were escorted by the battleship *Scharnhorst*, with the *Gneisenau* and the heavy cruiser *Admiral Hipper* in support. Once the troops on the destroyers had been landed in Narvik, these ships would then rejoin the battlecruisers and form a major task force to defend other parts of the invasion fleet heading for more southerly ports. Another force comprising the cruiser *Admiral Hipper* and four destroyers carrying 1,700 troops was going to seize Trondheim, and again once the troops were landed the warships would re-form with *Scharnhorst* and *Gneisenau*. It was an extremely well-thought-out plan.

In command of the northbound flotilla on the *Gneisenau* was Vice Admiral Günther Lutjens, a tall man with a serious, slightly introverted character, a veteran of the German Navy from the First World War. Lutjens knew that if the Royal Navy discovered his small fleet on its long journey north to the Norwegian Arctic, he would be seriously outgunned and the invasion would fail. But various pieces of intelligence about increased activity in German ports, and information from RAF reconnaissance flights, were never correctly interpreted by the Admiralty. Lutjens had a clear run.

A further landing was planned for Bergen with the light cruisers *Konigsberg* and *Bremse*, with 1,900 troops, and landings were also to be made at the towns of Kristiansund and Arendal. The Norwegian capital Oslo was targeted by 2,000 troops in the cruiser *Blucher* and the pocket battleship *Lutzow*. These German fleet movements heralded a full-scale invasion, for once the initial assaults were completed, planned reinforcements of another 3,700 troops would arrive by cargo vessel.

Equally important to the outcome of the invasion was the part played by the Luftwaffe. Five hundred transport planes carried troops into Norway as part of a second wave of reinforcements, and within a few days a further fifty thousand troops were in place. The operation was supported by 290 bombers, 40 dive bombers and 100 fighters. It was a brilliantly executed invasion, all the disparate forces carrying out their tasks with remarkable co-ordination.

Resistance by the Norwegian forces, who were unprepared and lightly armed, was sporadic, but they still managed to cause some casualties. *Blucher* was sunk by gunfire from shore batteries at Oslo, and *Konigsberg* was hit as she approached Bergen, although the occupying troops were only temporarily delayed. The damage caused to the *Konigsberg* by the Norwegians' defensive gunfire was enough, however, to prevent her from joining up with Lutjens' fleet, and she remained in the harbour at Bergen so that the crew could carry out repairs.

The British response to the invasion of Norway was confused. News that *Scharnhorst* and *Gnetsenau* had put to sea was slow to reach Admiral Sir Charles Forbes, Commander in Chief of the Home Fleet. He sailed late on 7 April but did not appreciate, and neither did the Admiralty, that the German force was part of an invasion attempt. Forbes believed that the German ships were attempting to break out into the Atlantic to attack merchant shipping, so he steamed a course to the north-east that meant he never made contact with the enemy fleet. Moreover, he did not take his aircraft carrier, HMS *Furious*, to sea with him, fearing that it would be sunk by torpedoes, just as *Courageous* had been a few months earlier. *Furious* was finally ordered to sea on 8 April by the Admiralty, but she left port without her squadron of Skua fighter aircraft.

On 9 April, Admiral Forbes's fleet was steaming north when it was attacked by a group of German bombers. *Furious* still had no fighter aircraft embarked, so the only defence available to the ships was their anti-aircraft guns, which of course, according to pre-war doctrine, were the best defence against air attack. Unfortunately this proved not to be the case, and despite some of the ships using up nearly half their ammunition stocks, bombs hit and sank the destroyer HMS *Gurkha*. Admiral Forbes had got off lightly, but he was shocked by this loss and ordered the Home Fleet to withdraw from the area controlled by German land-based aircraft. This was effectively the whole area south of Bergen, although, as the Germans strengthened their position, the reach of their aircraft spread ominously northwards up the Norwegian coastline.

The *Ark Royal*, of course, was in the Mediterranean taking part in exercises with the Mediterranean Fleet when the invasion of Norway started, and the Skua squadrons, 800 and 803, were based in Hatston in the Orkneys, defending the anchorage of the Home Fleet at Scapa Flow. One of the pilots from 800 Squadron, Lt Cdr Geoffrey Hare, had been loaned to the Royal Air Force to help with the identification of German ships. He spotted *Konigsberg* tied up at the mole in Bergen and the RAF staged an attack on the German warship with Hampden and Wellington bombers. They failed to score any direct hits on the target. When Hare returned to his squadron at Hatston, the two squadron commanders decided that the port of Bergen was within range of the Skuas, although the total journey time would be close to the limit of their endurance. There would be no spare fuel available to engage in a fight with enemy aircraft if they met any, and their navigation would need to be spot on.

On 10 April fifteen Skuas, each armed with a 500lb armour-piercing bomb, took off on the long flight over the North Sea.

Approaching from the south-east at 12,000 feet, they spotted the cruiser tied up at the mole. The key to dive-bombing a ship is to attack along the length of the vessel from bow to stern. The standard way to attack was to fly over the target until it appeared at the rear of the wing, on the port side, and then, as George Baldwin described it, 'You'd roll the Skua over the vertical until you were pointing at the target. And then you'd straighten up, and to get an accurate delivery of the bomb you had to pull the nose up a little bit to allow for the fall of the bomb. Which meant you didn't actually see the target when you pressed the button to drop the bomb. It was pure judgement, or guesswork – whatever you want to call it.'

The Skua pilots had decided to split their attack, to divide any anti-aircraft fire, but their arrival took the crew of the Konigsberg completely by surprise. As the Skuas passed, 8,000 feet machine gunners on the Konigsberg did start firing, but there was no response from the other heavier anti-aircraft guns on the cruiser. The first bomb to hit the ship probably destroyed the electrical power; other bombs, most of which were on target, caused further damage, and started fires. One of the pilots who had become separated on the flight to Bergen could see when he arrived late on the scene that the Konigsberg was sinking by the bows with flames and a column of thick black smoke rising into the sky. The attack had been a complete success, and nearly three hours after it ended the Konigsberg sank.

This was the first time a major warship had been sunk by air attack, and it was an important victory for the Fleet Air Arm. Whatever doubts may have been expressed about the Skua before the aircraft entered service, it had proved extremely effective in the skies above Bergen. Admittedly one aircraft went into a spin on the way back to Hatston and crashed, but all the other aircraft returned safely, though extremely low on fuel and with some minor damage from anti-aircraft fire. It had been a successful operation carried out with great daring, stretching the performance of the crew and the Skuas to their limit. However, this victory made little difference to the overall situation that now confronted the British government. The *Ark Royal* had still not been recalled from the Mediterranean and British forces generally were in no position to take quick advantage of the loss of the *Konigsberg*, or the demoralization it had brought to the German troops in Bergen.

Shortly after the outbreak of the war, Winston Churchill, as First Lord of the Admiralty, had been arguing that Britain should cut off supplies of Swedish iron ore to Germany by invading the Norwegian port of Narvik, through which the iron ore was exported. Plans were worked up for the Navy to transport troops across the North Sea and disembark them at Narvik, although the Army had no experience of or equipment for the extreme conditions of an Arctic winter. Troops were mobilized and ships were continually being loaded for an invasion that was constantly being postponed. The indecision of the Chamberlain government was mirrored by their French counterparts, who as allies in the war against Germany quite naturally insisted on being consulted about the invasion of a neutral country.

The German invasion had now made these concerns about access to Swedish iron ore completely irrelevant. There were much bigger issues at stake now, both strategic and political. Britain and France had been at war with Germany for seven months, and if they proved incapable of preventing Hitler from taking over two more neutral countries, there would naturally be enormous pressure on the Allies, both internationally and domestically, to seek a rapprochement with Nazi Germany. The more pressing strategic issue was the enormous advantage possession of the Norwegian harbours gave to the German Navy and its U-boat fleet. At a stroke Germany had outflanked Britain and made it much harder for the U-boat menace to be contained. The need to land troops in Norway and deny Hitler a total victory was more urgent than ever, but the conditions in which the Navy had to do this had been transformed.

As Admiral Forbes had already realized, the Navy was now highly vulnerable to German bombers based in Norway. British troops had been landed at Narvik on 14 April but had been unable to move forward to confront the German troops based in the town because of deep snow. Other landings by small contingents of British troops had taken place in Trondheim fjord, in preparation for a concerted assault from the sea on the town of Trondheim itself. The Luftwaffe, however, had occupied the airfields near Trondheim and Admiral Forbes realized that they presented a serious threat to any British landings, so on the night of 16 April he sent the cruiser HMS *Suffolk* to bombard Sola airfield.

The next day *Suffolk* was heavily bombed by the Luftwaffe for over six hours. In all there were thirty-three separate attacks, by a combination of high-level bombers and dive-bombing Stukas. One large 1,000lb bomb put the *Suffolk*'s rear gun turrets out of action and caused the rear of the ship to start taking in water. Even when the *Suffolk* came within range of the Skuas based at Hatston the attacks continued. She managed to struggle back to port in Scapa Flow, dangerously low in the water, her decks awash and her crew desperately fighting to keep the ship afloat. The rudder controls were destroyed and her hull was riddled with holes made by bomb splinters. Admiral Forbes now knew that any ships trying to land troops in Trondheim would be overwhelmed by the large number of bombers the Luftwaffe could put into the sky. The plans to seize Trondheim were abandoned, which left the small forces that had been landed to the north and south of Trondheim under attack. They slowly retreated to take up defensive positions at the towns of Namsos and Andelsnes.

If any progress was going to be made in Norway by British troops, the air support to the fleet and to the troops already on the ground needed to be strengthened. The Skuas based at Hatston had been at the limit of their range when they bombed the *Konigsberg*; only carrier-based aircraft could offer support to the troops further away at Narvik and Trondheim, men dreadfully exposed to bombing and strafing by the Luftwaffe. The situation was desperate, so the *Ark Royal* and the *Glorious* were finally ordered to steam out of the Mediterranean to form a carrier task force whose orders were to 'protect naval ships and convoys, to give cover to the troops at the landing places and to attack the German-occupied airbases in Norway'.

The *Ark Royal* was at Scapa Flow on 23 April, taking on stores and landing new pilots in Skuas and Rocs. The Roc, of course, was the version of the Skua which the Air Ministry had so urgently wanted to cancel at the last minute. George Baldwin was one of the air crew who flew onto the *Ark Royal* as she steamed north-east to meet up with Admiral Forbes's Home Fleet. The *Ark* arrived in Norwegian waters on 26 April, and it wasn't long before George was flying into combat for the first time. He discovered he had the naturally aggressive instincts of a fighter pilot. 'My first operational flight was on 27 April,' he said. 'I was sent up as number two to another Skua flown by a very senior pilot because I had no experience. We were flying at 8,000 feet, which was the standard way in, and we had only just got about 20 miles inland on the patrol line, which was above the German line at Andelsnes, when I saw a Heinkel bomber below me at about 2,000 feet. So I dived, did the attack I'd been taught to do, filled it full of lead, killed both the rear gunners, and then I was too close so I did the classic fighter school breakaway. I was only nineteen.'

The carrier task group stayed well away from the coast, sometimes by as much as 120 miles, hoping to avoid attacks from bombers based on the mainland. The *Ark Royal* wasn't fitted with radar so the only warning the ship's crew received of an impending attack by approaching enemy bombers was if they had been sighted by the defensive screen of destroyers. This left almost no time to launch a section of fighters before the bombers were above the *Ark*. Some of the escorting cruisers, like the *Sheffield* and *Curlew*, however, had been fitted with radar and could spot aircraft approaching up to 50 miles away.

Signalman Robert Elkington remembers that the air group on the *Ark Royal* was quick to understand how they could benefit from radar-equipped ships. The *Ark*'s air signal officer was Lt Commander Charles Coke, an observer in the Fleet Air Arm, and he and Elkington occupied a small office under the bridge on the *Ark Royal* where signals were received from the radar operators on the *Sheffield*. The ability to identify enemy aircraft 50 miles away allowed the *Ark* to launch her aircraft with enough time for them to reach altitude and intercept the bombers, though even with this advance warning the *Ark*'s pilots found themselves at a disadvantage because of the lack of power of the Skuas and Rocs. It was a rudimentary ad hoc arrangement, limited by the fact that in order to preserve radio silence the messages between the *Ark* and the *Sheffield* were passed either by flag signal or Aldis lamp.

On 28 April a series of attacks rained down on the *Ark* by Junkers 88 and Heinkel 111 bombers flying out of German bases on the Norwegian mainland. George Baldwin had been assigned to a Roc, and he attempted to pursue one of the bombers at low level. 'It was absolutely fucking useless,' he recalled. 'The Roc was a Skua with no front guns and a turret in the back. We chased the Heinkel at nought feet across the sea – it had just dropped a load of bombs; luckily they missed the *Ark Royal*. We chased him across the sea flat out and our full speed was exactly the same as his. And every time we managed to get close and the air gunner turned the turret, the drag on the four guns made us lose 20 knots of speed immediately.'

There was a massive Luftwaffe presence in Norway, and it soon became apparent that the carrier task force was not going to defeat it. The battle in Norway had been lost. The War Cabinet in London decided to move the troops out of Trondheim, and the role of the carrier group was now to cover the withdrawal.

On 1 May, the Luftwaffe made a concerted effort to sink the *Ark Royal*. The assault was heralded at eight o'clock in the morning by a surprise attack from a Ju88 bomber that arrived totally unnoticed and dropped its load of bombs, which fortunately for those on board missed the *Ark* by about 40 metres. This was followed by another attack in the afternoon by five high-level bombers all of whose bombs missed, then very shortly after that another unseen aircraft dropped a stick of bombs that fell in a straight line in the sea, miraculously just missing the bows of the carrier but so close that the whole of the forward flight deck was covered in spray. So far the *Ark*'s famous luck was holding out.

Three hours later another formation arrived, this time a combination of dive bombers and high-level bombers. The anti-

The massive bows of the *Ark Royal* dwarf the crowd gathered to see the launch in 1937.

Top: The boilers and the steam turbines were all manually controlled by the engine room staff.

Middle: Two of the *Ark*'s six boilers are hoisted on board in the fitting-out basin.

Bottom: Lady Maude Hoare swings the champagne bottle against the bow. It broke after four attempts.

The *Ark Royal* was the longest ship to be launched on Merseyside.

Xmas Menu.

1940

Breakfast.
Cornflakes.
Fried Bacon, Egg.
Marmalade.

Dinner.
Giblet Soup.
Roast Turkey & Stuffing.
Roast Potatoes.
Fresh Runner Beans.
Christmas Pudding & Sauce.
Figs, Dates & Nuts.
Oranges.

Tea.
Wholemeal Bread.
Christmas Cake.

Supper.
Cream of Tomato Soup.
Cold Ham.
Pickles.

Conditions on the *Ark* were better than most other warships. Even in wartime the Christmas menu promised turkey, and oranges, figs, nuts and dates. Captain Holland helps mix the plum duff *(top left)*. Chief Petty Officer King shows off his skills, and the officers' mess boasts tablecloths.

BRITAIN'S LATEST AIRCRAFT-CARRIER, WHICH REVIVES THE NAME OF LORD HOWARD OF EFFINGHAM'S FLAGSHIP AT THE DEFEAT OF THE ARMADA: THE "ARK ROYAL," A MEDIUM-SIZED VESSEL OF 22,000 TONS.

THE "ARK ROYAL'S" GREAT ELIZABETHAN NAMESAKE: HOWARD'S 800-TON FLAGSHIP, QUAINTLY PRAISED BY HIM AS "THE ODD SHIP IN THE WORLD FOR ALL CONDITIONS"

ON THE SPACIOUS FLIGHT-DECK OF THE "ARK ROYAL": A VIEW OF HER FUNNEL AND UPPER WORKS; WHEREON IS HER NAME-TABLET (CENTRE), BEARING THE BATTLE-HONOURS "ARMADA" AND "DARDANELLES." (Keystone.)

THE MODERN "ARK ROYAL," AN "ODD SHIP" IN THE MODERN SENSE OF THE WORD: THE GREAT OVERHANG SUPPORTING THE FLIGHT-DECK AT THE STERN; LIGHTS MOUNTED IN SPONSONS. (Central Press.)

wrote of her to Burghley, when he heard the Armada was about to sail "And I pray you tell her Majesty from me that her money was well give for the Ark Ralegh [she had originally belonged to Sir Walter Raleigh and wa purchased for £5000], for I think her the odd ship in the world for all con ditions." As regards the modern "Ark Royal," we regret that it was erroneousl stated in our last issue that she is the world's largest aircraft-carrier. Ther are, indeed, several larger carriers, both in our own and foreign navies, notabl the U.S.S. "Lexington" and "Saratoga," and the Japanese "Akagi."

The *Ark* was always a celebrated ship. The *Illustrated London News* ran a photo spread on the *Ark* when she was handed over at the end of 1938. Actors Michael Wilding, John Clements and Michael Rennie starred in a feature film shot on the *Ark* in 1940.

Above: A Blackburn Skua, ready for take-off. Designed as a fighter and dive bomber, it was slow and underpowered.

Left: A 500lb bomb is hoisted onto the flight deck ready for loading onto a Skua.

Above: A Fairey Fulmar fighter lands on, its arrestor hook down. This four-gun fighter replaced the Skua, but was still slower than enemy fighters.

Left: Torpedoes in their trolleys are lined up on the flight deck – the *Ark's* most effective weapon against ships.

Right: A Swordfish biplane and a Skua wait to be launched by the *Ark's* catapults.

Below: A Swordfish with its wings folded is taken down on the lift to the hangars below.

Air crew had their own ready rooms, and aircraft would be flying on and off the *Ark* throughout the hours of daylight.

Clockwise from left: John Moffat as a young sub-lieutenant. Ron Skinner looks pensively out to sea. John Richardson on the *Ark* in Gibraltar. Bill Morrison as a young rating.

Below: Val Bailey looks out of the cockpit of his Fulmar.

aircraft guns began to fire a barrage, particularly against the dive bombers which were potentially the more dangerous. Les Asher, the Royal Marine gunner in the rear starboard 4.5-inch anti-aircraft gun, remembers that on hearing the order 'Barrage to commence, commence, commence!' everyone 'went hell for leather. And the back of the 4.5-inch turret is open so there was always somebody looking outside to see what was happening. And all the information on the range and the fuse setting was done automatically. You lifted the shell up, put it on the tray, pushed it into a bracket and the range was set automatically, by information that came from the transmitting station that took their information from the range finder. It's rather surprising when the guns are firing. You get a really dry mouth. It's not fear, it's apprehension. There's so much going on you just get on with your job, and then you're glad when it's over. But when the guns are firing and the pom-poms start, there is always a lot of noise going on. And that, of course, is where I first lost my hearing.' The noise of that gunfire and the deep explosions of the bombs filled the air, and could be felt inside the hangars and engine rooms. Columns of water exploded all around the carriers and their escorts.

Ron Jordan, one of the armourers for 800 Squadron, vividly remembers those days the *Ark Royal* spent off Norway. 'Can you ever forget it?' he said. 'As the raids started the bugle sounded on the Tannoy and the fireproof curtains in the hangars would come down. And we could hear the 4.5's firing. Then of course the pom-poms started and we knew that we were warming up a bit. And then we hear one or two bangs, and shrapnel rattling against the sides. Just living there and waiting. I came to the conclusion that if we got hit we'd get killed, with all the petrol and explosives that were on board. One bomb in the hangar and I think we'd have gone. At times we thought, is it ever going to stop? Is it going to end?'

These sentiments were shared by Admiral Forbes. He believed that to keep the carriers on station off the coast of Norway was running an unacceptable risk. The army was evacuating from Namsos and the effort to get all the troops off would be finished by 3 May. The carriers were ordered back to Scapa Flow, to refuel and rearm, and to allow the crews to obtain some rest.

At Scapa, Captain Arthur Power, who had commanded the *Ark Royal* for all of her service life, and had prepared her crew for war, left the ship for promotion, and a post in the Admiralty. His replacement was Captain Cedric 'Hooky' Holland, who had spent the previous two years as the Naval Attaché in the British Embassy in Paris. Captain Holland would renew his acquaintance with the French Navy sooner than he expected, but his first, immediate concern was the continuing debacle in Norway.

The only British presence left in Norway now was the two small contingents outside Narvik, the most remote and northerly town on the coast. These troops became the focus of a renewed effort to salvage something, at whatever cost, from the failure of Norway. The British government and Winston Churchill had never been able to shake off their fixation with Narvik and its supposed importance to iron ore supplies to German industry and armaments. As a result, the troops in Narvik, rather than being recalled, were, under Churchill's aggressive prompting, brought up to a strength of 30,000 men. But Narvik was about to become a sideshow to the dramatic events unfolding in the rest of Europe.

The military catastrophe of the Norwegian campaign was a political disaster for the Chamberlain government in the UK. In a debate in the House of Commons on 7 and 8 May it became apparent how isolated Chamberlain was. Clement Attlee, leader of the Labour Party, put it most succinctly: 'Norway followed Czechoslovakia and Poland. Everywhere the story is "too late".' On 9 May, Chamberlain accepted that he should resign. The only question was, who should take his place? The next day, Winston Churchill was summoned to see the King and was asked to form a government. On that same day, the German Army, a massive military juggernaut that had paralysed the political leadership of Europe for years, invaded Luxembourg, the Netherlands and Belgium, and marched towards Paris.

With France, Britain's only ally, falling apart under the German blitzkrieg, Narvik was an irrelevant sideshow. More than that, it was a black hole that would have absorbed ships, resources and men's lives. It was now vital to recover as much equipment and as many troops as possible from Norway to help assist in the defence of France. On 24 May the War Cabinet gave the order to evacuate Narvik once and for all – but not before it had been captured from the German Army and made unusable as a port. As Ron Skinner remarked to me, 'I think Narvik was the only place where the evacuation had been planned before it had been captured!' Narvik was finally taken from the small German garrison in the town on 28 May, and after a brief assessment that confirmed it was no longer of any use as a port, preparations were made to abandon northern Norway.

The *Ark Royal*, the *Furious* and the *Glorious* were sent north of the Arctic Circle to provide air cover to the British troops in Narvik, and to escort the convoy returning to England. A squadron of Hurricane fighters had been transported to Norway by the carrier HMS *Glorious* to help defend the Allied troops against attacks from the Luftwaffe. Their commander, Squadron Leader Cross, did not want to abandon these valuable machines in Norway and thought that it was worth making an attempt to land them onto one of the carriers on station off the coast. The flight deck of the *Ark Royal* was 100 feet (30 metres) longer than that of the *Glorious*, which was an extremely important consideration to pilots who had never landed on a flight deck before, but the deck lifts on the *Ark* were too narrow to carry the Hurricanes with their full wing span, and the flight deck would quickly become congested. Cross decided it was better to use the *Glorious*, and the squadron of Hurricanes successfully landed on her flight deck – a remarkable achievement given the absence of an arrestor hook on the fighters.

The *Glorious* then left the *Ark Royal* and the convoy she was escorting and steamed back to Scapa Flow on her own. Officially the reason for this dangerous course of action was that she was running low on fuel, but the reality was that the senior command on the ship had collapsed. The captain had become mentally unstable and had removed the Commander Air from his position, and wanted to return to the UK as quickly as possible to institute a court martial against him. Such a move was the height of irresponsibility, and there has never been an explanation of why the captain of the *Glorious* was given permission by the senior officer of the task force, Admiral Wells on *Ark Royal*, to abandon the mission of escorting the convoy. It was to prove a fatal mistake.

At the beginning of the Allied troops' final assault on Narvik, the battleships *Scharnhorst* and *Gneisenau* had sailed from Kiel in Germany and headed north, to take the pressure off the German troops by bombarding the Allied positions. When these ships were underway, Admiral Marschall, the commander of this task force of German warships, was told that there were reconnaissance reports of large numbers of British troop carriers and warships heading west. Admiral Marschall was ignorant of the British retreat from Narvik, but he decided in any case that these ships were a more interesting target than the proposed attack on Narvik and changed course to search for them.

On 8 June, a lookout on the *Scharnhorst* saw smoke on the horizon. They had failed to intercept the British troop convoy. They had spotted, instead, the aircraft carrier *Glorious*, with an escort of just two destroyers. The *Glorious* had launched no reconnaissance patrols that morning and there were no Swordfish ready to be armed and flown off to attack the German warships, which were spotted by lookouts on board *Glorious* before they opened fire. Desperate efforts were made to put some Swordfish in the air armed with torpedoes, and three aircraft were brought up from the hangar deck and ranged at the end of the flight deck, but it was far too late. *Scharnhorst* opened fire with her 11-inch guns at 1632, shortly after tea time. Before the Swordfish engines could be started they were blown to pieces by the shells that ripped into the flight deck and exploded in the hangars. *Glorious*'s deck was not armoured, and the ship had almost no protection against the big guns of the German battleships. Explosion after explosion wreaked death and destruction throughout the carrier, and at 1740 the order to abandon ship was given.

The bridge had received one of the first incoming shells from the *Scharnhorst*, cutting off a radio signal that was in reality far too late to save the *Glorious* and her crew. A fragment of this desperate plea for help was received on the *Ark Royal* by Robert Elkington, who was in the communications room, earphones on, probing the ether for an unguarded signal, the rapid dots and dashes of a signalman's Morse key that might reveal the presence of an enemy aeroplane or a lurking submarine.

'Suddenly there was this burst of noise, "2PB" in Morse,' he recalled. 'Well, I knew what that meant – two pocket battleships – but that was all there was. It didn't last long enough for me to get a fix. I took the signals pad to the petty officer in charge, but there was no position, nothing.'

The *Glorious*'s two escorting destroyers, *Acasta* and *Ardent*, were also sunk by the *Scharnhorst* and *Gneisenau*, but not before they had steamed directly at the far more powerful battleships with guns blazing, *Acasta* managing to hit and damage the *Scharnhorst* with a torpedo. But it was all far too late to save the *Glorious*. Another carrier had been lost, and 1,519 sailors and airmen were dead or missing. The brave attack of the destroyers did, however, force Admiral Marschall to abandon his original mission to search for the troop convoys, and instead he headed east for shelter and repairs in Trondheim Fjord.

On 11 June, during a raid on Trondheim, the RAF spotted the presence of the German warships. The Admiralty came up with a plan for Skuas from the *Ark Royal* to mount a dive-bomber attack on the *Scharnhorst*, so the *Ark* was sent to avenge the loss of *Glorious*.

Skuas from the *Ark Royal* had carried out any number of missions over Norway during the evacuation from Trondheim and Narvik. Pilots from 800 and 803 Squadrons had shot down attacking bombers and broken up air attacks, but everybody knew that the Skuas were not capable of taking on German fighters. In the hands of determined and capable pilots, however, Skuas could get away from the fast, manoeuvrable and heavily armed Messerschmitt 109 fighters. George Baldwin described an incident to me when he had succeeded in doing just that. 'My squadron arrived over Bergen at 8,000 feet and started their dive bombing,' he said, 'and two Messerschmitt 109s arrived and shot four of them down. I decided to fly into the coast at nought feet, and it was only after I climbed up to height and dropped my bomb that they spotted me. This 109 was chasing me, and I thought two things: he won't like low flying at full speed, and he won't like flying over the open ocean. Most fighter pilots don't. I flew right down and my air gunner was saying he's getting closer and closer, so I flew at nought feet, absolutely nought feet, straight at the rocks in the island which lies just off the harbour, and turned, Jesus Christ as hard as I could, round the rocks and stayed very low and out to the open ocean, and he just gave up. So I knew about being chased by Messerschmitts.' Despite this escape, George had no illusions about the chances of survival in a fight. 'You really had no chance against them. They were infinitely more manoeuvrable, they had a better front armament, they were faster, they had been trained to shoot things down, and they were dying to shoot us down. Absolutely committed.'

What everybody hoped for with an attack on the *Scharnhorst* was a repeat of the brilliantly successful sinking of the *Konigsberg*. However, the *Scharnhorst* was a much bigger and more heavily armoured warship, and conditions were vastly different from just two months earlier. It was much later in the year for a start, and there was continual daylight; the weather was better, and visibility was greater. Furthermore, Trondheim had been occupied by the Wehrmacht for some time and the anchorage was well defended against air attack. A Luftwaffe air-base was located close to Trondheim, at Vaernes.

Fifteen Skuas were to take part in the attack on the *Scharnhorst*, nine from 803 Squadron and six from 800. Ron Jordan, the armourer from 800 Squadron, knew that something was up when they were ordered to load the Skuas with 500lb armour-piercing bombs – not a normal load for a combat air patrol or an attack on shore installations. 'To get two squadrons ranged together, we knew that it was exceptional,' he said. 'You see, we normally ranged three aircraft at a time on the flight deck. And of course with the 500lb armour-piercing bombs, you only use that against a warship. There was a feeling that it was going to be a very stiff job.'

At midnight on 13 June, the Skuas took off from the flight deck of the *Ark Royal*, formed up and headed towards Trondheim. A diversionary raid by the RAF on Vaernes was scheduled to take place at the same time, but they arrived early, and there was no common radio frequency between the RAF and the *Ark*. When the Skuas arrived over the target they were met with an enormous barrage of anti-aircraft fire, and the air crew discovered that rather than prevent the squadrons of Messerschmitt 109 and 110 fighters from taking off, the RAF raid had instead alerted them in advance so that they were already in the air, ready to pounce on the Skuas. The Skua crews attempted to carry out their attack, diving along the length of the ship from alternate ends to try to confuse the anti-aircraft fire, but it was a failure. Just one bomb hit the *Scharnhorst*, and it bounced off the thick armour plating. Eight of the Skuas were shot down by German fighters.

Ron Skinner remembers the increasing despondency as the *Ark*'s crew waited for the aircraft to return and land. 'We waited until the planes, if they were still flying, would have run out of fuel. I think we slowly realized that sixteen of our air crew were not going to return. It was a great blow, I think particularly for those involved in the flying operations. It affected us for days. We called it Black Thursday.' Some of the bodies of the air crew are buried in a cemetery near Trondheim, and Ron has just recently been there to put flowers on the graves of people he still remembers as nineteen- and twenty-year-old men. Ron Jordan recalled, 'In the mess we auctioned items from the people who had got killed for the relatives and wives. We all had a bit of a prayer and a get-together. It was very depressing. I'd never seen that before of course, but they said that was normal practice after an action.'

This last, almost suicidal mission ended the Norwegian campaign. The *Ark Royal* had survived a very intensive two months of war, acting not as an aircraft carrier in a major 'big fleet' action, but standing off the coast of a remote land war, providing reconnaissance and air cover for troops, and acting as a long-range bomber force. It was a role the Navy and RAF never thought would be necessary. The experience had welded the crew together, and they had shown that they were efficient and effective. Despite the *Ark Royal*'s lack of radar, some rudimentary form of fighter control had successfully been implemented. The loss of the air crew over Trondheim had been a tragic and unnecessary end to this short struggle. Hindsight, of course, is a remarkable thing, but if the *Ark Royal* and the other carriers had been better equipped, had they had more modern planes and had they been used correctly from the start, the war in Norway might not have been such an abject defeat for Britain.

Still, the incompetence and failures that bedevilled the British response to the German invasion of Norway paled almost into insignificance compared to the catastrophe in Europe that overwhelmed Britain in June 1940.

5

DEATH TO THE FRENCH

On the same day that Winston Churchill became Prime Minister, 10 May, the fascist government of Italy under Mussolini joined the war against Britain and France. Things were going very badly for the two allies. British and French armies had failed to hold the German advance in France, and with the growing prospect of military defeat a political crisis enveloped the French government. On 14 June the German Army marched into Paris; two days later Paul Reynaud, the French Prime Minister, resigned, handing power over to Marshal Henri Pétain. On 22 June Pétain, whose government had moved from Paris to Tours, then from Tours to Bordeaux, sought an armistice with Germany. From that date France was split into two: the northern half of the country, including the whole of the Atlantic coastal area, was under German occupation, and the southern part was under the control of the Vichy government, an administration nominally independent from, but an ally of, the German government.

HMS *Ark Royal* had returned to Scapa Flow after the heavy losses over Trondheim. She then sailed for Gibraltar with HMS *Hood*, the largest ship in the Navy, an elegant and fast battleship, 'the pride of the fleet'. With three destroyers for an anti-submarine escort, the two large ships arrived in Gibraltar on 23 June.

The events of the last two months had thrown British strategy in the Mediterranean into absolute chaos. It was the end point of a process that had started in 1935 with the Italian invasion of Abyssinia and the attempted imposition on the Italian government of League of Nations sanctions, which Britain and France had undertaken to enforce. This international crisis, of course, had prompted the move of the headquarters of the British Mediterranean Fleet from the island of Malta to Alexandria in Egypt – much further away from Italian airbases in Sicily and the main Italian port of Taranto. In the years since then, in an attempt to create a modern navy that could enforce Italian interests in the Mediterranean and Africa, Mussolini had poured money into building new battleships and submarines – an expansion that was naturally viewed as a threat by both Britain and France, who agreed that in the event of a conflict with Italy, Britain would assume responsibility for the eastern Mediterranean while the French Navy would seek to control the western basin from its base in the port of Mirs el Kebir at Oran in Algeria.

The collapse of France raised crucial questions about this strategy, and they were discussed at a series of crisis meetings in the Admiralty and in the War Cabinet. Should Britain pursue an active war against Italy? Germany and Italy had helped install the Franco regime in Spain; would Franco remain neutral or throw in his lot with the fascist axis? Was Gibraltar capable of being defended? The chiefs of staff took the view that neither Malta nor Gibraltar was capable of being defended, and Sir Dudley Pound, the First Sea Lord, contemplated abandoning the Mediterranean.

Churchill refused to consider this course of action. From his point of view there were very great issues at stake. A withdrawal from the Mediterranean would weaken British ability to defend the Suez Canal and ensure continued access to the Middle East oilfields. Also of prime importance was the way such an abandonment of the Mediterranean would be interpreted, not only by Britain's enemies but in the neutral countries of the area, such as Turkey, Greece and Spain, that might yet be won over to a coalition against Germany. Withdrawal would also have ramifications on opinion in the United States, where there was a great deal of discussion about the wisdom of backing Britain, a country that, it was believed, would inevitably be forced to seek terms with Germany. Churchill was convinced that after the defeat in Norway and the occupation of France it was absolutely necessary to demonstrate that Britain had made a break with the policies of negotiation, even though in the Cabinet there were still senior figures like Lord Halifax, the Foreign Secretary, who thought it wiser to maintain a dialogue with Italy and Germany. To win the day, Churchill needed to provide concrete proof of his determination, to Parliament and to the population of Britain.

The Mediterranean, then, was not going to be abandoned, and with this decision the *Ark Royal*'s fate was sealed. She would form the nucleus of a force based in Gibraltar to be known as Force H, and the Admiralty appointed Admiral James Somerville to lead it.

Somerville was, on the face of it, a strange choice. From a solid and respectable family, part of the Somerset squirearchy, James Somerville had gone to Dartmouth Naval College in 1897 at the age of fifteen. He saw action in the Dardanelles in the First World War, and developed an interest in radio telegraphy and signals. By 1936 he had been appointed Rear Admiral (Destroyers) in the Mediterranean Fleet, and during the Spanish Civil War he had several brushes with the Italian Navy, whose submarines often targeted British ships. His active career had, however, been cut short in 1939 when he was diagnosed with tuberculosis and placed on the Retired List. When war started, he was called back to the Admiralty, to the Signals Division, and became responsible for the development of shipborne radar. His return to active service was made permanent when he became assistant to Admiral Bertram Ramsay, who was in charge of the evacuation of the British Expeditionary Force from Dunkirk. Somerville was an intelligent and witty man with a strong independent streak in him. He was not afraid to speak his mind. In 1939 he gave a talk for the BBC Home Service about the Royal Navy, and this was the first of regular broadcasts over the next few years about the conduct of the war and the *Ark Royal*.

Somerville's orders for Force H were, initially, short and to the point. In order to guarantee the Royal Navy's position in the Mediterranean, the priority task was to prevent the French Mediterranean Fleet anchored in Oran harbour, and in the naval port of Mirs el Kebir a few miles along the coast, from falling into the hands of Germany or Italy. If necessary, the French ships would be sunk. During his journey down to Gibraltar, Somerville received several messages from the Admiralty refining the plans for Operation Catapult, as it was now called. On 30 June the Admiralty signalled, 'As we desire to prevent ships getting into

German or Italian hands, with as little trouble and bloodshed as possible, it is under consideration to give [the French] these alternatives:

1. To steam their ships to a British port.
2. To sink their ships.
3. Have their ships destroyed by gunfire.

Your plan should be based on giving them the three alternatives. You will be informed as soon as possible which alternative HMG [His Majesty's government] decides to give them.' There were also indications that the role of Force H was going to be wider. Somerville intercepted an Admiralty signal to Admiral Sir Dudley North, the Commanding Officer of North Atlantic Station in Gibraltar, asking for his opinion about what Force H could do to neutralize any bombardment of Gibraltar if Spain became hostile. Somerville's comment was, 'I was somewhat surprised at receiving this message, since I understood . . . that Gibraltar as a naval base would be completely untenable.'

Somerville arrived in Gibraltar in the early evening, and held a meeting with all the senior naval figures and the Commanding Officers of Force H. The French ships that most worried the Admiralty were the two modern battleships *Dunkerque* and *Strasbourg*, and another older battleship, the *Bretagne*. They would seriously affect the balance of power in the Mediterranean if they fell under the control of the Axis navies. The captain of the *Ark Royal*, Captain Cedric Holland, had been the naval attaché in the British Embassy in Paris shortly before the war and had a very good knowledge of the policies and personalities of the current French government, and more importantly the French Navy. He, like Somerville, North and the other officers present, was strongly opposed to the use of force. Their proposal was that there should be a show of force, if necessary, and that the French ships should only be sunk after they had been evacuated. There was a serious worry that shelling the ships in Oran and Mirs el Kebir could only be achieved with a great loss of life. It was the view of almost everyone at the meeting in Gibraltar, and also in the Admiralty in London, that the French admirals would be bound to see that they had no alternative but to give in to British demands.

The date set for Operation Catapult was 3 July, and Somerville proposed that Captain Holland should go to Mirs el Kebir as an emissary to Admiral Gensoul, the French commander in chief. Captain Holland arrived off Mirs el Kebir in the destroyer *Foxhound* early in the morning of 2 July and he was allowed to enter the harbour. A little later Force H, which was now a significant fleet with not only *Ark Royal* but the battleships *Valiant*, *Resolution* and *Nelson*, and the flagship *Hood*, two cruisers and eleven destroyers, arrived to take up position outside the harbour at Oran. A reconnaissance aircraft had flown off from the *Ark Royal*, and it reported that the French battleships and cruisers were raising steam and taking down their canvas deck awnings, indicating that they might be preparing to put to sea. At one o'clock that afternoon, Swordfish aircraft flew off from the *Ark Royal* with an escort of Skua fighters and laid magnetic mines in the mouth of the harbour, putting further pressure on the French admiral.

What the Admiralty, Somerville and Captain Holland had failed to foresee was that the French Naval High Command saw no reason to hand over its ships to Britain. The general opinion was that Britain was not going to be able to hold out for much longer without following the French down the path of negotiating with Germany. Moreover, the French equivalent to a First Sea Lord, Admiral Darlan, had accepted a post in the Vichy government of Marshal Pétain, and Admiral Gensoul saw Darlan as his legitimate superior officer and the Vichy regime as the legitimate French government. In addition to that, the terms of the armistice between France and Germany had been drafted with some sensitivity towards the French Navy. Hitler had no desire to drive the French admirals into the arms of the British and had agreed that the French fleet should remain under French control. Darlan had sent secret signals to Gensoul and French admirals in other ports in the French colonies instructing them to sail to neutral ports in the United States if there were any moves by Germany or Italy to take possession of French warships. As far as Gensoul was concerned the British had no cause for alarm, and there was no excuse for the Royal Navy to blockade his ports and mine the entrances to his harbour. These feelings were vigorously made known to Captain Holland when, finally, after several ultimatums, Gensoul agreed to meet him.

The terms of the agreement between France and Germany were known to the British government, but as far as Churchill and the First Sea Lord Sir Dudley Pound were concerned the word of Hitler was worth nothing. That fact had been amply proved by the fate of Czechoslovakia, Poland, Belgium, Norway, and now France itself. As for the signals from Darlan to Gensoul, the Admiralty was worried that the Germans had obtained the ciphers to the French naval codes, and that the authenticity of messages from Darlan could not be trusted.

In the afternoon of 3 July, the Admiralty received reports that other French warships were heading to Mirs el Kebir to relieve Gensoul. They signalled to Somerville – 'Settle matters quickly or you will have reinforcements to deal with' – and Somerville had no alternative but to signal to Gensoul that if the terms of the British ultimatum were not agreed to, Force H would open fire at 1730. Now Captain Holland, still in heated discussions with Gensoul, sent a message to Somerville on the *Hood* saying that the crews of the French ships were being reduced and that the ships would proceed to Martinique or the USA. It was a last desperate effort by the captain of the *Ark Royal* to prevent an attack on the French fleet, but it was too little and too late. The officers who had so vehemently opposed the use of force against the French, and who had believed utterly that it would not be necessary, had been driven by the determination of Churchill and the Admiralty, and the complacency of French admirals, to a course of action they abhorred.

Holland was allowed to leave Mirs el Kebir in the motor boat in which he had arrived. He was picked up by HMS *Forester* at about a quarter past seven in the evening. Twenty minutes after he left Mirs el Kebir harbour, Force H opened fire. The massive guns of the *Hood* and the *Valiant*, *Nelson* and *Resolution* erupted with yellow gun flashes and thick smoke, and shells whistled through the air to land in the harbour.

Val Bailey was a lieutenant on the destroyer *Active*, and had had a ringside seat all day. *Active* had been patrolling outside the boom that controlled the entrance to Mirs el Kebir, keeping watch on the movements of the ships inside the harbour. 'I had had absolutely no idea what was going to happen,' he said, 'and as we scuttled back to the fleet the guns started firing and went whistling over our heads. I'd never seen big guns firing before, and suddenly there I was in the middle of a big ship action. It was startling, I can tell you.' When the guns started firing, *Active* lost no time in getting back to the main body of Force H, but shells from the French shore batteries and the battleships in the harbour were finding the range of the British warships. The French used coloured dye in their shells to help identify each ship's fall of shot, and Bailey was covered in pink water from one very near miss.

Three minutes after Force H started firing, a huge explosion took place in the harbour and an enormous column of smoke billowed into the air, rising for several hundred feet. This was the battleship *Bretagne* blowing up, taking the lives of over 900 French sailors with her. A shell had penetrated her decks and exploded in a magazine. She capsized slowly.

Two Swordfish had taken off from the *Ark* and were circling over the French ships, carrying out their classical role of spotting the fall of shot, but with three battleships firing into such a closely confined area it was impossible to tell whose shells were falling where. Clouds of thick oily smoke from fires and explosions blanketed the harbour, and at 1812 Somerville ceased firing, just seventeen minutes after the onslaught had begun. The damage to the French ships was catastrophic. Shells had not only hit the *Bretagne* and destroyed her, but the *Dunkerque* and the *Provence* were also badly damaged. The former was holed, and had been slowly beached on the mainland near the village of St Andre; the latter had been set on fire, and with flames and smoke pouring out from a massive shell hole on her superstructure she too was slowly driven ashore to stop her from sinking.

However, the most modern and powerful battleship in Mirs el Kebir, the *Strasbourg*, had managed to cast her moorings and was heading for the entrance to the harbour when the first incoming shells detonated. One of them hit one of her escorting destroyers, which completely lost her stern, but *Strasbourg* continued through the harbour bar, with some other destroyers, and escaped into the Mediterranean. At high speed they headed east, towards the *Ark Royal*.

The *Ark Royal* had taken very little part in the destruction of the French ships in Mirs el Kebir harbour, but her flight deck had seen an enormous amount of activity throughout the day. Two Swordfish aircraft had flown off the *Ark* at five o'clock that morning on a dawn patrol, and then, as the darkness lifted, had acted as an anti-submarine air patrol. Within the next hour and a half six more Swordfish flew off to search for Italian or French warships that might be at sea in the area, as well as three Skuas to act as a fighter escort for Force H and another Swordfish to reconnoitre Mirs el Kebir and Oran harbours, and to provide assistance for *Foxhound*, the destroyer carrying Captain Holland to his meetings with Admiral Gensoul. As the day wore on these aircraft landed on to refuel and were replaced by others. Some twenty aircraft were landing and taking off at roughly two-hour intervals. In addition to these regular aircraft movements, plans had been made to bomb the heavy ships in Mirs el Kebir, and the submarines and smaller craft in Oran harbour. A torpedo attack on the battleships in Mirs el Kebir had also been prepared. And of course both harbour mouths were mined by two flights of Swordfish aircraft.

Several aircraft were lost during the day as the flying programme became disrupted and they ran out of fuel. The original plan to bomb the battleships in Mirs el Kebir had been scheduled to take place at five thirty in the afternoon, but it was postponed because of Somerville's desire to see a resolution to the conflict without firing on the French fleet. As a consequence, the bombed-up Swordfish were ranged at the end of the flight deck for over an hour while aircraft returning from patrols landed on. Eventually, six Swordfish, heavily laden with four 250lb armour-piercing bombs and a further eight 20lb anti-personnel bombs, rolled along the flight deck and heaved into the air. As they circled the carrier and formed up, three Skuas were flown off to act as a fighter escort. Then they set course for the harbour at Mirs el Kebir, but it was too late: the *Strasbourg* had already cleared the bar.

The *Strasbourg* now became the main target, and the Swordfish and escorting Skuas on their way to the harbour at Mirs el Kebir were radioed with instructions to divert from their bombing attack and head for the French battleship. She and her escort were soon spotted by a Swordfish reconnaissance plane and their course, which was directly the carrier, was reported urgently to the *Ark*. She immediately went to full speed and steered a course in the opposite direction, but the *Strasbourg* and her destroyers were intent on reaching the safety of a French port and continued to head north-east with HMS *Hood* in pursuit.

Within minutes of the six Swordfish and three Skuas taking off from the *Ark*, the Skuas had seen five French fighters attacking the spotting Swordfish flying near the starboard quarter of the carrier. The Skuas drove them off, but one Skua, flown by Petty Officer Airman Riddler, spun into the sea. The plane and its crew were never recovered so it was impossible to say whether the Skua had been shot down or whether Riddler and his air gunner had been the victim of the Skua's tendency to dive into an irrecoverable spin. So it was only two Skuas that flew with the Swordfish towards the *Strasbourg*. At 12,000 feet another group of French fighters attempted to attack the Swordfish, and the Skuas once more took on a superior force. The nine French fighters and the two Skuas went into a dogfight, and two of the French fighters were hit and dived away. During this fight both the Skuas had problems with their forward firing guns jamming. Three more French fighters appeared, but again the Skuas intercepted them, allowing the Swordfish to make their

bombing attack on the *Strasbourg*, which they did by approaching from the north and diving at the battleship from a height of
4,000 feet. By this time the *Strasbourg* was firing its heavy anti-
aircraft guns at the planes. There were no hits observed on the
Strasbourg, although a 250lb bomb would have only slightly
damaged an armoured battleship. The flight returned to the
carrier, but two of the Swordfish had to ditch in the sea on
the way back when they ran out of fuel. The two Skuas then
encountered a French flying boat, and Sub Lt Brokensha made
an attack and put one of its engines out of action.

It had been a long and stressful mission, with three aircraft lost
and two crew members dead, but the *Strasbourg* steamed on
untouched. Her escape had taken Somerville totally unawares.
He had failed to foresee that the French ships would attempt to
leave harbour while under fire from his battleships and make a
dash for safety. He admitted to his wife later that his personal
antipathy to the whole operation, certainly to the use of force
against the French, had affected his judgement. 'To you I don't
mind confessing I was half-hearted,' he said, 'and you can't win
an action that way.'

The raid on the *Strasbourg* led by the *Ark Royal* was not, however, the last attempt to sink the French battleship that night.
Before the Swordfish and Skuas had returned from their bombing
attack, another six Swordfish aircraft from 818 Squadron had
been armed with torpedoes. With the light fading, at ten minutes
to eight they took off to launch a torpedo attack on the French
warship.

The Swordfish aircraft that flew off into the dusk looked completely anachronistic, with two sets of wings supported by struts
and wire, an open cockpit, huge wheels on struts that didn't
retract, and a skin that was largely canvas. The whole affair was

pulled through the air by one large radial engine that appeared to be stuck on the nose of the fuselage. The Swordfish looked like a relic from the First World War. It was in fact designed in the early 1930s, and had first entered service in 1936. It had a very slow speed, and could land and take off quite easily from the deck of the carrier. Its large wing area enabled it to carry heavy loads, and it was extremely stable, which was an advantage when dropping torpedoes. Almost every pilot who flew it regarded it as a safe, reliable aircraft. It was easy to repair, and could take enormous damage and stay flying. It did have some disadvantages, though. The engine was started with a flywheel, mounted behind the engine. Two ground crew would have to turn a crank and get the flywheel spinning as fast as possible, then the pilot would engage a clutch, the primed engine would turn over and fire, and the propeller would become a lethal disc just feet away from the two ground crew. It was not an easy thing to do in safety on a pitching deck.

It took a variety of qualities to be a Swordfish pilot. Patience and stoicism were virtues on long, slow patrols over the empty ocean in an open cockpit, hoping that the observer in the rear could correctly calculate the return course back to the carrier. Courage was also necessary. A torpedo was essentially aimed at a ship by pointing the Swordfish at it and flying low and steadily towards the target while gunfire was pouring towards you. The pilots of six of these aircraft were now going to do exactly that as they headed towards the *Strasbourg*.

Screened by six destroyers, the *Strasbourg* was heading towards Toulon at a speed of about 26 knots. By the time the Swordfish had made visual contact with the battleship the sun was low on the horizon, and the Swordfish made their initial approach from the west, out of the setting sun. The crew of the ship were at action stations, and when the pilots of the Swordfish approached to identify the ship they immediately put up a heavy anti-aircraft barrage. The agreed plan of attack was to fly into a position so that the aircraft were ahead of the *Strasbourg* and its destroyer screen, and on their starboard side, so that the battle-ship was silhouetted against the afterglow of the setting sun in the west. Splitting into two flights of three, the pilots flew at 50 feet above the sea in a wide sweep across the course of the French ship and its escort. Thirty minutes after their first sight-ing, the Swordfish pilots were in a position to start their attack.

Dropping to a height of 20 feet, the two groups headed between two of the escorting destroyers at the starboard quarter of the ship. The general principle was to judge the speed of their target by the size of the bow wave, and to set the sights to make allowances for that speed when launching the torpedo. Flying very low above the sea, the pilots set their sights for speeds of between 22 and 30 knots. As they flew between the two escort-ing destroyers they were fired on by both ships, but were not hit. The two section leaders started the attack together, their sections following them in line astern, planes in each section launching simultaneously. The conditions were now so gloomy that the attack went ahead unseen by the lookouts on the *Strasbourg*, and very little anti-aircraft fire was directed at the Swordfish from the battleship. It was also too dark to see any hits, although the estimate of the pilots was that one or two may have been obtained. In fact none was. The attempt to stop the *Strasbourg* had failed again.

It had been an extremely long day, with the first aircraft launched at 0500 hours and the last Swordfish landing back on the carrier at 2310. Throughout that time the *Ark*'s aircraft had played an extremely important role in the attack on the French fleet, and this was the first time that the *Ark* had attempted an attack on a warship steaming at speed. But the *Strasbourg* had escaped.

Somerville had, of course, objected in the strongest possible terms against opening fire on the French fleet. In that letter to his wife he expressed his anger. 'The thought of slaughtering our former allies was repugnant,' he wrote; 'we all felt thoroughly dirty and ashamed that the first time we should have been in action was an affair like this'. And it was not only the morality of his actions that concerned Somerville. The action had released the French from their armistice agreements, and Somerville was concerned that they would now be an active enemy in the Mediterranean, making his task to secure the western Mediterranean more difficult. He saw no reason why he should go out of his way to make another enemy when the Italians already had superior air and naval forces in the area. Moreover, the attitude of the Spanish government could become more hostile, and Gibraltar was impossible to defend against a determined air attack. Force H was still untrained, and the destroyers based in Gibraltar had limited range. The main enemy was Italy, and so far Force H had not fired a shot in anger at them.

The French fleet affair was not yet over. The following day, 4 July, the *Ark Royal* readied an attacking force of Swordfish and Skuas armed with semi armour-piercing bombs in order to carry out a dive-bombing attack on the beached *Dunkerque*. Force H ran into thick fog, however, and by 0600 hours the *Ark* decided to abandon the attack because of the danger to planes from anti-aircraft fire if they made their attack in broad daylight. Force H returned to Gibraltar. Somerville received orders to make sure that the *Dunkerque* was out of action by means of a further bombardment of the harbour. He was convinced that this would lead to even more casualties, particularly among the civilian population in the small villages north of where the *Dunkerque* lay. He asked for permission to attack the ship with torpedoes and bombs from the air, and this wish was granted.

Force H set out again, and on 6 July were once more to the west of Mirs el Kebir. Permission to use the Swordfish aircraft in a torpedo attack was received by Somerville at three that morning, so there was little time to plan the operation and prepare the aircraft. At 0520 the armed Swordfish were flown off the *Ark Royal* with an escort of Skua aircraft.

The attack was to be made by a first wave of six aircraft, and then two more waves of three aircraft each. The attack was complicated by the position of the *Dunkerque* because she was beached so close to the shore, near a battery of anti-aircraft guns, making a beam attack very hazardous. It was hoped that the aircraft could approach out of the rising sun to achieve an element of surprise. This was successfully completed by the first wave, which flew along the coast at about 7,000 feet, and as the sun rose above the horizon the flight leader, Lt Compton, led the aircraft in a shallow dive over the breakwater. They dropped all their torpedoes without any opposition. The flight claimed five out of the six torpedoes were successful in hitting the ship.

The next waves were not so lucky. The defences had been warned, and the air crew of the three Swordfish came under heavy anti-aircraft fire from the batteries. They had to take violent avoiding action, the black bursts of exploding shells as close as 80 yards. Captain Newson, the pilot of the lead Swordfish, reported that the sound of the explosions could be distinctly heard, and the concussion felt. They attacked the ship from the same direction as the previous flight, heading over the breakwater and launching their torpedoes at the starboard side of the *Dunkerque*. Captain Newson's air gunner fired at a group of sailors running to man a machine gun on the mole. As the three Swordfish made their getaway, behind the headland at Mirs el Kebir point, they saw a large explosion, and they assumed that one of the magazines had exploded. In fact a lighter had been moored next to the *Dunkerque* to offload ammunition, and it was this that had exploded, though it caused considerable damage to the hull of the battleship. The final wave took a different approach, attacking the port side by flying over land and coming in over the town of Mirs el Kebir. They too were fired on by the anti-aircraft guns, and scored a direct hit on a tug that completely disintegrated but they caused no other damage.

While making their getaway, the pilot of one of the Swordfish, Sub Lt Pearson, saw splashes on the sea in front of him and he realized that they were caused by machine-gun fire from above. The observer, Lt Prendergast, then saw a fighter breaking away, and almost immediately saw another fighter approaching out of the sun. Pearson turned very hard to the right, narrowly avoiding a burst of machine-gun fire, then doing the same to escape a third burst of fire from the French fighter. The fighter returned for a third attack from astern, and Pearson made a 180-degree dog-leg turn and dived beneath the fighter. The Swordfish was hit this time: a hole appeared in the port side of the engine cowling, the rear gun, torpedo release gear and radio were smashed, the tail controls and the right aileron were damaged, and several ribs in the lower right wing were destroyed. Despite this the Swordfish stayed aloft and the dogfight continued, Sub Lt Pearson extracting every advantage he could from his plane's low speed and manoeuvrability by flying along 100 feet above the sea. A third French fighter moved into the attack, and Pearson again executed a hard right turn, this time getting the fighter in his sights and firing off about fifty rounds with his front-mounted machine gun. The French fighters then abandoned the chase and Pearson returned to the *Ark Royal*.

The attack on the French fleet had been a bloody one, with a death toll of over two thousand and several warships completely disabled. The *Ark Royal*'s aircraft, the Skua fighters and the Swordfish torpedo bombers, had constantly been in the air and had shown how quickly they could make a variety of attacks. Somerville was grateful for their presence. Attacking the *Dunkerque* with torpedoes rather than using the *Hood* and the other battleships to shell her had saved a lot of civilian lives, and the pilots had shown that they were capable of making a successful attack in a well-defended harbour, and taking on land-based fighter aircraft. The attack on the *Strasbourg*, however, had not been decisive. The torpedoes, with their Duplex war-heads, were prone to failure, and their target, unlike the stationary *Dunkerque*, had been steaming along at 30 knots – a very different proposition.

For Somerville, however, this was a minor issue. He had made his objection to this unilateral declaration of war against the French quite obvious, not only to his fellow admirals but to Sir Dudley Pound and the Prime Minister. It didn't go down well with them. Churchill spoke in the House of Commons a few days later to answer his critics and justify his actions against the French fleet. He made it plain that in his view the operation had been a success. It had demonstrated to the world that Britain, under his command, was prepared to be ruthless and to take whatever action was necessary to fight the war in which it was engaged. In a way the shelling of the French fleet had been Churchill's personal declaration of war, a signal that there would be no going back. The first shots in Britain's war against

Germany and Italy, the fascist axis of Europe, had been fired in the Mediterranean, albeit against the French, and Force H and the *Ark Royal* were in the front line.

6

THE *ODIN FINDER*

My plan to search for the *Ark Royal*, which was meant to be the focus of a story about the Royal Navy in general and what I was increasingly thinking of as the battle of the Mediterranean in particular, had so far gone very well, but it was not without its difficulties.

I had worked out the logical place to search for the *Ark Royal*, and in collaboration with Rick Davey of C&C Technologies, the Louisiana-based surveying company, I had calculated how to do it, but it took another six months before I was able to put any of these ideas into effect. We had decided to survey the sea floor in the part of the Mediterranean where the *Ark Royal* sank using a hull-mounted sonar device on a boat called the *Odin Finder*. Rick had been working with the company that owned the boat, and it seemed the most economical way to search a large area. The plan was to make use of the *Odin Finder* in the few days available between major surveying contracts. The months went by, however, and that summer there were gales in the Mediterranean that reached speeds of over 70 knots, making survey work impossible. I waited and waited. The pipeline survey the *Odin Finder* was carrying out dragged on and on. Finally, one morning in July, Elisabetta Faenza, a director of the company GAS that owned the boat, telephoned me. The *Odin Finder* would be putting into Almeria on the southern coast of Spain in a week's time, and would be ready to take me out to sea. I couldn't have been happier.

As I boarded my plane at Heathrow I was relieved that at last I was going to see some concrete action after all the research, planning and telephoning that had gone on over the past few months. It was now over half a year since I had first discussed searching for the *Ark Royal* with Hugh McKay, the salesman at Kongsberg Simrad in Aberdeen. I had raised some money for this search on the understanding that it would be the centrepiece of a television series about the history of the Royal Navy. Even with these funds we would be dependent on companies like GAS and C&C Technologies providing time and equipment at well below their commercial rates. But finding enough money to produce the whole series had not been going very well. Documentaries can be quite expensive to make, particularly if they involve filming underwater, and it was vital to raise more cash from foreign broadcasters. For the BBC, that meant the Discovery Channel in the United States, and not surprisingly they questioned why a US audience would be interested in British history. The upshot was that the BBC couldn't afford to make a series about the Royal Navy because it was too British. There was little I could do about this, but I was banking on the fact that success in finding the *Ark Royal* would put fresh life into the TV series. There was a lot resting on this trip.

In retrospect, even at this early stage I should have considered whether it was wise to continue the search, but I had already invested too much of my time and energy. What had started out as a slightly romantic dream of finding the wreck of a very famous ship had become something too tangible to walk away from. At the start of my research, with the sixty-year-old documents recording the sinking, I had become doubtful about the prospects of success. The process of looking closely at all the findings of the Board of Inquiry and working out how the search would be accomplished had, however, restored my confidence. The evidence I had gathered, including the various contradictory positions I had seen written down the edge of some aerial photo-graphs taken at the time, had to be viewed in perspective. Their accuracy, I reminded myself, was important only to me. It had not been important to the pilots and seamen at the time, for whom errors of a few miles could easily be corrected. Navigation sixty years ago was a question of using a compass, a chart and an assessment of wind and currents. For hundreds of years ships had navigated thousands of miles across the oceans; pilots and observers of the Fleet Air Arm patrolled over the sea for hundreds of miles and managed to locate their aircraft carrier again even though it might have moved 70 or 80 miles from the point where they took off. Occasionally pilots did get lost, but it was rare – testimony to the fact that their navigation skills were very good.

The *Ark Royal* had been torpedoed, and it was close to Gibraltar when it happened – there could be no doubt about that. We had worked out a number of different possible positions for the wreck's location, but I had my own hunch where we were going to find it. I felt sure it was going to lie on a line that connected the position where the torpedo struck the *Ark* to the furthest point to which the *Ark* could have been towed. Rick Davey and the people at GAS had looked over my evidence and seemed satisfied with my analysis. It was not therefore something I could easily abandon.

I arrived late in Almeria and went to meet the technicians from GAS who would do the survey. They were still in their hotel, because the *Odin Finder* had suffered another delay and was not due to arrive in port until the following day. It was the very first time I had met any of the people who were going to carry out the search. The chief surveyor, Massimo Magagnoli, was in his forties, with dark curly hair and a flamboyant, confident air about him. Elisabetta Faenza, the co-owner of GAS, had also come to Almeria and she was charming and elegant, although I got the impression that she did not often go to sea. Perhaps she felt it wiser to be on hand because of the unorthodox nature of the survey, and the customer. Over dinner I got on well with Massimo, Elisabetta and the three other young technicians, Alessandro, Sergio and Giorgio, and I realized that they had a long acquaintance, and clearly would work well together. It was reassuring. Massimo had worked out that we could travel at a rate of about 4 knots over the search area and that this would take about fifty hours, allowing us time to investigate any targets that we found. It would take a day to travel to the search area and then return, so we should be able to do everything we wanted in the three days we had agreed. I mentioned my concern about the accuracy of the sonar signals in the depth of water we would be working in, partly to show that I was not completely ignorant, but Alessandro had no doubts that the sonar on the *Odin Finder* could locate the wreck. 'It's a big wreck,' he reassured me. 'If it is there, we will find it.'

I hadn't realized that part of our search area was in Spanish waters and Elisabetta had had to obtain a licence to carry out the survey. She had said that the survey was for experimental purposes. The area was part of a busy shipping lane, and was also used as a submarine exercise area. The Spanish maritime authorities had suggested that an alternative area be used for the 'test', but had not insisted. So everything was in order, and all we needed now was the boat.

The next day, as promised, the *Odin Finder* cruised slowly into the port of Almeria. The area of the town closest to the old port is dominated by a covered elevated conveyor that once carried minerals and ore to the ships in harbour. But most of that industry has finished and the port is now mainly devoted to ferries taking passengers to North Africa and other destinations along the Mediterranean coast. The *Odin Finder* had a lonely berth on the far side of the harbour, but she was easy to spot. At 600 tons and about 50 metres in length she was much smaller than a car ferry, and had a distinctive 'A' frame winch on the rear deck. Fuel and fresh food were being loaded when we got to her, garbage was being thrown into containers on the quayside, and the captain was talking to port agents. Massimo took me to the canteen for a glass of wine and a plate of pasta, negotiating the narrow stairs and passageways of a working boat.

It was summer, and because of the busy ferry traffic out of the port of Almeria we could not get a pilot to take us out until seven that evening. But on time, with the pilot on board, we finally headed out past the lighthouse at the end of the mole. As I felt the bows lift to meet the swell of the open sea my heart filled with a sense of relief and anticipation. I was at last, after many months of waiting, starting the search for the wreck of the *Ark Royal*.

Before we had finalized our search area, Rick Davey had

asked some of the surveyors in his company, C&C Technologies, to make an assessment of the operation. Their view was that at best it had a fifty-fifty chance of success. I thought that was too pessimistic. I had sat at the desk in the Public Record Office and read and touched again the documents and drawings that had been produced sixty years ago. I believed that they held the key to finding the *Ark*. I was sure my calculations would prove correct, and I anticipated success. The line along which I believed the *Ark* lay crossed two of our planned survey lines, and I looked forward to locating the wreck on one of these survey lines by the end of the first day. We were due to start our first line of search, which would be the southernmost edge of our box, at about seven the next morning.

We headed west out of Almeria. Darkness fell, until the only things visible were the lights of ships on the horizon and the beams of distant lighthouses. Content that my search would soon be over, I went to my bunk and fell asleep.

The next morning I awoke to find that the noise of the engines was muted, and the boat was pitching and rolling. My view of the sky through the porthole was obscured every so often by white-capped waves surging past. I made my way to the bridge and discovered from the first officer that a storm had blown up in the night and we were sheltering near the coast, off Malaga. We could not conduct a survey in these conditions. In answer to my question of when the wind and the rough seas would ease, he shrugged. 'A few hours, maybe more.'

Finally, after several excruciating hours, we picked up speed. The weather was abating and there was the prospect that by the time we got to the search area it would be calmer. Over lunch, Massimo said that on our present course it would be quicker to start our search on the eastern edge of the survey area, head south, then run our first line on the southern side. Then we could go back to our original plan, gradually working north. Eager to make a start, I agreed. The eastern edge of our box was determined by the recorded position of the torpedo impact. I believed it was highly unlikely that we would find the wreck there, but who knew?

When a vessel is working on a survey, the ship is not really controlled from the bridge. The captain is responsible for maintaining a course and speed, and for the safety of the ship, but the ship is really directed by the survey team below decks. Because a survey ship has to follow a predetermined course and speed it has a right of way, and special lights and flags are hoisted at the masthead to warn other ships to alter course.

The survey team works in what is known as the lab. It isn't a laboratory at all, of course; it's a large room that can accommodate technicians, surveyors and representatives of companies hiring the boat. Around the room at various work stations are a variety of computer screens which are duplicates of the radar and Decca navigator screens on the bridge, but they also display, in various ways, visual interpretations of the sonar echoes returning from the sea floor. These echoes can be represented in a colour display as a plan or sideways view, each image gradually moving across the screen every second or so as the returns are processed. In the lab of most survey ships there is nothing to indicate that you are on a boat. On the *Odin Finder* there was one small window at the rear of the room that looked out over the rear deck. For the next two days, there would be two technicians on duty here day and night as we carried out our hunt. This was the nerve centre of the boat, and it was here that the first evidence of the wreck would be seen.

As soon as the *Odin Finder* entered our box of co-ordinates and turned south on the first leg, the big sonar machine in the hull switched on. From that point on I could not stay away from the lab. I forgot that this search might go on for two days and nights and that, although the survey technicians would be working in shifts, I had no-one to relieve me. But I could not bear the possibility that I would miss that revelatory moment of finding the *Ark*.

Within an hour the *Odin Finder* had suddenly slowed and gone off track. The images on the screen no longer depicted a steady increase in area. Instantly, Massimo was on the telephone to the bridge. I could not understand the Italian conversation, so I went out of the door onto the rear deck. A large bulk carrier with four giant cranes rising high above its deck was steaming past within a quarter of a mile of us, a big bow wave indicating its speed. It had paid scant attention to the signals at our masthead. I looked around and went up to the bridge. The radar there showed a lot of ships all around us, their projected courses crisscrossing our own. In the excitement of the search I had momentarily forgotten that we were crossing one of the busiest shipping lanes in the world. We were trying to cross the nautical equivalent of the M25. The captain had now taken over from the first officer on the bridge. He looked at the large ship passing close to us and shook his head. 'We cannot raise anyone on the bridge,' he said. 'Never mind. In half an hour we turn, head west and stick to the pattern. There should be no problems.'

Andrea Pupa, the captain of the *Odin Finder*, was a tall, quietly spoken, urbane man in his late forties who had been too busy while we were in Almeria to do anything but shake my hand. Now he turned and asked me if I was comfortable, and if I had slept well. We talked, and he was clearly curious about what I was trying to do. I filled him in on some of the background.

'But tell me, why do you think you can find this wreck?' he asked. He pulled the chart of the area out of a drawer and spread it on the table. 'Show me.'

I explained to him what I knew, and as I went through the story he drew little crosses on the chart, repeating what I had done a few months ago. Then he roughly drew a box around them. 'Mike, you know that the chances are slim,' he said. I explained that there were some discrepancies but that in a sense they had to cancel each other out. We knew the *Ark Royal* had sunk. We had drawn our search area large enough to accommodate any errors. Where else could the wreck be?

He pulled a fax out of a drawer that had been sent to him from C&C Technologies. It was the analysis that had been done for Rick Davey, which I had already seen. Andrea had highlighted the assessment that there was only a fifty-fifty chance of success. 'You know, I must say I agree with this,' he said. 'In my experience things are never where you think they are at sea. All these things happened sixty years ago.' I explained to him that I had seen the assessment and pointed out what I really felt about the Board of Inquiry, that it contained fresh evidence from eye witnesses. He looked sceptical. 'You know, people in circum-stances like a boat sinking, like any accident, they never remember very much.'

Then he asked an extremely difficult question: 'Do you know what you will do if you don't find it?'

I was silent. This was a question I had lived with for some time, but for which I had no answer. All I could say was, 'I have gone over all of these positions. I think we have made a lot of allowances for errors.'

Andrea was quiet for a moment. He was a sensitive man, and he realized he was touching a very delicate nerve.

'OK, very good. You know, Mike, we will do whatever we can to help you. If you have any problems, ask me.'

I believed him. The bread and butter work of underwater surveying can be extremely monotonous. Most of the people in the industry are intelligent and well educated and welcome the opportunity to search for something like the *Ark Royal*. It engages their intellectual curiosity in a way their daily work does not. Andrea's offer was heartfelt, I was sure.

But he had raised an issue that was very sensitive, and which I, for whatever reason, had refused to acknowledge. What I was trying to do was a huge gamble. I knew nothing about this business. I barely understood the technology, and others who had tried to locate the *Ark Royal* had failed in the past. There was no reason why I should succeed. I had been given enough money to pay for the *Odin Finder* for just three days. I had warned people that if three days was not enough I would probably ask for another day's surveying, but it had been made plain to me that this was not going to be popular. In the months since the idea of making the series about the history of the Royal Navy had first been proposed, it had proved expensive and difficult to fund. If I returned to London empty-handed having spent so much of the licence fee payers' money, I could not expect much mercy.

I went back to the control room. We had returned to our southerly track and had nearly reached the point where we were going to turn west and survey our first line along the southern edge of our search area. We had passed over the point where the *Ark* had been torpedoed and, as I'd expected, nothing had been picked out by our sonar. The captain's question had triggered a level of anxiety in me that nobody seemed to share. As the hours of searching passed, the excitement and tension grew. Sergio and Alessandro, the technicians on watch, were talking animatedly, occasionally glancing at the screens to make sure that we were on course, at the right speed, and that the sonar was working properly.

The *Odin Finder* travelled west, into the sunset silhouetting not the Rock of Gibraltar but Ceuta on the North African coast, the westerly current growing stronger as we approached the Straits. Then, at the end of that survey line, we turned and headed east, on our second line, and I stayed glued to the sonar screens. I was behaving irrationally, unable to tear myself away from the lab and its hypnotic screens in case I missed some discovery, not trusting the technicians on duty, whoever they were. Eventually, Massimo persuaded me to go to my bunk and sleep.

The next day I woke extremely early. Today we should be covering lines four and five, the area where I was convinced we would find the wreck of the *Ark Royal*. The weather was fairly calm but grey, a close mist hanging on the sea, obscuring the horizon. I went on deck. A school of pilot whales was slipping in and out of the waves just off the port side, dark grey and glistening, keeping pace with the boat then vanishing and reappearing a few hundred metres away. I went into the survey room, which was now becoming fetid with cigarette smoke and the smell of people who had stayed awake through the early hours. The two technicians on duty were playing rock music and talking animatedly. I looked at the screens. We were on our third line across the search area and nothing had so far been seen. Despite the fact that everything was being recorded by the computers I assiduously marked the stages of our survey on my own chart of the area. The next line of our survey would cross one of the lines I had plotted from the torpedo's impact to the point where, according to the Board of Inquiry, the tow had been abandoned. Over the next twelve hours we should be passing over a cluster of positions, one of which had to be the final resting place of the *Ark*.

I had a late breakfast in the canteen, walked around the deck, and on to the bridge. The *Odin Finder* was heading into the morning sun which was slowly burning off the haze over the sea. A small boat, workmanlike with its blue hull, white super-structure and orange day-glo patches, sailed sedately where sixty years ago great battleships, destroyers and the *Ark Royal* herself had sped out to war. I thought of the comments of Admiral Somerville, who remarked several times on the very difficult conditions the Straits of Gibraltar presented to his sonar operators hunting for enemy submarines. Huge differences in temperature and salinity caused by a mixture of Mediterranean and Atlantic waters created enormous blind spots, while often whales, rather than submarines, had been the recipients of depth charges dropped by patrolling Swordfish aircraft. Our sonar was far more sophisticated, or at least I hoped it was, and the pod of pilot whales whose fins could still occasionally be seen breaking the surface was safe now from sudden death.

All was quiet on the bridge, apart from the animated conver-sation between Elisabetta and the captain. Every so often Andrea would scan the horizon, check the screen that showed our position and the course of other ships moving around us, then resume the conversation that seemed to have no beginning and no end. He had a coffee brought up from the galley for me.

I felt slightly uneasy whenever I was out of the lab, but I knew that this was irrational. I couldn't understand why the technicians showed only a cursory interest in the screens that charted the progress of the survey, but I knew they would realize very quickly if there was any sign of anything out of the ordinary, even though in the event they would continue the line until the end. Most likely we would finish our survey of the whole area before returning to any target that seemed to require further investigation.

I returned to the survey room. We were about to start line four of our survey, and Sergio told me that nothing had been recorded on line three. This wasn't quite true. He showed me indications of two or three depressions in the sea floor, but in his view they were purely geological. I was surprised. When I had started discussing our survey with Rick Davey, we had both assumed that there would be several targets we might need to investigate further with the AUV that C&C Technologies had developed.

Still, I felt certain that the crucial area of our search was now approaching, the northern part of our search box. However irrational it was, at this point in the survey nothing could take me away from the computer screens. The *Odin Finder* proceeded slowly along the allotted course, the sonar returns appearing on the screens with metronomic regularity. Line four eventually finished. Nothing.

We turned into line five and slowly headed towards Gibraltar. Halfway along we started to see a sudden change in the sonar returns, the colour of the graph-like pattern on the screen changing from green to yellow, then a bright red. Yes! But Massimo, after glancing at the screen, returned to his conversation. Almost in disbelief at his indifference, I asked what he thought it could be. He looked again. 'It's very high,' he said. 'Almost 50 metres.'

'Is it the *Ark*?' I asked eagerly.

'I think it's a hill.'

As the returns continued, his analysis was confirmed. The object was 60 metres high and almost 300 metres in width. It was nothing like the *Ark*.

Eventually line five finished too and we returned for line six. The journey along this line became almost unbearable for me. The fate of the whole enterprise rested on what we would find over the next few hours. But apart from more returns from the hill we had located on the previous line, again we saw nothing.

As we neared the end of line six, I went out on deck. This trip over a balmy Mediterranean had lost its charm. The sun was silhouetting the Rock of Gibraltar, and once again the pod of pilot whales was keeping the ship company. I was exhausted, from tension and lack of sleep. The rear deck was noisy with the clang of chains against the 'A' frame and the pounding of the diesels, and there was no escaping the fumes from the engine room uptakes. I waited for the ship to turn, then went into the survey room again. This was the last chance. The next four hours had to bring success.

My tension produced a chilling effect in the survey room. The sociable conversation between the team members ebbed away as we slowly proceeded east. Massimo disappeared halfway through the line, but I paid little attention. Minor changes in the sea bed would raise my hopes, only to see them dashed as they became another part of the sea bed's undulations. As we neared the end of line seven, and the most northerly part of our search area, I experienced a sudden onset of extreme depression. Before we got to the end I knew I had failed.

I sat in the lab not knowing what to do. I had made some miscalculation but did not know what it was. There were disjointed discussions going on behind me, and I felt the ship turn. The phone in the survey room rang and Giorgio handed it to me. It was the captain.

'Mike, can you come to the bridge?'

I knew what he was going to say. I had come to the end of the period we had contracted for, and Andrea obviously wanted to discuss the logistics of our arrival back in port.

I went up to the bridge. Massimo was already there, and it was clear that he and Andrea had already been talking to each other. This must have been the reason he had left the survey room earlier. They had several charts spread out on the table in the bridge.

'So, nothing, eh?' Andrea said.

'Massimo,' I said, 'are you sure the equipment is working OK?'

He looked at me and smiled, although in retrospect he could have been forgiven for being angry. 'That's what everyone says, Mike. Listen, last year we searched in the Adriatic for a Jaguar aircraft that had crashed in the sea. The air force guy was certain he knew where it was. The pilot had got out, they had a GPS position, and they knew exactly where the plane crashed. But we did not find it, and they blamed our equipment. But we found it quite a way away. And here you have no GPS, and it is sixty years ago.'

'Mike, why are you looking here?' Andrea asked.

I knew the assessment from C&C Technologies was at the back of the captain's mind. I went over the story once again, from the torpedo to the eye witness report of the sinking, marking the points on the chart.

'But what about the sinking? How did it happen?'

I recounted what I had read in the evidence. The ship had capsized sufficiently for the hole in her side to be identified, suggesting to me that the *Ark* had turned completely over. Andrea then said that the *Ark* could have drifted for some time, just below the surface. 'What goes on below the surface is strange,' he said. 'Ships don't necessarily sink straight away. She may have just hung in the water and drifted for some time.' He looked at the chart. 'The question is, where?'

'It is unfortunately a very big sea,' said Massimo.

'This is where the currents go,' Andrea continued, pointing at the chart, 'so if she was sinking slowly and drifting, that means we should look in deeper water. That is what I would do. But it is your search. We can give you another day, but you must decide what to do with it.'

'We will finish the eastern line,' Massimo added, 'then in one hour you must decide what to do. Where shall we go – north, east, west or south?'

I was stunned. Andrea and Massimo had decided that they wanted to find the *Ark* if they could, to the extent that the *Odin Finder* was mine for another twenty-four hours. No mention had been made of an additional fee, so Elisabetta must have agreed to the extension, although she was nowhere to be seen.

I went down to the lab and pored over my own charts. The meeting had banished my sense of isolation, and I felt a wave of gratitude for their support, though I had no idea what to do. Andrea's advice was probably sound, but I had little to go on. Massimo had retrieved a chart of the surface currents in the Mediterranean. We knew from our search that currents changed throughout the day, becoming faster as the day wore on. But Andrea believed that the *Ark* had drifted below the surface and we knew nothing about the behaviour of the sea at depth.

Massimo entered the survey room. The time to make a decision was approaching, and nobody was going to make it for me. I looked again at the chart, drew a deep breath and said, 'We'll go this way.' I drew two lines that extended the search area by another 32 square miles. After a brief conversation with the bridge the *Odin Finder* changed course, and the deed was done.

Elisabetta, Andrea and Massimo had thrown me a lifeline – or had they merely extended the agony? I thought there was a lot of sense in what Andrea had said, and certainly he and the survey crew had more experience than I. But if the *Ark* had drifted for some time below the surface, she could have ended up fifty or more miles away, in any direction. For the next few hours I paced backwards and forwards on the rear deck, staring at the darkening sea and the pinpoints of light on the southern coast of Spain. A small voice in my head persistently told me that I had taken the wrong decision, that I was headed in the wrong direction, that if there were any errors then they were in the recorded position of the *Ark* when she was torpedoed, and that she had headed further north than I had calculated.

I went to the galley for a meal and a glass of wine. Massimo and Andrea were there, and I joined them. Their obvious commitment to the success of this search had removed any reservations I had about revealing my doubts, and I told them that I was anxious that we were heading in the wrong direction. Andrea was emphatic: if the currents and the sea bed were to be taken into consideration, then it didn't matter where the *Ark* had been torpedoed; we were searching in the direction she *had* to take. Of course, he added, if we were out by 50 miles then we were lost.

Later that night, at about two a.m., I went to the darkened survey room. We had covered another line and drawn another blank. Every second the screens depicted another line of sonar echoes, getting slightly bluer as the depth increased. I stayed for an hour, but then the fatigue of the past few days really hit me. I was convinced now that I had failed, and that tomorrow I would need to think about where I went from here. I did not know how I was going to explain my failure. It seemed obvious that with nothing to show for the amount of money that had been spent the series on the history of the Navy was never going to see the light of day. Yet, depressing as this was, I knew that my failure to find the *Ark Royal* would have far more serious personal consequences. I had done all that I could to work out the area we had so fruitlessly searched. If I had made an egregious mistake then I could perhaps better come to terms with my defeat, but I could not see where I had gone wrong. Yet I had failed, and I knew that nobody would be more critical of that than I. I knew that when I got back to the UK I would feel seriously demoralized. Then again, I have always been blessed with a somewhat fatalistic temperament.

Once more I retired to my cabin. I was so exhausted that despite the heat I went straight to sleep. At eight o'clock in the morning I woke up, showered, and went to the lab.

Massimo was there. 'Mike, we have a contact,' he said.

'What do you mean?'

'We saw something about two hours ago. There is something there.'

'Why didn't you wake me?' I spluttered. I couldn't believe they had let me sleep.

'It was on the edge of the track. We will finish this line in half an hour and then we will go back. Then we can be certain. But look at this.'

I looked at the picture Massimo brought up on the screen from two hours ago. Sure enough, right on the edge of the swathe of our sonar beam a sudden blip of red showed in the blue. It lasted for two pulses, then it was gone. I reminded myself that we had been fooled like this before, by holes and the edges of sea mounts in other parts of the search area. I stared at the screen. Could I dare to raise my hopes this time? Massimo turned the screen back to real time. He had a very good idea of what was going on in my mind.

'Mike, go and have breakfast,' he said. 'In two hours we will have a better view.'

He was right. There was only one way to do this and that was the methodical, professional way in which the crew of the *Odin Finder* normally worked. If it was there, we would find it. Excitement wouldn't change anything.

I went for coffee and some fresh pastries, and after that for a walk on deck. The sky was grey, a mist hanging over the sea, a pale yellow sun threatening to burn through in an hour or so. I steeled myself to stay calm, to be prepared for a false alarm, and went to the lab.

The ship was on the next track, heading in the opposite direction. As we approached the point where we had seen the anomaly we now had an overlap, and there was the hard red blip again, slap bang in the middle of the swathe of sonar pulses. Massimo was intent now. 'It's 20 metres high,' he said.

'Is it a rock?' I asked.

He twiddled a few knobs and changed to a different representation on the screen. 'I think it is man-made.' Then it was gone again. 'We will finish this line,' he said, 'then come back and take another angle.'

'Do you have the time?' I asked.

He grinned. '*Certo*. Of course.'

Two hours later, we were looking at the anomaly again. The EM 3000 sonar mounted on the *Odin Finder* was not the most up-to-date piece of equipment, but the computers on board could still extract a lot of information from the reflected sound beams, and Massimo interpreted it for me. 'It is 20 metres high and maybe 200 metres long. I think it is the right size.' Those were the dimensions of a wreck the size of the *Ark Royal*, resting on its keel. Massimo was certainly treating the signals as though this were a significant object.

I looked at the screen, though it was hard for me to understand what he was investigating. The objects seemed relatively insignificant in the kilometre swathe of sonar signals. It was only the sudden change in height above the sea floor that indicated something was there. And there was another puzzling thing about the contact. There were in fact two targets, the large one and a smaller one, separated by almost a kilometre. Massimo's analysis was that both targets were reflecting as though they were metallic and man-made, with sharp, definite edges. It *was* a significant object, the first one we had found in over three days of endlessly probing the sea floor with our sonar beams.

The *Odin Finder* had done its job, and the crew made preparations for the trip back to Almeria. All the technicians crowded into the survey room, and there was a sense of achievement and satisfaction that they had done the job. Elisabetta also came down and congratulated me. 'Mike, well done, you have found it. I am so pleased for you,' she said. I thanked her, profoundly, and I went off and thanked Andrea as well.

But as we headed back to Almeria and the results of the survey were downloaded and printed off in the various forms underwater surveyors use (I still have a chart of 289 square nautical miles of the Mediterranean sea floor contoured in rich blues and magentas), I realized that there was much still to do. All we had found was a target that needed further investigation. I was slowly appreciating that I was working in a profoundly abstract world. The object of my search was deep on the ocean floor, so deep that I would most likely never be able to see it with my own eyes, certainly never touch it. Furthermore, I had no idea what it looked like. We had ascertained the shape and position of this target with at best a hundred individual sonar echoes, but when I looked at the hard copy coming out of the chart printer that was located in the lower decks of the *Odin Finder* it was just a black and white pattern that looked like the interference on a television screen. Lines running across the frame correlated with dates and times and the position in degrees, minutes and seconds, and there in the middle were two solid black square shapes, one larger than the other.

It was not a great deal to show for our efforts, or, I thought, to assuage the almost crushing sense of defeat I had experienced just hours earlier. I had my doubts about whether it was enough to persuade the powers-that-be in the BBC to go ahead with more investigation. I had a target, but was it really the *Ark Royal*?

7

THE MEDITERRANEAN WAR BEGINS

Force H under Admiral Somerville had carried out their attack on the French fleet and had permanently disabled the battleships *Dunkerque* and *Bretagne*, but the *Strasbourg*, the most modern battleship in the fleet, had escaped and had managed to seek sanctuary precisely where the Admiralty did not want her, in the French home port of Toulon.

Somerville now had to consider how Force H could replace the French fleet as the gatekeepers of the western Mediterranean. It was unclear in July 1940 just how aggressive an enemy the French would be. There was no doubt, however, that the fascist government of Italy would seek to increase its influence in the area. Somerville had already experienced the combative attitude of the Italian Navy during the Spanish Civil War, when he had been in command of the Destroyer Flotilla of the Mediterranean Fleet.

Italian forces in the western Mediterranean were numerically far superior to anything Somerville could command. Their warships were all modern or modernized, fast and well armed, with several bases and full repair facilities in important ports like Taranto and Genoa. They could shift their forces fairly easily from the eastern to the western Mediterranean, and they had a string of agents in sympathetic or neutral countries bordering the sea who constantly monitored the movements of the British fleet. After the *Hood* was withdrawn from Force H to the Home Fleet, on the fourth of August, all that Somerville could command was his usual flagship the *Renown*, modernized but slow when compared to the modern Italian battleships, the *Ark Royal*, a radar-equipped cruiser like *Sheffield* and a flotilla of destroyers. In addition, the Italian Air Force had bases that stretched from the north of Italy to Sicily and Sardinia, and could assemble concentrations of both high-level and torpedo bombers with fighter protection throughout the central Mediterranean. In Norway, *Ark Royal*'s aircraft and the Royal Navy generally had experienced the dangers of operating against an enemy that could call on modern land-based bombers and fighters. They had never fought against the Italian Air Force, but the *Ark Royal*'s air crew were still flying the Skua fighter bombers that had proved so vulnerable to the Messerschmitts over Trondheim harbour in May.

One of the problems the *Ark* faced was that its deck lifts were narrow and could only accommodate aircraft built with folding wings. In July, Captain Holland had asked the Admiralty for work to be done to widen the lifts so that RAF planes like the Hurricane could be used, but the *Ark* had been designed with the flight deck as the main strength deck, and any modifications would need a major refit in a shipyard. The *Ark* could not be spared for this length of time. So Somerville had to rely on the three squadrons of Swordfish reconnaissance torpedo bombers and the two squadrons of Skua fighter bombers the *Ark* normally carried. They were Force H's aggressive force against the Italian Navy, and other targets, and its defensive shield against submarines and attack from the air.

Knowledge of how they would survive in this new and hostile environment arrived quickly. Churchill and the Admiralty wanted to take advantage of any surprise British aggression against the French fleet might have caused, and ordered a strike against the mainland of Italy. Three days after Force H returned to Gibraltar from the second attack on the *Dunkerque* it sailed once again, this time to attack the Italian base at Cagliari in Sardinia. Somerville had been urged by the Admiralty to take the *Hood*, *Valiant* and *Resolution*, the battleships still under his command, to bombard the port and the Naval Air Station at Elmas in Sardinia. Somerville demurred, believing that the bombardment would force the ships to steam too close to the Italian bases, leaving them vulnerable to mining and submarine attack. Instead, he planned to launch an air attack with Swordfish bombers.

On 8 July, Force H sailed from Gibraltar. It was a significant force, comprising the *Hood*, the *Valiant* and the *Resolution* as well as the *Ark* and the cruisers *Arethusa*, *Faulkner* and *Delhi*. Eight hours later three waves of Italian bombers flew over the fleet and started their bombing run. The struggle between the Royal Navy and the Italian Air Force, which had been anticipated for several years, had finally arrived. The hostile aircraft were not detected by the cruisers' radar and the first wave of aircraft were seen only a few seconds before their bombs fell. They exploded with loud cracks and the accompanying spouts of water but did not cause any damage. A second wave of aircraft was then observed by radar, and by 1750 hours the anti-aircraft guns of the fleet were blazing. A third wave also managed to approach without being detected, but were fired on before they could release their bombs.

Forty aircraft attacked Force H, dropping over a hundred bombs, which Somerville thought were 500lb high-explosives. Had they hit a ship they would have caused some damage but would not have managed to sink it. They could, however, have caused chaos on the *Ark Royal* if one had penetrated the flight deck. The *Ark*'s Skuas were in the air during the attacks and their pilots claimed that two enemy aircraft had been shot down and two damaged by anti-aircraft fire, although they thought that the anti-aircraft fire was generally not that accurate. It was Somerville's opinion, and presumably of those on the *Ark* who had experience of the Norwegian campaign, that the accuracy of the high-level bombing was close to that of the Luftwaffe.

The Norwegian experience was still very much on the Navy's mind, and Somerville was very unhappy about the situation that was developing in the Mediterranean. In his Report of Proceedings, he wrote quite clearly: 'As a result of this, our first contact with the Italian Air Force, it appeared to me that the prospects of the *Ark Royal* escaping damage whilst operating within 100 miles of the coast the following morning were small. I therefore decided the Force should withdraw to the west and proceed at its highest speed in order to increase the range from Sardinian aerodromes.' Somerville had retreated. The Italian Air Force had caused no damage to the British fleet, but had won a victory nevertheless.

To compound Somerville's failure, on 11 July two destroyers attacked an Italian submarine on the surface. While one of the destroyers was attempting to ram the submarine, the other was torpedoed, and it later sank. In the ensuing hunt for the submarine, Italian aircraft scored some near-misses on the destroyer *Foxhound*. It was a chastening experience for Somerville, and it showed quite clearly that the Italian Navy and Air Force were not going to let the Royal Navy do what it wanted in the Mediterranean.

In a letter to the First Sea Lord, Somerville set out his fears. 'Calling off the attack on Cagliari was a most distasteful decision to make,' he wrote, 'but I felt it was most improbable you would want *Ark Royal* put out of action in view of our limited objective.' It was clear that the lack of warning of air attack from radar was a major problem. *Valiant*, one of the battleships in Force H which had radar, was able to report the presence of aircraft, but it was impossible for the operators to tell which were hostile and which were the defending Skuas. 'The Skuas failed to locate any enemy aircraft until late in the afternoon,' Somerville continued, 'when they shot one down. The first bombing attack at 1630 was unobserved until the bombs fell.' Then, commenting on the destroyers' failure to sink the submarine (their depth charges were set to safe), he wrote, 'This shows how essential it is for the units of this force to be properly worked up. Until they are I can have no confidence that they are ready to do their stuff.'

Over the next two weeks Somerville did start to work them up. Ships in harbour were given daily exercises in communication, height finding, target spotting and other air defence procedures. Practice gun firing with live rounds, of both main armament and anti-aircraft guns, was also carried out at sea to the east of Gibraltar.

It was not long before Force H again had to put to sea and face the Italian Air Force. Malta had been abandoned as a naval base in 1936 during the crisis over the Italian invasion of Abyssinia, but the decision to attempt to maintain British control of the Mediterranean meant that the island now had to be defended, and more fighter aircraft were needed to ward off attacks by Italian bombers over Malta's towns and harbours. Operation Hurry was the plan conceived to achieve this – the delivery of Hurricane aircraft from the UK to Malta. No-one knew at the time how massive these operations would become; several hundred aircraft would eventually be taken to the island. Malta became the base from which all offensive operations against the Italians, and the Germans in North Africa, were mounted. The maintenance of this island in a hostile sea was to absorb an enormous amount of the *Ark*'s war effort.

The plan was that the old First World War aircraft carrier the *Argus* would sail from England with twelve Hurricane aircraft on deck, escorted by four destroyers. On reaching Gibraltar, the *Argus* and the destroyers would form up with Force H and sail for Malta. When the *Argus* had reached a safe distance from the island the Hurricanes would fly off the flight deck to Malta. It was thought that the RAF pilots could not fly and navigate at the same time, particularly over the sea, so they were to be led to their destination by two Navy Skua aircraft.

The mission to bomb Cagliari was now to be incorporated into this overall operation, with the intention of preventing the use of the airfield by the Italian Air Force and misleading them about the true purpose of Force H's departure from Gibraltar. Somerville assumed that the Italians had spies in the Spanish town of Algeciras, constantly monitoring British ships arriving and departing from Gibraltar. In order to mislead these watchers, Force H often left Gibraltar and headed west, steaming into the

Atlantic for several hours before changing course and passing east into the Mediterranean through the Straits under the cover of night.

As they made their way eastwards, the *Ark Royal* and Force H were on alert for the expected presence of the Italian Air Force. At eight in the morning of 1 August, one day into the mission, a section of three Skuas took off from the *Ark* to intercept Italian aircraft that were shadowing the fleet.

Robert Elkington, the telegraphist, put his experience in the Mediterranean before the war to good use. 'One of my duties was direction finding, and the Italians used a frequency very close to that of our aircraft. I heard this peculiar un-English Morse – I swung my compass coil and got him nice and true and clean. I kept reporting it, and the Communications Officer plotted a rough position and fighters were sent and before long we got "Tally ho" on the radio. It was a three-engine Cant and it was immediately shot down of course. From then on, almost as soon as we left Gib, a search would be on all the time by radio or radar, for Italian reconnaissance planes.'

Later in the day, the anti-aircraft gun crews went to action stations and six more Skuas took off to form a defensive air patrol over the fleet. Sure enough, thirty minutes later the first wave of Italian aircraft was seen approaching. The ack-ack started, but despite the training Somerville had given the gun crews over the last two weeks it still appeared to be inaccurate. However, it was more concentrated and made a more effective barrage, and when a second wave of nine bombers attacked from a different angle the fleet was able to make a rapid change of course and continue firing at both waves of bombers. One of them was hit, and most of the bombs fell short.

About eighty bombs were dropped by the Italian aircraft, but

Somerville was of the opinion that the attack was much less determined than the previous one in July. Whether this was due to more effective anti-aircraft fire or the fact that the *Ark*'s pilots were in the air waiting for the bombers was hard to say. One of the Italian bombers was shot down by a Skua, of 803 Squadron, and no more attacks from the Italian Air Force took place that day.

The *Ark Royal* and the *Hood*, with a cruiser and a group of destroyers, then separated and set off for the position where the Swordfish would fly off to attack the aerodrome at Cagliari, leaving the main fleet with *Argus* and its Hurricanes to continue eastwards. At two thirty in the morning of 2 August, a group of Swordfish, nine carrying bombs and three armed with mines for the harbour, flew off the deck of the *Ark Royal*. One aircraft crashed into the sea, and its crew were lost; the rest headed off into a westerly wind that threatened to slow them down and delay their arrival over the target.

This attack was a crucial event for the *Ark Royal* and its air crew, and indeed for Admiral Somerville. He was in charge of a still untrained fleet operating against a still untested enemy with the awareness that he was responsible for the *Ark Royal*, an extremely valuable ship he could not afford to lose. He had abandoned this mission the previous month because he had judged that it was not worth the risk to the carrier. That risk had not really diminished, and in a letter to his wife he revealed his very human anxieties about the operation:

At 2.30 a.m. in the pitch dark on Friday as we were mucking about only 100 miles or so off the Itie coast I thought of all the possibilities – destroyers, MTBs [motor torpedo boats], submarines, cruisers, bombing attacks at daylight, etc. – and began to feel that it was all a bit sticky and the temperature of my feet dropped appreciably.

And then in the pitch dark I saw a small shadow separate itself from the great shadow of the *Ark*. The first Swordfish taking off. And then I thought of those incredibly gallant chaps taking off in the pitch dark to fly 140 miles to a place they've never seen, to be shot up by A/A guns and dazzled by searchlights and then, mark you, to fly over the sea and find that tiny floating aerodrome with the knowledge that if they don't find it they're done. Well, that shook me up and I realized how small my personal difficulties were compared to theirs.

It was daylight when the Swordfish reached their target. They were met with heavy anti-aircraft fire, and one of the aircraft was badly damaged and had no choice but to land on the enemy airstrip. But the two hangars were hit and in flames, four aircraft were blown up, and several buildings were destroyed or badly damaged. In addition, three mines were dropped in the harbour at Cagliari. The *Ark*, meanwhile, had changed course to meet up with the remainder of the fleet after the Hurricanes and their Skua guides had flown off the *Argus*, and by eight in the morning the Swordfish had returned to the *Ark* and both groups of ships had re-formed into one fleet.

Throughout the day the *Ark*'s Swordfish and Skua squadrons maintained patrols as part of the anti-submarine screen, and as fighter cover for the fleet. At midday, a reconnaissance aircraft was located by the radar set on the *Valiant*; a Skua intercepted it and shot it down. By the afternoon of 4 August all the ships of Force H were back in Gibraltar. There had been some casualties among the Swordfish squadrons on the *Ark* but the operation was a great success. A squadron of Hurricane aircraft had reinforced

Malta, an Italian aerodrome had been bombed, and an attack on the fleet by Italian bombers had been repulsed by a combination of anti-aircraft fire and the *Ark Royal*'s fighters. Operations were possible against the Italian mainland, and the Italian Air Force was not as deadly as Somerville had feared. The planning and the training he had introduced as a matter of urgency had apparently paid off, and Force H had begun to establish itself in the Mediterranean.

Admiral Somerville left Gibraltar on the *Hood* on 4 August bound for Scapa Flow, and then went by train to London. He had been called to a meeting at the Admiralty to discuss the next major operation the *Ark Royal* was going to carry out, Operation HATS, or 'Hands Across the Sea', which was designed to reinforce the Royal Navy's Mediterranean Fleet under Admiral Cunningham in Alexandria. A modern aircraft carrier, *Illustrious*, and the battleship *Valiant* with two cruisers and some destroyers were to be escorted from Gibraltar to Malta, where guns were going to be unloaded from the *Valiant*; from there the ships, to be known as Force F, would make for Alexandria, the main British base in Egypt. This fleet of warships could travel fast enough through the Mediterranean to avoid attacks from submarines, and both *Illustrious* and *Ark Royal* would be able to launch enough fighters to repel any attack from the air.

The operation was complicated, however, by the desire of Churchill and the War Cabinet to use the opportunity to transport tanks to Alexandria to reinforce the British Army under General Wavell. Wavell was planning to launch an offensive against the Italian Army in Tripoli and needed to build up his forces. Somerville objected to the inclusion of heavy tank-carrying ships on the grounds that the transports would inevitably slow the fleet down and make it more vulnerable. Most of the reinforcements for Alexandria and the British Army in Egypt went via the Cape Route, although this added weeks to their journey time, but in Somerville's view this was by far the safest route. Admiral Cunningham had also sent a written memo to Sir Dudley Pound, the First Sea Lord, backing up Somerville, and their combined objections carried the day. Churchill, however, thought that they and the Admiralty were being far too cautious. He was to return to the question later.

Somerville travelled back to Gibraltar in HMS *Renown*, the ship that was to remain his flagship for some time, and he was accompanied on this journey by the *Illustrious* and the other ships that were going to reinforce the fleet in the eastern Mediterranean. On 30 August they set out from Gibraltar. *Illustrious*, unlike the *Ark Royal*, carried her own radar, and three other ships, the cruisers *Coventry* and *Sheffield* and the battleship *Valiant*, were similarly equipped. With four radar sets at his disposal Somerville would be able to steer the fighters on to approaching bomber formations, and at the same time keep an eye out for other incoming enemy aircraft.

On the second day out of Gibraltar radar detected a shadower, and the standing patrol of three Skua aircraft was directed towards it by radio. After a 55-mile chase, Lt Spurway, the leader of the Skua section, fired a burst of machine-gun fire into the Cant floatplane, which caught fire and started to break up. Two of the crew managed to bale out. Four hours later the radar operators detected another Italian reconnaissance aircraft, and the standing air patrol of three Skuas was again successfully directed to shoot it down.

Diversionary attacks on the aerodrome and seaplane base at Cagliari were planned again, but this time there were to be two of them on two separate days. The first attack on Elmas aerodrome took off at five minutes past three in the morning of 1 September. Nine Swordfish aircraft armed with four 250lb bombs formed up over a floating flare dropped in the sea ten miles from the *Ark*. Their attack was made at six in the morning. When they dived to their bombing height of 3,000 feet they were fired at by anti-aircraft guns, but they succeeded in dropping their bombs and starting several fires and were able to rendezvous with the *Ark Royal* by eight o'clock. The second attack took place the next night, although this time the target was obscured by low cloud and fog. The Swordfish dropped several flares but could not identify any targets. They fired at some searchlights, but jettisoned their bombs into the sea before returning to the *Ark*.

Somerville reported that the force had remained in effective bombing range of Italian airbases for at least forty-eight hours. The crew had been at Action Stations for long periods of time. Heavy air attack had been anticipated, and indeed hoped for, because he was confident that with the number of fighters available to him and the number of anti-aircraft guns mounted on the ships he would be able to deliver a blow to the Italian Air Force which might have a telling and lasting effect. Somerville thought that the absence of any aggressive move by the Italians against the fleet could be accounted for by the quick destruction of reconnaissance aircraft on the first day, and the first attack on the aerodrome at Elmas, as well as nervousness on the part of the Italians at the concentration of fighters the carriers could launch.

The *Ark Royal* and its air crew had proved their worth to Somerville. In little more than eight weeks since retreating in the face of an overwhelming air offensive, Force H supplied Malta with a badly needed squadron of Hurricane fighters having escorted a fleet of reinforcements through one half of the Mediterranean. Aircraft from the *Ark Royal* had carried out two attacks on Italian airbases and had accounted for several Italian bombers and reconnaissance aircraft with the loss of only one of their own aircraft. The *Ark* and Somerville could be justifiably proud of their achievements.

It wouldn't last.

The *Ark Royal* was detached from Force H and went to West Africa to assist in the attempt to persuade the French African colonies to switch their allegiance from the Vichy government to the Free French Forces under General De Gaulle. When this mission ended in failure, the *Ark* sailed north to Liverpool, where she spent some time in dock for a refit. Apart from repairs to parts of the main machinery, she was fitted with a new flight deck barrier that would help to speed up the process of aircraft landing.

Many new members of the ship's crew joined her at this time, and one of the squadrons of Skua fighter aircraft was replaced with a squadron of Fairey Fulmars, a fighter that was a variant of the Fairey Battle bomber. The plane had failed as a bomber in the RAF, being slow and unable to carry a significant bomb load. It was, however, faster than the Skua, and it carried more guns. As far as the Fleet Air Arm was concerned it was a stopgap machine over which they had little choice. As far as the pilots were concerned, the plane had strengths and weaknesses. Val Bailey, who had by this time managed to transfer to the Fleet Air Arm and was undergoing flying training, thought that the Fulmar was a marked improvement on the Skua. It had eight guns, just like the Hurricane, it was a solid, safe plane to deck-land, and it was very comfortable, like flying an armchair. But it just wasn't fast enough. The Swordfish squadrons were also new to the *Ark* and comprised newly trained air crew, many of whom were from the Volunteer Reserve, or hostilities-only servicemen who had joined the Navy because of the war and were not career naval officers.

Liverpool was under constant attack from the Luftwaffe during the time the *Ark Royal* was in Liverpool docks. Many of the crew believed that the *Ark* was as important a target as the city, so it was a disturbing time for all of them. They had endured air attacks in Norway and in the Mediterranean, but it was shocking to realize that Britain was also being bombed nightly, and that their relatives and sweethearts were also facing danger. The realities of the total war in which the British people were engaged were extremely harsh.

On 3 November the *Ark Royal* sailed from Liverpool and arrived in Gibraltar three days later. Almost immediately, on the 7th, she sailed with Force H on another mission to Malta, Operation Coat. This time the reinforcements were troops and warships for the Mediterranean Fleet. A total of 2,150 troops were embarked on the battleships *Berwick* and *Barham*, the cruiser *Glasgow* and six destroyers.

Force H had changed slightly by the time of the *Ark*'s return. The *Ark* was still under the command of Captain Cedric Holland, but the Vice Admiral (Aviation), Admiral Wells, who had been a flag officer on the *Ark*, had gone and not been replaced, so Somerville could exercise slightly more direct control over her. The cruiser HMS *Sheffield* had also joined Force H, and she had experience of working with the *Ark* as her radar direction ship during the Norwegian campaign. This collaboration was to be developed further over the next few months, and the relationship between the radar operators on *Sheffield* and the signals department and fighter direction officer on the *Ark* was to become an extremely proficient one. The disadvantages were that not only were the pilots on the *Ark* 'pretty green', as Somerville wrote to his wife, but the crews of many of the other ships had not had experience of working together and fighting off air attacks.

They were in action almost straight away. On the first day out of Gibraltar, at six o'clock in the evening, south of Sardinia, three Fulmar aircraft from 808 Squadron were preparing to land on the *Ark* when a Savoia Marchetti 79, a three-engine bomber, was identified by the *Sheffield*'s radar. The Fulmars were directed by radio telegraphy, Morse code, from the signallers on the carrier. The Italian aircraft was sighted by the leader of the Fulmars at 3,000 feet and they climbed to 6,000 feet where they themselves were spotted by the gunner of the Savoia Marchetti, whose pilot immediately dived at full speed down to sea level. The Fulmars chased the Italian bomber but they took some time to get within range because they had a relatively narrow margin of speed, and they were slowed by the drag from their landing hooks, which had already been lowered. When they reached sea level, the three Fulmars attacked the bomber from the rear in succession. The Italian aircraft crashed into the sea.

Yet another raid on Cagliari was planned to act as a diversion from the main force of ships. Nine Swordfish aircraft took off in the dark at 0430, their exhausts emitting blue flames and sparks in the dark. They formed up on a flame float dropped in the sea near the *Ark* and then headed for Elmas aerodrome. The Swordfish were armed with 250lb bombs, some fitted with delayed-action fuses, incendiary bombs and small high-explosive bombs. On their way to the target the planes passed through thick cloud, but all managed to arrive at roughly the same time, dropping their bombs from a height of 3,000 feet and causing some heavy fires to start. There was little enemy gunfire

German claims that they had sunk the *Ark* in 1939
were a godsend to the British Ministry of Information.
The claims were graphically illustrated in the *Nazi
Volkischer Beobachter* and broadcast by German
radio, giving the *Ark* international renown.

The *Ark* was everywhere. The German pocket battleship *Admiral Graf Spee* explodes off Montevideo harbour *(right)*. A stick of bombs narrowly misses the *Ark* off Norway *(below left)*. The air crew were not so lucky. Many were lost, and some are buried near Trondheim *(below right)*.

Bottom: The *Strasbourg (inset)* tries to escape. French sailors struggle to rescue their shipmates at Mirs el Kebir.

THE ILLUSTRATED LONDON NEWS

The World Copyright of all the Editorial Matter, both Illustrations and Letterpress, is Strictly Reserved in Great Britain, the British Dominions and Colonies, Europe, and the United States of America.

SATURDAY, JANUARY 6, 1940.

A COLUMN OF SMOKE SHOOTING HUNDREDS OF FEET INTO THE AIR PROCLAIMS THE IGNOMINOUS END OF THE "ADMIRAL GRAF SPEE": AN AMAZING AERIAL PHOTOGRAPH UNIQUE IN NAVAL HISTORY.

Above: Italian bombs again just miss the
Ark, and explosions obscure the *Ark* in the
Mediterranean *(inset).*

Right and below: Rear Admiral Somerville
congratulates the crew after another
successful convoy, and Spanish dancers
entertain them in Gibraltar. The censor
pencils out the warships in the
background.

Admiral Günther Lutjens *(right)* had commanded
several successful naval operations, and he was
rewarded with command of the *Bismarck*, the
most modern and powerful battleship afloat. Its
enormous firepower – it is pictured here firing at
night *(below)* – was a match for any British
warship. But when the *Bismarck* was spotted and
photographed by one of the *Ark*'s Swordfish
(bottom) Admiral Lutjens and most of his crew
had only a few more hours to live.

OPPOSITE PAGE:
Desperate oil-covered survivors from the
Bismarck struggle for life in the icy Atlantic *(top)*.
Just one week earlier, German Stuka dive
bombers had failed to halt the *Ark* in the
Mediterranean.

The *Ark* listed heavily almost immediately. Most of the crew abandoned ship directly onto the decks of HMS *Legion*. Black smoke poured out of the funnels as the engine room crew struggled to relight the boilers. The popular version of events described in the illustration proved to be highly misleading.

The Ark Royal sank within 25 miles of Gibraltar.

"She toppled over like a tired child
Her stern reared up for a moment & then gently she sank beneath the waves"
14 hours after being struck

"A powerful little tug appeared on the scene & proceeded to take the Ark Royal in tow."—a period of 12 hours.

"Gradually became less "Steam & sm evidence th Ark Royal w to help herse harbou

"The Ark Royal was listing alarmingly to starboard"

"I could see men sliding down ropes to the Destroyer's deck"

"Others leaped into the sea from a height of 70 feet—Carley floats were bobbing about the carrier's hull.

Destroyer takes off greater part of ship's company.

Below: This dramatic photograph shows the first crew members climbing down to the deck of the *Legion*. Ron Skinner in a white cap stands by a railing and watches the destroyer approach. To the left, further along the hull, Val Bailey and Percy Gick have started to lower a boat. All of the crew except one made it back to the UK *(left)*.

and all the planes and their crews were able to return to the *Ark Royal*, landing at 0745.

Two hours later, the combat air patrol of three Fulmars was again directed by radar to intercept another Italian spy plane, this time a Cant seaplane, that appeared at 0950. The three Fulmars were 5,000 feet above the Cant and dived to overtake it, using clouds as cover. They attacked in a V formation to the side of the aircraft, and then made another attack from the rear. The seaplane burst into flames and crashed.

It was a more serious situation two hours later on the same day when twenty-five Italian bombers attacked Force H and the troop-carrying warships. The formation of bombers approached at a height of 13,000 feet and were located by the radar on the *Sheffield* when they were 50 miles away and on a course towards the fleet. The three Fulmars on patrol were told to climb to 15,000 feet and the pilots saw the approaching bombers when they were 5 miles away from the Fulmars and about 10 miles away from the *Ark Royal*. The bombers were flying in a wide circle, so the Fulmars attacked the leader from the beam, their eight machine guns firing simultaneously, then breaking off and firing at any other bomber that appeared in their sights. This made no impression on the bombers, which continued their steady approach until they were in position to drop their bombs. They fell across the fleet in a straight line. There were explosions on both sides of the battleship *Barham* carrying its 700 soldiers, then on either side of the *Ark Royal*. Miraculously they all missed.

Three Skuas had also been flown off the *Ark* to assist the Fulmars, and they flew into a position to attack some of the rear sections of the bomber group. Lt Spurway, the leader of the section, said that all guns on the Skuas were fired until they stopped working. In all, over four thousand bullets were sent into the formation of bombers, but again this did not disrupt the attack. Lt Spurway commented bitterly, 'Our aircraft were at a great disadvantage as the speed of the enemy in formation was slightly higher than the top speed of the Skua. This lack of performance in our aircraft made it extremely hard to carry out effective attacks.' Somerville agreed with Lt Spurway's remarks, and added some worrying words of his own to the Report of Proceedings, the weekly report he was obliged to send to the Admiralty. He remarked that the fighters had seemed unable to break up the bomber attack, moreover that the anti-aircraft fire was again inaccurate, bursting too low. He went on to say that many of the pilots had very little experience, and the form of attack, from the beam, was probably not well judged. Furthermore, the observers in the new Fulmars wanted a gun, which of course they'd had in their previous aircraft, the Swordfish and the Skua, mounted in the rear cockpits. Trials were taking place with a sawn-off Lewis gun, reported Somerville.

The *Ark Royal* and Force H returned to Gibraltar on 11 November. Four days later the *Ark* again set sail, this time on Operation White, to cover the old aircraft carrier *Argus* which was ferrying twelve Hurricane fighters to reinforce the defences of Malta. But the winds started to increase in speed and the sea started to get rougher, so many of the flying operations were cancelled, though a section of fighters was kept at readiness in case any hostile aircraft were detected by radar.

Admiral Somerville then received reports that some Italian warships were in the area south of Naples. Assuming that the Italians knew of the current operation of Force H, and that the Italian Navy might try to intervene, Somerville wanted to launch the Hurricane aircraft as far to the west as possible. The winds were still from the west, and the pilots of the Hurricanes and the captain of the *Argus* calculated that the aircraft could be flown off from a position about longitude 6 degrees east, which gave a flying distance of 400 miles to Malta. This was a long way for a single-engine fighter to fly over a featureless sea, but the Hurricanes were to fly off in two flights of six, each accompanied by a Skua aircraft. To ensure that they were successfully guided to their destination the two flights would also be met by a Sunderland flying boat and a Martin bomber from Malta, with experienced navigators on board. The Hurricanes would carry sufficient fuel to give them a range of 520 miles, and they had the added advantage of a tailwind behind them.

While the Hurricanes took off from the *Argus*, at first light, aircraft from the *Ark Royal* provided fighter cover, and sent reconnaissance patrols to the east. All the aircraft were successfully launched from the *Argus* by eight in the morning. From that point the operation started to unravel. The Martin bomber never succeeded in meeting up with its flight of Hurricanes, and only four Hurricanes and one Skua managed to reach Malta. The rest either couldn't find Malta or ran out of fuel because of an unexpected headwind. Somerville was particularly angry to discover that the observer of the second Skua, whose flight failed to find Malta at all, was a sub-lieutenant in the Royal Navy Reserve who was on his very first operational flight. Operation White was a tragic failure.

The next mission Force H took part in raised even more doubts about the experience of the pilots who had left Liverpool on board the *Ark Royal*, and gave Churchill the opportunity to attack Somerville, about whose instincts he had harboured severe doubts ever since the assault on the French fleet at Oran. The mission's aim was to reinforce the British Army and other forces in Egypt with another convoy to Malta and Alexandria. This time it was a combination of Operations HATS and Hurry, and it had an extra sense of urgency because of the invasion of Greece and the decision to move some of the British Eighth Army to support the Greek government.

The convoy was going to be made up of three mechanized transport freighters, the *New Zealand Star*, the *Clan Forbes* and the *Clan Fraser*, carrying a cargo of tanks and armoured equipment, and a contingent of Royal Air Force personnel who were needed in Alexandria. The vessels carrying the armoured equipment would sail from Britain and would not call at Gibraltar; instead, their escort of corvettes and destroyers would join them as they passed Europa point, the southernmost tip of Gibraltar. The RAF personnel arrived in Gibraltar in a transport ship, the *Franconia*, and were transferred to the cruisers *Manchester* and *Southampton* for passage through the Mediterranean. Force H would meanwhile sail to the north of the cruiser and motor transport ship convoy, providing air cover and surface protection from attacks by the Italian Air Force and Navy. At a point roughly south-east of Sardinia, Force H would meet a fleet from Malta comprising the battleships *Ramillies* and *Berwick* and some cruisers, who would then continue to protect the convoy on its journey to Alexandria.

Somerville was concerned about the distinct possibility that the convoy would be intercepted by the Italian Navy. An attack on the Italian fleet in its harbour at Taranto by Swordfish aircraft flying from HMS *Illustrious* had been a blow to the Italian forces in the Mediterranean, severely damaging as it did three of their battleships. The rest of the fleet was moved from Taranto and directed to ports in Naples and La Spezia. However, British intelligence had lost track of the rest of the battleships.

Somerville believed that the obvious strategy for the Italian Navy was to reinforce the western part of the Mediterranean and force a fight with the slow convoy. He stressed to the Admiralty that in his view the Italians could concentrate three battleships and several cruisers in the period between Force H leaving Gibraltar and the time when they were accompanying the convoy on its journey south of Sardinia.

On 26 November, Force H set off from Gibraltar, and by the end of the day had located the convoy and taken up position sailing on a course parallel to them at a distance of twenty-five miles to the north. The next day, the *Ark Royal* flew off nine Swordfish aircraft to act as long-range surveillance for the convoy, covering an area 100 miles to the north and west of the convoy and Force H. At the same time, anti-submarine patrols were launched, and so was a standing patrol of fighters. In addition, a squadron of Swordfish had been armed the night before with torpedoes and were standing by in case there was any contact with a force of Italian warships.

At ten in the morning, the patrolling Swordfish saw that the situation Somerville had been most concerned about had in fact occurred. Sixty miles to the north-west of the *Ark Royal* and Force H was a substantial fleet of Italian warships comprising two battleships and a destroyer escort; 10 miles away was a further force of three cruisers and destroyers. They were steaming directly for the convoy.

Somerville told the *Ark Royal* to launch a strike force of Swordfish torpedo bombers, and at the same time ordered Force H, now comprising his flagship *Renown* and her escorts, to make full speed to meet up with the *Berwick* and *Ramillies*, which were approaching from Malta. They met up just before noon, and the combined force altered course to confront the Italian fleet, although various reports from the patrolling Swordfish left Somerville in some doubt as to how big the enemy fleet was and what ships were in it. Moreover, it is quite likely that the Italian battle fleet changed course to the east when they realized they had been observed by reconnaissance aircraft, because they were sailing to the east, away from the convoy, by a quarter past eleven.

The first strike force of Swordfish was flown off the *Ark* at 1130 hours. The air crew were the most experienced available, what Captain Holland of the *Ark* later described as 'our first team', but out of nine aircraft only five had ever previously dropped a torpedo in action. Some had had perhaps two practice drops, some as many as eight. The Swordfish approached the battleships from the west, out of the sun, at an altitude of about 6,000 feet. They dived over the destroyer screen and went low to make their attack. There was no attempt to split up the flight so that torpedoes could be launched from different positions, to split the anti-aircraft defences and make it difficult for the target ship to manoeuvre and comb the tracks of the torpedoes. All the pilots launched at the same point, to the front of the leading battleship on the starboard side, except for the leader, Lt Commander Mervyn Johnstone, who launched his torpedo at the rear of the two battleships. The battleships and the destroyers were firing a lot of anti-aircraft fire at the planes and it was, according to Johnstone, heavy and accurate fire, causing damage to three of the aircraft.

Two torpedoes were seen to explode in the sea, but one explosion with a lot of brown smoke was observed on the far side of the leading ship. A considerable amount of AA fire continued to be directed at the planes as they made their escape, twisting and turning, keeping as low as possible, and as Johnstone said, 'it is very difficult in an attack of this sort to get any idea of what is going on until you get a report from everyone in the squadron. It is extremely difficult to observe anything on a low-level attack. You are never on a steady course for more than about five seconds. It is very difficult when you are manoeuvring to get out of gunfire to look around and see what is going on.' It wasn't until the flight of Swordfish had landed back on the *Ark Royal*, almost an hour after the start of the attack on the Italian fleet, that the air crew formed the conclusion that one of the Italian battleships might have been damaged.

In the meantime there had been an exchange of shells between the Italian cruisers and Force H, and one of the patrolling Swordfish observers reported that an Italian cruiser had come to a standstill, a fire burning in the rear turret. The pilot, Sub Lt Henry Mays, said, 'I noticed she was burning furiously aft, and after having looked at my silhouettes and another careful look at this ship I decided she was of the San Giorgio class. I stayed over her for nearly half an hour and then returned to the *Ark Royal*. This cruiser had been stationary for the whole of the time I had been shadowing her and she opened fire with short-range armament on one occasion.'

Somerville's main forces were struggling to maintain speed to overtake the Italian ships, who were now clearly returning to the Italian mainland as fast as they could, and Somerville was also getting dangerously close to the enemy coast, which was now just 30 miles away. He decided at this point that the protection of the convoy was the more important task and broke off the pursuit of the Italian ships, although in fact neither *Renown*, *Ramillies* nor the convoy's escorting cruisers were capable of making enough speed to intercept the Italian ships. On receiving the report of the burning Italian cruiser, Somerville instead ordered the *Ark Royal* to make an air attack and attempt to sink her.

When Captain Holland had been told that the first strike force had probably hit one of the Italian battleships, he had ordered a second Swordfish strike force into the air with orders to locate a damaged battleship, or, if this proved impractical, to attack any other target. The leader, Lt Commander James Stewart Moore, approached the retreating Italian ships on a course of 30 degrees. He realized that in order to attack the battleships he would have to pass close to the cruisers before reaching the main target, thus allowing the crew of the battleships ample warning of their approach. The alternative was to fly around the fleet and attempt to approach the battleships from ahead, but this would take some time. As Moore was considering his options he saw Italian fighters manoeuvring over Sardinia, and he reasoned that he would have to get the attack over with quickly or accept the risk of seeing it disintegrate under enemy fighter attack. Another consideration that weighed on his mind, he reported, 'was the very untrained personnel in the striking force. It seemed that if I gave them a difficult target I would probably have no hits at all, whilst the rear cruiser, quite unscreened, seemed much more promising. I decided to attack the single cruiser.'

Moore led his nine Swordfish into the attack at 1320, and his torpedo and that of his wingman dropped almost simultaneously. They then turned and zigzagged to avoid anti-aircraft fire. The cruiser started to turn into the torpedoes, and as she did so Moore saw a mound of water about 30 feet long and as high as her forward deck appear under the bridge. The ship continued her turn and was then attacked by another sub flight, but the cruiser continued on her way, completing a circle and rejoining her companion ships. The last group of Swordfish attacked not the last cruiser but the leading one, and no hits were observed.

While this attack was going on the *Ark* had launched a force of seven Skua aircraft with orders from Somerville to locate the burning cruiser and attack it with 500lb bombs. They took off at 1500 hours. They could not find any trace of a damaged cruiser, but their leader, Lt Richard Smeeton, saw three cruisers of the Condottiere class steaming north in close formation at about 25 knots. He climbed to 8,000 feet so that he could begin his attack out of the sun. He led his flight into a bombing run on the last ship of the line, and all the aircraft except one released on target at about 900 feet, but no definite hits were seen. They were completely unopposed, having achieved outright surprise, but as they made their getaway they received some heavy anti-aircraft fire.

Meanwhile, the Italian Air Force had very belatedly flown to the assistance of the Italian ships, and at 1635 fifteen bombers concentrated their attack on the *Ark Royal*, getting within range despite the patrols of Fulmars and Skuas. Around thirty bombs fell close to the *Ark*, but she emerged through the clouds of smoke and spray unscathed, with all her guns firing. That was the last effort by the Italians to attack the convoy, and it achieved its aim of transporting the armour and personnel to Alexandria.

However, twenty-five British aircraft had attacked the Italian fleet on three separate occasions throughout the day and had achieved precisely nothing. Taking into account the failure to obtain any hits when the *Ark*'s Swordfish had tried to stop the *Strasbourg* escaping, the success against shipping at sea by carrier-borne aircraft was far less than pre-war exercises had forecast.

As John Moffat, a Volunteer Reserve Swordfish pilot, described it, the training he had received was rigorous. It included judgement of the speed and course of a ship from observation of its bow wave and wake, and he had practised dropping dummy torpedoes in the Clyde against moving ships, every drop recorded by a camera mounted on his aeroplane's wing. But it was hard enough to judge speed, distance and height during an exercise; it was another question altogether to do it when the ship you were attacking was firing every gun it could bear at you in a desperate effort to shoot down your aircraft and kill you. Some of the attacks carried out by the *Ark*'s air crew were relatively unopposed, but many had been met with heavy gunfire.

Part of the problem may have been the fuse fitted to the warhead of the torpedoes carried on the *Ark*. A normal old-fashioned contact fuse relied on an impact with the target to detonate the explosive in the warhead. In order for this to work the torpedo had to hit the target fair and square, on the side of the hull, the place where most modern warships had their thickest armour and were often invulnerable to the small warhead of the 18-inch torpedoes carried by the Swordfish. To overcome this, a fuse known as the Duplex fuse had been developed that was triggered by the influence of the magnetic field of a ship. The theory was that a torpedo with a Duplex fuse could be set to run deeper so that it would explode directly underneath a ship, causing greater damage. There was a great deal of scepticism about the reliability of these new fuses, particularly on the part of the Swordfish crew, but their orders were to continue to fit them.

There were other problems too, such as the lack of communication and poor reporting, that needed addressing. It seemed clear as well that initial planning of the attack was not very thorough, and that little attention was paid to tactics to divide the enemy fire.

Admiral Somerville and Captain Holland of the *Ark Royal* had little time to address these failings when they returned to Gibraltar. The escape of the Italian fleet had been immediately noticed by the Admiralty, and before Somerville could make a proper report of the incident he was told that a Board of Inquiry had been set up and Admiral of the Fleet the Earl of Cork and Orrery was arriving in Gibraltar to conduct it. Somerville now had two Boards of Inquiry to deal with, one investigating the failure of Operation White, which had seen the loss of over two thirds of those Hurricanes flown off to reinforce Malta, and now a far more serious inquiry into his handling of Operation Collar.

The second Board of Inquiry was in a sense pre-ordained. It had been ordered by Winston Churchill, who had of course objected to Somerville's quite outspoken opposition to the attack on the French at Mirs el Kebir. Churchill's view that Somerville was lacking in the fighting spirit needed to win the war had not been diminished by his constant unwillingness to take further action against French shipping. He had as well been outspoken in his defence of Admiral North, in charge of the North Atlantic Station in Gibraltar, who had been unjustly blamed and forcibly retired for failing to stop French warships leaving the Mediterranean. He had also, of course, vigorously stated his opinion that the HATS convoy would be running an unacceptable risk if it tried to escort cargo vessels carrying tank reinforcements. Churchill wanted to remove him, and Somerville's failure to intercept the Italian fleet was his chance.

But Somerville was saved, essentially for three reasons. The first was that he was unambitious, and saw his current position as a postscript to a career that had effectively ended when he was invalided out of the Navy in 1938. This was why he was prepared to be outspoken – a trait he himself realized sometimes made him difficult to deal with. In this particular instance he had absolutely no qualms about criticizing the Admiralty and its peremptory decision to hold an inquiry. Secondly, Somerville was a well-known figure, a broadcaster and the Admiral in Charge of Force H and the *Ark Royal*, which also had a high public profile. He would not go quietly, a fact he made very clear; his sacking would create political problems for the government and the Admiralty. Somerville was saved as well by the fact that many of his fellow admirals, including those in charge of the inquiry, believed that it was unjustified. They would go ahead with the inquiry but make sure it was favourable to Somerville. In a letter to Somerville, the chairman of the Board of Inquiry said, 'These people impatient for results exist both in and out of the Admy and in high quarters (I speak from personal experience) and no doubt have raised their voices on this occasion, and the most expeditious way of silencing them has in this case been adopted. As a result I do not think you need anticipate hearing anything further. This is as far as I can judge and sincerely hope.'

And so it turned out, although Somerville remained angry at the slur on him and the men under his command. He thought it an underhanded way to save him. Somerville had written lengthy letters to the Admiralty, pointing out that he had been faced with a dilemma during Operation Collar. If he had abandoned the merchant ships to pursue the Italian fleet they would have been left defenceless against air attack and other units of the Italian fleet. Moreover, there was a serious possibility that the *Ark*'s safety would have been jeopardized. The Admiralty prevaricated on the question of what he should have done, refusing to address the point. Even after the subject was closed, Somerville continued to raise this question, pressing the Admiralty for clarity before every operation in the Mediterranean.

When the inquiry was completed, Somerville paid a visit to the *Ark Royal*. A series of training exercises had been initiated on board the carrier, and Somerville was able to take part in some of them – torpedo exercises, practice dive-bombing flights, and exercises in fighter interception and combat. It was clear that he intended his visit to help remedy some of the deficiencies brought to light during the attack on the Italian fleet. He talked to the air gunners and emphasized the importance of regular communication with the carrier, and other aircraft. As he toured the ship, he gave encouragement and praise as well as gently highlighting the need to maintain a high level of efficiency.

Somerville's nephew Mark was a lieutenant observer in Fulmars in 808 Squadron, flying with Lt Commander Tillard, the squadron's commanding officer, who had been responsible for shooting down several Italian aircraft. Mark Somerville penned a letter to his uncle that was full of praise for the tour. 'The general view about the visit is that the ship is now operating under a Flag Officer who not only understands the general aspects of Naval Aviation but who has also taken the trouble to investigate the practical and personal side of it,' he wrote. The visit certainly did an enormous amount to boost morale on the *Ark* after the critical interrogation by the Board of Inquiry. Somerville could not resist another jibe at the Admiralty in his Report of Proceedings for the period. Remarking on his visit, he wrote, 'I am convinced that when opportunity serves, it is most desirable that Senior Officers should take part in such practices that they may acquire a full appreciation of the problems which face the FAA pilots and observers.'

Somerville's criticism of many of the tasks Force H was asked to carry out was based partly on a lack of clarity about the purpose of Force H, and also on Somerville's assessment of the strategic situation in the Mediterranean. Force H was originally set up to control the western exit to the Mediterranean, and to carry out offensive operations against the coast of Italy. Subsequently, to these were added the passage of reinforcements to the eastern Mediterranean; control of all major units of the French fleet; the tracking down of raiders in the Atlantic; preparations for the defence of Gibraltar should the Spanish enter the war on the Axis side; the capture of the Azores, to pre-empt a German seizure; and possible forays into the Indian Ocean in the event of war with Japan. It was a lengthy list, and as Somerville was always keen to point out there were no substitutes for either the *Renown* or the *Ark Royal*. So weak were his forces that the destroyer flotilla in Gibraltar could not find the ships to mount anti-submarine patrols of the Straits and provide an effective destroyer screen for Force H on its forays into the Mediterranean.

Somerville's assessment was that he simply did not have the resources constantly to monitor French shipping in the Mediterranean, as he was asked to do; he certainly could not afford to create a situation that might turn the Vichy government into an active enemy. Gibraltar was far too vulnerable to air attacks from the French bases in North Africa, and he would never be able to deal with a combined French–Italian fleet. His attitude towards seeking a conflict with the Italian fleet was also governed by his view of the balance of forces in the Mediterranean. The task of destroying the Italian fleet was secondary to the need to maintain the RAF and the military in Egypt, and now also in Greece. The Admiralty never in his view gave enough weight to the fact that the Italian Navy, as well as being numerically superior, had the advantage of air support from a shore-based air force. The Italian air and naval forces had been poorly co-ordinated during Operation Collar, but they might get it right next time. Somerville argued that for forthcoming operations in the Mediterranean Force H should be enlarged, if not by additional cruisers, then by another battleship. The Navy was, however, being stretched by the war in the Atlantic as well as in the Mediterranean. It was unlikely that Force H would receive significant reinforcements in the short term.

Indeed, the fact that the *Ark Royal* was stationed at Gibraltar, the gateway between the Mediterranean and the Atlantic, meant she was now in a perfect position to fight on both fronts. Rather than Force H being reinforced and strengthened for the tasks of supporting the military offensive in the Mediterranean, it now found itself being called upon to reinforce the Home Fleet in the Atlantic. Already feeling extreme pressure from the Italian forces in the Mediterranean, the demands placed on Force H were threatening to push them to breaking point. Events over the next few weeks would only increase this. The Luftwaffe were about to join the war in the Mediterranean with dramatic effect. The role of the *Ark Royal* would become increasingly significant in shaping the ensuing conflict.

As Christmas and the New Year approached, events were to take an even more desperate turn, and the demands on Somerville, Force H and the *Ark Royal* would be even more acute. To understand why, it is necessary to look at events in the Eastern Mediterranean at the end of 1940.

8

SHOWING THE FLAG

HMS *Illustrious* was one of the most modern carriers in the fleet, built after the *Ark* and designed specifically for combat in areas like the Mediterranean, where air attack from shore-based aircraft was to be expected. As a defence against bombs the *Illustrious* had been constructed with an armoured flight deck, and because this affected her weight distribution, the ship and all the carriers that were built to the same design sat lower in the water than the *Ark*, and therefore had just one hangar deck, which limited the number of aircraft that could be carried. The trade-off was thought to be necessary, and certainly the *Illustrious* and its new Fulmar fighter aircraft operated aggressively in the eastern Mediterranean, supporting supply convoys to North African ports and to Greece.

The commanding officer of the Mediterranean Fleet, Admiral Andrew Cunningham, was less concerned about the threat from the Italian Air Force than that posed by the Italian Navy. It was a significant force, with several modern battleships and cruisers and a large number of destroyers and submarines. This fleet was based in the port of Taranto in Puglia, inside the 'heel' of Italy, and its presence was a constant anxiety to Cunningham. The Italian fleet had so far avoided a direct confrontation with the Royal Navy, and if Cunningham could eliminate them and reduce the threat they posed to his ships and convoys, then several of his battleships could be freed for duty in the Atlantic. The question was, how to do this if the Italian Navy wanted to avoid a major fleet action?

Taranto's location, deep in the Gulf of Taranto surrounded on three sides by the Italian mainland, made an attack from the sea impossibly risky for Cunningham. However, as a consequence of the Italian invasion of Abyssinia in 1936 and the possibility that Britain would be at war with Italy in an attempt to enforce League of Nations sanctions, the Royal Navy had worked out a plan to attack the Italian fleet in Taranto, not with surface ships but with torpedo-carrying aircraft. The captain of the *Illustrious*, Denis Boyd, and the ship's flag officer Rear Admiral Lumley Lyster had been a part of the planning staff back in 1938 and knew a great deal about the plan. It was a simple matter for them to dust it off and rework it for the present situation.

Taranto had two natural harbours, a small inner one that was accessed by means of a short canal from a much larger one that was shielded from the sea by two large moles. The bigger warships of the Italian fleet moored in this harbour, while the smaller destroyers and cruisers docked in the inner harbour. The final plan presented to Cunningham by Captain Boyd and Rear Admiral Lyster called for the *Illustrious* and the smaller HMS *Eagle* to steam to a position in the Ionian Sea about 170 miles from Taranto, and then to launch twenty-four Swordfish armed with torpedoes and bombs to make a night attack on the fleet. The main targets would be the battleships in the outer harbour, but bombs would also be dropped on the destroyers and a seaplane base in the inner harbour. It was an audacious and very risky plan. The port of Taranto was well protected by anti-aircraft fire, the ships were protected by torpedo nets, and there were fighter aircraft based at airfields a short distance from the port. But the attacking force would have the advantage of surprise, and the cover of darkness.

Shortly before the scheduled day for the raid there was a fire in the hangar of the *Eagle*, so only the *Illustrious* could take part in the attack. Some Swordfish from the *Eagle* were taken on board *Illustrious*, and on 11 November twenty-one Swordfish aircraft took off from the flight deck of HMS *Illustrious* on this extremely hazardous mission. Three of the Italian battleships moored in the harbour were sunk, and three cruisers and two destroyers were badly damaged. In addition, the Swordfish managed to destroy the seaplane base on the shores of the inner harbour, and the port's oil storage tanks were left blazing. Only two of the aircraft were shot down. It was a remarkably successful attack, and, as we have seen, it forced the Italian Navy to remove the rest of its fleet to the port of Naples. Admiral Cunningham's problem had been solved. Moreover, having lost three battleships while in the safety of one of their most important harbours, the Italian Navy had suffered a massive blow to its morale.

Yet the enormous strategic advantage that the raid on Taranto gave to the Royal Navy in the Mediterranean was relatively short-lived. In January 1941 units of the German Army landed in North Africa to reinforce the Italian Army, and a large element of the Luftwaffe, the Tenth Air Corps, or Fliegerkorps X, was moved from Poland to Sicily. This small, self-contained air force specialized in anti-shipping attacks and mine-laying and boasted 150 Heinkel 111 and Junkers 88 bombers alongside an equal number of Stuka dive bombers. There were also fifty Messerschmitt 109 fighters and several squadrons of the long-range twin-engine fighter, the Me110. Their presence was as threatening to the Allied war effort in the Mediterranean as the build-up of the Afrika Korps under General Rommel in North Africa. Fliegerkorps X was a well-integrated force that had already proved, in Norway, that it could wreak devastation on warships. Indeed, within a few months the German Army would be rolling the British Army before them in Greece and North Africa, and Rommel and his Afrika Korps would be holding daggers to the throats of British troops around the Nile, Alexandria and the Suez Canal.

The withdrawal of the Italian fleet from Taranto was quickly seized upon by the Admiralty as a perfect opportunity to pass another convoy from Gibraltar to Alexandria with reinforcements for the Eighth Army. The plan was to take 4,000 tons of ammunition, 3,000 tons of seed potatoes and a squadron of Hawker Hurricanes to Malta, with another ship continuing to Alexandria. The convoy's journey down from the UK was disrupted by the presence of the *Admiral Hipper*, a German cruiser, in the Bay of Biscay, which forced the *Ark Royal* to put to sea on Christmas Day and almost caused a mutiny among the crew (as we shall see in the next chapter). The *Ark* escorted the convoy to Gibraltar, but it was not until 6 January that the convoy headed east towards Malta and the Sicilian channel.

This stage of the journey was marked by an attack by ten

Italian bombers, which were driven off. The fleet had adopted a tactic of firing its anti-aircraft guns in a co-ordinated barrage, a system where shells were fired at set heights, forcing attacking aircraft to fly through a wall of explosions. The Fulmar aircraft from the *Ark* also took off to break up the attack, and Lt Commander Tillard, the commanding officer of 808 Squadron, shot down two of the Savoia Marchetti bombers. On the evening of 9 January, the *Ark* and Force H left the convoy having, in the words of Admiral Somerville in a letter to his wife, 'seen them to the front door of the next parish'.

It was at this point that the complicated manoeuvres to cover the safe delivery of the ships to Alexandria started to go wrong. *Illustrious*, with her escort of battleships *Warspite* and *Valiant*, was waiting to meet the convoy after it had passed through the Sicilian channel by the island of Pantelleria. They had taken up a position further to the west than normal, and on the morning of 10 January *Illustrious* was steaming to the north-west of Malta. The weather was fair, and visibility was excellent. Sailing this close to Sicily was extremely risky, and both Captain Boyd and Rear Admiral Lyster had pointed out to Admiral Cunningham that *Illustrious* could provide air cover for the convoy from a much safer position, further away from the Italian airbases on Sicily. Cunningham, who was never as intelligent about the use and vulnerability of his carriers as Somerville was when it came to the *Ark*, had overridden their objections, saying that the presence of the carrier had an excellent effect on the morale of the fleet.

Shortly after midday, two Italian torpedo bombers flew low over the sea towards the *Valiant*, dropping two torpedoes that fell behind the warship as she steamed east. Then the radar on the *Illustrious* detected two large formations of aircraft approaching from the north. As they got nearer they were identified as German aircraft, a combination of twin-engine Junkers 88 medium bombers and the notorious Junkers 87 or Stukas, the single-engine dive bombers with a highly distinctive V-shaped crank in their wings whose banshee-like screams had come to symbolize the terror of the German blitzkrieg on Poland and France.

Admiral Cunningham recorded in his diary that 'a very heavy, determined and skilful dive-bombing attack developed on the fleet, mainly directed on *Illustrious*, and lasting for some ten minutes'. The pilots of the Stuka squadrons had spent many hours practising their dive-bombing technique on targets drawn on the runway of their base in Sicily which reproduced the shape of the *Illustrious*'s flight deck. She was quickly hit by six large 1,000kg bombs, dropped on the flight deck by Stukas whose pilots flew so low over the ship that they were often level with the compass platform on the carrier's island. The handful of Fulmar fighters on the *Illustrious* were simply overwhelmed by the numbers of German aircraft, and the carrier's armoured flight deck offered little defence against such large armour-piercing bombs. Both deck lifts were hit, and fires started in the hangar deck, killing many of the air crew who had taken part in the attack on Taranto just two months earlier. The steering gear was damaged too, and the ship steamed in circles for some time before the damage control parties managed to free the rudder again. All the time the attacks continued. The fountains of water from near-misses sometimes completely obscured the carrier.

Illustrious eventually managed to steam to Malta and put into the dockyard in Valletta for emergency repairs. The Luftwaffe did not stop, however. The next day, 11 January, a wave of Stukas attacked the cruisers *Southampton* and *Gloucester*, destroying the former and badly damaging the latter. Attack after attack also rained down on the *Illustrious* while she was in dock, but after several weeks she was patched up sufficiently to steam to Alexandria and head, via the Suez Canal, for an American shipyard to be rebuilt. She had not been sunk, but she was lost completely to Cunningham and the British war effort in the Mediterranean.

Any advantage Britain had achieved in the Mediterranean as a result of Taranto had now been completely wiped out by the Luftwaffe. There was no question of any more convoys being sent through the Mediterranean, and as Cunningham said, 'the fleet itself would operate by day within the range of the dive bombers only at considerable risk. In the absence of a modern aircraft carrier it therefore became necessary to abandon any idea of offensive operations against the enemy's coast.' This, of course, had an immediate effect on the *Ark Royal* and her crew. The Admiralty had been planning to replace her with the *Illustrious*'s sister ship *Indomitable*, but now *Indomitable* had to replace *Illustrious* herself in the eastern Mediterranean, as soon as it became possible to get her there, and the *Ark* would have to stay in Gibraltar. A badly needed refit for the ship and home leave for the crew were now indefinitely postponed.

But there were bigger problems now facing Cunningham in the aftermath of the loss of the *Illustrious* than lack of home leave for a ship's crew. The Luftwaffe's onslaught led to a serious loss of prestige for the Royal Navy, and it wasn't clear how that would affect the two most important neutral countries at either end of the Mediterranean, Spain and Turkey. Their attitude to Britain and the Axis powers was crucial to Britain's ability to continue the war in North Africa and the Mediterranean. The *Ark Royal* and Force H now had the task of demonstrating to

Spain that Britain was still a potent force to be reckoned with. This was a really pressing issue, because there were rumours that the Spanish were considering their position about the British presence on the Rock of Gibraltar, and a summit meeting between Mussolini and General Franco was due to take place in February. The question of Spanish assistance to Italy was certain to be discussed between the two dictators.

Admiral Cunningham was also eager to see an attack on northern Italy, because it would dissuade the Italian fleet from returning to Taranto now that the threat from *Illustrious* had been removed; it should also make the Italian Air Force shift some of its squadrons to the north. In the event the Admiralty proposed a two-pronged attack: the bombardment by the warships of Force H of Genoa and, along the way, an attack on the Tirso Dam in Sardinia by Swordfish aircraft. The dam had been built in front of Lake Tirso and was responsible for supplying a third of the island's electricity. The Admiralty supplied an intelligence assessment, which said that the dam was only three feet thick at the top and could easily be breached by a torpedo.

Somerville discussed this operation with his senior officers and the captain of the *Ark Royal*, most of whom opposed the plans. It was not hard to see why. The mission to bombard Genoa would take the *Ark Royal* and Force H past Sardinia, very close to the Italian mainland and well within range of the Italian Air Force; moreover, the attack on the Tirso Dam would alert the Italian defences at an early stage in the operation. *Illustrious* had been lost because the risk from shore-based aircraft had been ignored. It seemed foolish to do the same thing with the *Ark*, especially as she was now the only lifeline to Malta. As for the attack on the dam itself, launching torpedoes required that the Swordfish fly low and steady for some time, and if the raid was to be successful all the aircraft would have to fly predictably on a line down the lake towards the dam. They would make a perfect target for anti-aircraft guns whose crews would have the benefit of a lengthy arc of fire from dry land. The Admiralty had suggested, however, that the defences of the dam were light, and that the aircraft would have the benefit of surprise.

Somerville had, of course, often objected to missions that in his opinion jeopardized the safety of the *Ark Royal* and its air crew. There was no question that these two operations, Result and Picket, were extremely risky, but he knew that the arguments for the combined operations were, in the circumstances, fairly compelling. For a start, he was extremely conscious of the vulnerability of his base at Gibraltar and knew that a change in the Spanish policy of neutrality would lead to its evacuation. He also knew that Cunningham in the eastern Mediterranean needed help to take the pressure off his depleted forces.

Result and Picket were given the go-ahead, and on Saturday, 1 February, the *Ark Royal*, with *Renown*, *Malaya* – a battleship sent as reinforcement by Cunningham to Somerville at the end of 1940 – *Sheffield* and a screen of destroyers, was steaming at high speed towards Sardinia where, very early the following Sunday, a group of Swordfish aircraft would fly off to attack the dam.

The weather worsened. By 0200 hours, as the *Ark Royal* approached the take-off position 60 miles off the coast of Sardinia, there was a 37-knot wind blowing from the west. The Swordfish would be flying into this wind when they returned from the raid, and the *Ark* would have to remain in the same position to give them any chance of making it back safely. This would not only delay the attack on Genoa, it would also increase the risk to the whole force if the *Ark Royal* was spotted by enemy reconnaissance aircraft while loitering in the flying-off position.

But there was no alternative, and the Swordfish aircraft were brought up on the hangar lifts their torpedoes mounted, and they were ranged at the end of the flight deck.

The *Ark* pitched in the rough sea amid sudden squalls of rain, and in the dark of early morning the deck was extremely hazardous. In such high winds and with a heaving ship there was always the danger of a collision between aircraft, or an accident involving ground crew. The mechanic turning the handle to start the engine was only ever a few feet away from sudden death. The flight deck was slippery with oil and moisture, and the powerful wash from the spinning propellers combined with the gale-force wind threatened to blow the mechanics and aircraft handlers off their feet. Albert Arnell was an aeroplane rigger on the Swordfish aircraft, and he gave me this graphic description of his job when a squadron was being launched: 'When it came to take-off time we would get the order to start engines as the ship was turning into wind. If you're on the chocks at the back then it's a hell of a wind. You can't look into it and open your mouth because if you do it will blow your cheeks right out here. You're lying on the deck holding onto two chocks and they're flying off in front of you. It comes to your turn and you hang on for grim death. If there's a white line painted on the deck you hang onto it if you can. If you keep low you will go under the propellers so it's a matter of keeping your nerve. It's quite something to see a plane launched. It disappears over the bows, and you're on the flight deck and you look at everybody's neck going up about another six inches to see if it's gone off all right.'

Despite the conditions, by six o'clock eight Swordfish aircraft had taken to the air and were on their way to the Sardinian coast. The weather was too rough to launch the Skua fighters, so a patrol of Fulmar aircraft was kept in the air from seven in the morning. The Swordfish formed up in sections on their way to the coast, where the weather was dark and it was raining hard. Seven of the pilots turned out to sea to wait for light, but the eighth, flown by an inexperienced crew, entered cloud at about 5,000 feet and was unable to see land. The cloud thickness varied between 5,000 and 9,000 feet, and this pilot never managed to locate the target.

Before long, the seven other Swordfish flew inland to the Tirso Dam, and the first to attack made an approach along the length of the lake. It immediately came under heavy fire from anti-aircraft batteries set up on either side of a bridge crossing the foot of Lake Tirso. It abandoned its attack, turned and tried another approach, but again was met by very heavy ack-ack. The pilot reckoned he would never get through such a thick barrage, so he abandoned the attack and jettisoned his torpedo.

The rest of the strike force, now down to six aircraft, made individual approaches. Two aircraft, the first flown by Lt Godfrey Fausset, the pilot who had led the attack on the Italian cruisers at Spartivento, avoided the anti-aircraft batteries at the foot of the lake and turned to make their run towards the dam. They were also met with heavy ack-ack but managed to drop their torpedoes before taking violent evasive action to avoid getting hit. As a result they were unable to see whether they had hit the dam or not. The third Swordfish to attack flew at extremely low level all the way in from the coast, following the river that fed the lake. Flying at 50 feet the whole way, the pilot, Sub Lt Charlier, took the crews of the anti-aircraft batteries totally by surprise, made his drop and was only fired at when he was making his getaway. As the Commander (Air) on *Ark Royal* remarked, his method showed thought and initiative. It was unfortunately to no avail. Only one other torpedo was launched at the dam, by Sub Lt Ken Pattison, who lost his leader in the clouds, dived and found himself almost above the target. Too high, he turned, and again under a heavy barrage launched his torpedo at a height of 150 feet travelling at 145 knots.

The dam remained intact.

Seven Swordfish returned to the *Ark* – the eighth was shot down, its crew taken prisoner – and had landed on by 0905 hours. The weather was getting even worse, so the *Ark* signalled to Somerville that it would probably be impossible to carry out the second part of the mission. The present wind and sea conditions meant that aircraft could not be flown off in the dark, and the low cloud that was forecast would make an attack difficult. If there was any further increase in the wind, it would be impossible to carry out deck landings. At ten past seven that evening it was still blowing a gale and the attack on Genoa was abandoned. The *Ark* and Force H returned to Gibraltar.

On the way they carried out a series of training exercises that covered the spectrum of operations the *Ark* had to deal with. Four Skuas practised dive-bombing attacks on the other ships in Force H, Swordfish crews practised torpedo attacks on the escort destroyers, and another Skua dived at the *Ark* for an hour for a gunnery training class. The lessons of the failed attack on the Italian fleet had been taken to heart and every opportunity was being taken to hone the skill of the air crews, which were now often joining the ship with little experience.

It seemed to Somerville and the captain of the *Ark Royal* that the Italian forces had been forewarned about the attack on the dam. The information from the Admiralty that the dam was lightly defended had certainly proved wrong. Somerville believed there had been a serious breach of security. In the circumstances, the *Ark* had been lucky to lose only one

Swordfish and crew. From this point on, to prevent information being leaked in the run-up to sensitive operations, the *Ark* and the other ships in Force H were kept at one hour's notice for steaming, preventing the crews from taking shore leave.

The most important part of the mission, the attack on Genoa, might have been cancelled because of poor flying conditions, but the reasons for carrying it out – the need to influence both the Spanish government and the Italian Navy – had not gone away. A week later the *Ark Royal* and Force H was again steaming to the east in order to carry out the bombardment. This attack on the Italian mainland still posed enormous risks to the *Ark* and Force H, and the anti-submarine and fighter patrols were instructed to avoid being seen by merchant ships and radio warning of their course so that Force H could take avoiding action.

Aircraft from the *Ark Royal* were detailed to mine the entrance to the harbour of La Spezia and bomb an oil refinery at Livorno. At five in the morning on Sunday, 9 February, fourteen Swordfish flew off carrying four 250lb bombs each, followed by four aircraft carrying magnetic mines. John Moffat of 808 Squadron was one of the pilots in that mine-laying force. Their main aim was to achieve surprise by making a very quiet low-level approach over the town of Spezia itself. With engines throttled back, flying into the prevailing wind the Swordfish were virtually silent. The town already had some of its lights on; Moffat's observer remarked that the people must be going to mass. All four aircraft dropped their mines. Meanwhile, eleven of the fourteen Swordfish that had the Azienda oil refinery at Livorno as their target succeeded in making a rendezvous over the town and dropped their bombs, causing a large explosion. Two of the three aircraft that had lost the target made their way to Pisa where they bombed the marshalling yards. Unlike the previous operation, the raiders from the *Ark Royal* had achieved almost complete surprise; the anti-aircraft fire only started once the raid was underway. One Swordfish was shot down and the crew were taken prisoner, but by a quarter to nine in the morning all the other aircraft had landed back on the *Ark*'s flight deck.

The bombardment of Genoa was carried out by the big guns of the *Renown* and the *Malaya*, and they opened fire at a quarter past seven. Somerville, on the *Renown*, was uncomfortable about the whole operation. He knew it was inevitable that civilians would be killed, and in a letter to his wife he wrote, 'War is lousy. For half an hour we blazed away and I had to think of Senglea, Valletta, London and Bristol to harden my heart.' The bombardment was devastatingly effective. Salvoes from the *Renown* ripped up the railway track at the marshalling yards and damaged factories on both sides of the River Polecevera. A shell in the vicinity of the power station caused a large explosion in an oil tank. The dry docks and warehouses were also hit, but one of the observers from the spotting Swordfish remarked once he had landed back on the *Ark Royal* that he'd seen whole rows of houses knocked down like a pack of cards by a single shell.

Their job done, Force H left the scene and by half past nine had rejoined the *Ark Royal*. Now was the most dangerous part of the operation. The Italian defences had been well and truly notified of the presence of the *Ark Royal* and Force H, and it would require eight hours' steaming before the ships were out of range of the Italian Air Force. The small fleet was quickly located by reconnaissance aircraft, and two shadowing aircraft were shot down by the *Ark*'s combat air patrol. Just over an hour later the first attack was made. Two bombers targeted the *Ark*, but their aim was off. With remarkable luck, Force H was covered by a deep haze that effectively obscured the ships from aircraft above. For several hours the ships sailed on, and Ron Skinner remembers that the noise of bombers circling overhead created enormous tension on board the *Ark*, where the crew stood at action stations expecting the enemy aircraft at any minute to burst through the clouds. But they never did, and the *Ark Royal* returned safely to Gibraltar.

Somerville was astounded that so remarkably audacious an operation had achieved such complete surprise, particularly in light of the previous adventure on the Tirso Dam. The raid received considerable publicity in Britain and was an enormous boost to the government after the loss of the *Illustrious*. The war in North Africa was not going well, and the losses in the North Atlantic to the German U-boat campaign were mounting. Once more the *Ark Royal* and Force H had pulled off another coup and given the country some very welcome good news. Moreover, the talks between Mussolini and Franco did not result in any change in Spanish policy towards Britain and Gibraltar.

It had been a turbulent few weeks during which the Royal Navy's power in the Mediterranean had waxed and waned, but after the successful attack on Genoa confidence aboard the *Ark Royal* was again at a high. But harder challenges lay ahead.

9

OPERATION TIGER

It is hard to appreciate today the extent to which the size of the Royal Navy was reduced during the decades before the start of the Second World War. The global obligations and ambitions of the Royal Navy at the height of the British Empire's power were by 1939 impossible to sustain. War quickly started to expose the cracks in the façade. Churchill's decision to wage war against Italy and to seek to maintain control of the Mediterranean despite French capitulation was stretching the Royal Navy to the limit. The *Ark Royal* found itself at the heart of the unfolding events, moving rapidly from theatre to theatre, strengthening weaknesses in the fleet wherever they occurred.

The Commander in Chief of the Kriegsmarine (the German Navy), Admiral Erich Raeder, had spent a considerable time in the 1920s analysing German naval doctrine and strategy during the First World War. He had come to the conclusion that the most effective part of the German naval offensive was not the giant battle in the North Sea between the German High Seas Fleet and the British Grand Fleet, but the efforts of the commerce raiders that roamed the South Atlantic and the Pacific, attacking merchant shipping and tying down large numbers of British warships. Raeder had pursued this policy in the current conflict, and it had proved to be just as effective. The *Graf Spee* had not sunk a large amount of commercial tonnage, but it had forced the Royal Navy to send the *Ark Royal* and *Renown* to the South Atlantic, and other task groups of carriers and battleships to other oceans. Once there they spent weeks fruitlessly scouring the area for the German pocket battleships.

The French defeat in 1940 had allowed the Kriegsmarine access to the Atlantic ports on the French coast, and this gave Raeder's strategy a new lease of life. That year had in fact proved to be one of the most tumultuous in history, the German blitzkrieg overwhelming all opposition throughout Europe. The *Ark Royal* had been extremely active throughout the year, in Norway and in the Mediterranean, and by the end of the year she was tied up in harbour in Gibraltar.

Christmas Day 1940 started like any other on the *Ark Royal*. Engine room artificer John McCrow described the atmosphere at six o'clock in the morning in the ERAs' mess: 'It is early morning and the mess decks are still dimly lit with the shaded blue night-time lighting. Rows of oatmeal-coloured canvas hammocks are gently swaying with the motion of the ship. There is a soft creaking sound coming from the ropes securing the hammocks to the rails fixed to the deck head above. From the scuttles in the metal ducting of the ventilation system comes the swishing sound of the air passing through. Someone murmurs in his sleep and there is an occasional snore. These are the sort of noises of the night. At six o'clock, halfway through the morning watch, the stillness is shattered by the loudspeakers blasting our reveille. The main lighting comes on and a voice shouts, "Wakey wakey, rise and shine, you've had your time, now I'll have mine. Lift up and stow!"'

You could normally tell the day of the week on the *Ark* by the lunchtime menu. 'Sunday was the crème de la crème day, always tomato soup, roast beef, Yorkshire pudding, roast potatoes, and custard with tinned sliced peaches. There was a soup served every day. On Thursday it was mulligatawny, and then I think Irish stew was the main dish on a Tuesday. The amount of bones always outweighed the meat. On a Friday we usually had fish for the main course. The plate of lovely golden battered fish and chips was not all that it seemed. When cutting through the batter a piece of salted cod with a black skin would be revealed.' But on Christmas Day 1940 the crew were looking forward to a day of rest and a slap-up Christmas dinner. The menu had already been printed and it promised giblet soup, a proper roast turkey and chipolatas, Brussels sprouts and roast potatoes. The captain, 'Hooky' Holland, had been photographed stirring the Christmas pudding mix in enormous basins, and after dinner a women's concert party was scheduled to come on board to entertain the crew in the hangar decks.

By one thirty in the afternoon the Christmas dinner had been eaten, and on the various mess decks illicitly saved bottles of the daily rum ration were being passed around. 'It was about two o'clock in the afternoon, when we were thinking about the afternoon show, when over the Tannoy came, "Red watch below!" So we said to ourselves, "They're joking," but it was repeated. "At the double!" Nobody moved. Then the senior chief engineers got going, and then the chief stokers are coming out – their mess was further along from us. But no-one on the stokers' mess deck would move. They were not going down below; they were having their Christmas Day. And the senior engineer came along and he was up on one of the mess deck tables shouting a few rude words, and they were shouting them back at him. Eventually they managed to get the stokers down below. But it took two and a half hours before we were underway.'

The *Admiral Hipper* was threatening a convoy 700 miles east of Cape Finisterre; she was a sister ship of the *Prinz Eugen*, a heavy cruiser armed with 8-inch guns. Hit by shells from the warship that was escorting the convoy, HMS *Berwick*, the *Hipper* retreated and put into Brest harbour for repairs. By the time the *Ark* arrived on the scene the convoy had scattered, and the carrier spent three days locating and shepherding the merchant ships back on to their course, under the protection of another escort ship. A further three days later the *Ark* was back in port in Gibraltar.

Raeder had proved his point. It was clear that access to the French Atlantic ports was of enormous benefit to the Kriegsmarine, and that the rapid deployment of two commerce raiders could bring the *Ark Royal* out of the Mediterranean. For the Royal Navy, this was a grave situation. German armed forces were starting to threaten British positions in the eastern Mediterranean. The Luftwaffe had attacked the *Illustrious*, Malta itself was under continual air attack, and there was a build-up of German armed forces preparing to come to the assistance of the Italian Army in Greece. The Royal Navy was being stretched by the need to fight from Alexandria in the east through the entire Mediterranean, into the Atlantic and up to the north of the Arctic Circle off Norway.

In February 1941 Admiral Somerville signalled to the

Admiralty his proposal for a series of operations in the western Mediterranean to threaten enemy positions on the Italian coast and relieve pressure on the fleet in the east. The Admiralty replied that he was not to do so, as Force H was going to be deployed on the protection of trade routes in the Atlantic.

There was a pressing reason for the Admiralty's message to Somerville. On 5 February those veterans of the Norwegian invasion of 1940, the German battleships *Scharnhorst* and *Gneisenau* under the command of Vice Admiral Günther Lutjens, had slipped into the Atlantic and were heading for the convoy routes. Their campaign was proving highly successful. Working in collaboration with a fleet of U-boats, the *Scharnhorst* and *Gneisenau* accounted for over twenty six cargo ships either sunk or captured, and the torpedoing, by a U-boat, of the battleship *Malaya*. Now every convoy had to have a battleship escort, with its own anti-submarine escort. The *Ark Royal*, with Force H, was detached from the Mediterranean once again to patrol the Atlantic in search of German surface raiders.

Ark Royal and Force H put out from Gibraltar on 8 March and headed west towards the Canary Islands. Their orders were to relieve the *Malaya* from escort duty of a convoy and allow the damaged battleship to proceed to port in the United States for repairs. It was near the Canaries that the *Scharnhorst* and *Gneisenau* had been operating, and liaising with the U-boat flotilla. The *Ark* tried to keep a force of Swordfish torpedo bombers ranged on the flight deck in permanent readiness in case of an encounter, and during the first few days of their patrol the Swordfish were kept on the flight deck overnight, but the wet weather affected the aircraft. Night-time rain put the radios on the Swordfish out of action, and damp affected the engines. After that the aircraft were moved down to the hangar decks.

On 10 March, Force H made contact with the convoy. *Malaya* departed and the *Ark Royal* increased its readiness for action. The Skua squadron on board was kept armed with 500lb semi armour-piercing bombs, despite the fact that these had proved ineffective against the heavy armour of the *Scharnhorst* during the last attack against it in Trondheim Fjord. For the next seven days the *Ark* had the responsibility of escorting the convoy on its course across the Atlantic. An intensive flying programme was carried out. Three quarters of an hour before sunrise an anti-submarine patrol of three Swordfish armed with depth charges was flown off. After patrolling around the convoy, they took up a position 15 miles ahead. A relief patrol of anti-submarine Swordfish also armed with depth charges was kept ranged on deck at readiness, the pilots' observers and telegraphist air gunners waiting in the squadron ready rooms. In the afternoon all-round searches were carried out by nine aircraft, patrolling as far ahead as 120 miles, and during this time a torpedo armed force was kept at readiness throughout the day, as were relief shadowing aircraft should a surface raider be spotted.

Such operations took their toll on both aircraft and men. Sub Lt John Moffat remembers the excruciating routine. The crew would come out onto the flight deck and climb into the cockpit up the small metal steps inset into the Swordfish fuselage, taking care not to put a flying boot through the canvas covering. The engine was started by two flight mechanics inserting a huge starting handle in the side of the cowling and, when everything was ready, turning it as fast as they could. This rotated a flywheel in the engine, and when it was at sufficient speed they would yell and the pilot would press the ignition switch, firing up the radial engine. John would sometimes mistime the ignition switch, and 'they would have to start all over again. There would be curses and God knows what else – which I was not meant to hear of course.' Then the Swordfish, at full throttle, would roll down the flight deck, lift off and head out over the sea on patrols that according to John 'were excruciatingly boring, lasting for three hours or more, over the broad expanse of empty ocean'. The pilots on these patrols would fly over 100 miles away from the *Ark* in a set pattern over the sea, then they would return to the carrier that would in the meantime have moved to a new position. Navigation was by dead reckoning most of the time, the observer hoping to keep an accurate plot of the aircraft's course, with any variations in wind direction and speed accurately recorded.

It was intensely monotonous, lonely and dangerous, and there were casualties. On 15 March a Swordfish failed to return to the carrier from a long-range patrol. There was no signal, although radio silence was the norm so it was unlikely any distress message would have been sent. A Swordfish and three crew members had just silently disappeared. The pilot could have taken the wrong course and run out of petrol, or crashed because of mechanical failure. John Moffat recalled, 'I parcelled up his clothes and belongings, addressed them to his family and handed it in for posting when we got back to Gib. And then you put it out of your mind. There but for the grace of God.'

On the twelfth day of the mission the *Ark Royal* sighted HMS *Kenya*, the cruiser detailed to take over the protection of the convoy. The *Ark* then concentrated on a search for German supply ships that might lead Force H to the *Scharnhorst*. Six Swordfish aircraft and three Fulmars were flown off and three supply ships were finally spotted, the *Bianca*, the *San Casimiro* and the *Polykarp*. Swordfish were sent off to shadow each of them in the hope that eventually they would liaise with the

German warships. However, it soon became obvious that the crews had been given orders: on being spotted they should abandon their ship and scuttle it. The pilots' instructions were to prevent this, if necessary by opening fire with their forward-mounted machine guns.

John Moffat was sent to shadow the *San Casimiro*, and when he arrived he found that the crew were preparing to lower the ship's boats prior to scuttling her. He flew at the ship and fired at the lifeboats, but the forward machine gun was designed to fire through the propeller, and the interrupter mechanism that prevented the bullets from damaging the propeller blades made the rate of fire extremely slow. John believes he could have fired faster with a revolver. While he was trying to damage the ship's boat on one side, the boats on the other side were being lowered, and the crew set fire to the ship before abandoning it.

Another patrol, trailing the *Polykarp*, was having more success. Five Swordfish and three Fulmars had been flown off the *Ark* at four in the afternoon in the belief that the Fulmars with their greater speed would take less time to establish contact than the Swordfish. One of the Fulmars was piloted by Lt Commander Tillard, and his observer was Lt Mark Somerville, Admiral Somerville's nephew. As they searched for the *Polykarp*, they saw below them two German warships steering north. They had spotted the *Scharnhorst* and the *Gneisenau*. Unfortunately their radio chose this vital moment to break down; they could do nothing else but fly at maximum speed back to the *Ark Royal* with the news of their sighting. They landed at half past six.

Captain Holland considered his options. He had seven Swordfish aircraft on patrol, and ten left on board. He immediately had one Swordfish prepared to head to the last reported position of the *Scharnhorst* and *Gneisenau*, which because of the radio failure on the Fulmar was now an hour old. The nine remaining Swordfish were armed with torpedoes and were ready on the flight deck at 1845. In the meantime the captain was calculating ranges and flying times, for the enemy battleships were some 140 miles away and dusk was falling. It would be impossible for the Swordfish to make contact with the two German warships before nightfall. Lt Commander Tillard and Lt Somerville argued that as they had first spotted the *Scharnhorst* and *Gneisenau*, they should take out a Fulmar and search again, which they did, but after an hour on patrol with the light fading they gave up and returned to the *Ark*, landing on at night. The next morning a thick fog lay over the sea to a height of 3,000 feet. Contact with the *Scharnhorst* and its sister ship had been lost completely.

That day, a Swordfish was catapulted off the flight deck on an anti-submarine patrol. The catapults or accelerators were trolleys mounted on the forward part of the flight deck which were fastened to the fuselage of the aircraft being accelerated. When the order to launch was given, the aircraft's engine would be running at full speed and a hydraulic piston under the flight deck would propel the trolley forward, releasing the aircraft at the end of its run. This time, however, the Swordfish did not release from the trolley, and the fuselage broke up. The front part, including the cockpit with the crew and the depth charges under the wing, hurtled into the sea. The crew were seen swimming away, but the great bows of the *Ark* ploughed over the aircraft. The depth charges sank to their predetermined depth and then exploded. Robert Elkington was in his mess at the time, level with the water line in the bows. 'It was an enormous crash,' he recalled, 'and I was sitting with my back to the side of the ship.

I was thrown onto the floor as if a horse had kicked me in the back, and I thought my back was broken.' The impact of the explosions under the hull caused the ship to whip into the air, and on the *Ark*'s eventual return to Gibraltar several splits in the hull had to be repaired with concrete.

Despite the accident, efforts to search for the *Scharnhorst* and *Gneisenau* continued, but Lutjens evaded them and headed safely for Brest, the French port on the Atlantic coast. He had had a very successful and bloody cruise.

The *Ark* had been in the Atlantic almost without a break since early February, when she finally docked in Gibraltar on the first of April. Admiral Raeder's strategy was really paying off. The continuous air patrols, totalling on some days as many as thirty-seven flights, had taken its toll on the men and machines. In the two weeks from 10 March the number of serviceable Swordfish on the *Ark* dropped from a total of twenty-seven to fifteen. Meanwhile, back in the Mediterranean things were also rapidly deteriorating for Britain.

Rommel had opened an offensive in North Africa and was advancing towards Egypt. The German Army, which had been concentrating in Albania, invaded Greece on 6 April and began to drive back the Greek and British armies. By the end of the month it was clear that Greece was lost. Troops and artillery taken from General Wavell's Army of the Nile had been unable to stop the German 12th Army from overrunning the entire country. Those men would now need to be evacuated. In North Africa, the British Army, weakened by the loss of the men and materiel sent to Greece, was now unable to withstand the Afrika Korps' attacks. Cyrenaica, with the exception of Tobruk, was once more in enemy hands.

Wavell had reported to the War Cabinet in London that a German Panzer division had been identified in North Africa. He told them that he urgently needed tank reinforcements to deal with this threat. Even before the evacuation of Greece had been completed, a convoy of five mechanized transport ships left England for Egypt carrying the new tanks that would bolster Wavell's forces. Since the Luftwaffe's entry into the war in the Mediterranean most supplies to the British Army of the Nile had travelled the long route around the Cape of Good Hope. The Admiralty was again extremely reluctant to attempt to run a convoy through the Mediterranean, but Churchill was impatient with these anxieties. 'The fate of the war in the Middle East, the loss of the Suez Canal, the frustration or confusion of the enormous forces we have built up in Egypt . . . all may turn on a few hundred armoured vehicles,' he said. He would brook no opposition, and ordered the convoy to go by the shortest route.

Operation Tiger was the result, which would, if successful, deliver 307 tanks to Alexandria and forty-three Hurricane fighter aircraft, in crates, to be assembled by the RAF in Egypt. HMS *Breconshire*, the special supply ship, would transport fuel and munitions to Malta, and the battleship *Queen Elizabeth* and two cruisers would also travel the length of the Mediterranean under the protection of Force H to reinforce Cunningham's fleet in the eastern Mediterranean. On 5 May the *Ark Royal* sailed west to meet this convoy. Somerville called these transport ships 'ships that passed in the night', because they never stopped at Gibraltar, passing instead under cover of darkness through the Straits with Force H.

There had been some changes in the *Ark Royal*. Captain Holland's health had been deteriorating in the year that he had commanded the carrier, and he left the ship to recuperate, and then became a staff officer in Gibraltar. The new commander was Captain Loben Maund, fresh from a post in Combined Operations, where he had been responsible, among other things, for working up plans to invade the Italian island of Pantelleria. His knowledge of the strategic situation in the Mediterranean was now going to be severely tested.

The *Ark Royal*'s squadrons of Skuas had now been fully replaced by Fulmar fighters, and there were two squadrons of these planes on board, 803 and 807, though out of the nominal number of twenty-four aircraft only twelve were serviceable and fit to fly. If the Luftwaffe attacked the convoy their tactics would be similar to those deployed on *Illustrious*, whose Fulmars were swamped by a far greater number of Stuka dive bombers and Messerschmitt fighters. There was almost no chance that the small number of Fulmars on the *Ark* could stand up to a Luftwaffe onslaught.

It was impossible to know whether the complicated manoeuvres carried out by Force H and the components of the convoys ever fooled the Italian spies in Algeciras, although they may have assumed that the Navy would never, now, dare attempt to pass another convoy down the length of the Mediterranean. Admiral Cunningham's fleet in the eastern Mediterranean was heavily engaged in the evacuation of the British Army from Greece, and his sailors were paying the price for pre-war decisions that left the fleet bereft of fighter protection. On 8 May, in the waters off Greece, two destroyers, *Diamond* and *Wryneck*, came to the assistance of a troop ship that had been bombed and was struggling to reach safety. Between them they took off seven hundred troops and headed at top speed for Crete. They were, however, still in range of the German Stukas, and both destroyers were bombed and sunk. Just one officer, forty-one ratings and eight soldiers survived the deadly attack.

Almost simultaneously, at the other end of the Mediterranean, Force H and the Tiger convoy was spotted by an Italian reconnaissance aircraft. They were three days out from Gibraltar and they had so far evaded detection, but it couldn't last. The presence of this enormously tempting target, a convoy of five large transports with a maximum speed of 14 knots with the *Ark Royal*, the *Renown* and other major warships for company, caused a rapid mobilization of the Italian and German air forces.

At 1345 on 8 May eight aircraft were sighted approaching very low on the starboard bow of the *Ark Royal*. 'They were wicked-looking brutes,' Somerville recorded, and they were also dangerous: Italian S79 torpedo bombers whose pilots had a reputation among the sailors on the *Ark* for pressing home an attack despite a barrage of anti-aircraft fire. One bomber was shot down and crashed into the sea in an eruption of water and wreckage, but the others continued doggedly on their course through gunfire from machine guns and rapid-firing cannon, heading for the two big ships. They dropped their torpedoes inside the destroyer screen designed to protect the *Ark* and the *Renown*. Each aircraft launched two torpedoes simultaneously, and the *Ark Royal* took immediate evasive action to comb the tracks, two torpedoes passing down the port side and the other two avoided on the starboard bow. Admiral Somerville saw one of the torpedoes heading straight for *Renown*, his flagship. 'Now we're for it, I thought, but would you believe it, the damn thing had finished its run and I watched it sinking about 10 yards from the ship.' Two more of the torpedo bombers were hit by the hail of close-range weapon fire as they flew low over their targets, and crashed into the sea.

The torpedo bombers had been accompanied by a squadron of CR42 fighters, and their formation had been spotted by *Sheffield*'s radar ten minutes before they were seen from the *Renown*. The two Fulmars that were already in the air, flown by Lt Commander Tillard and Lt Hay, saw the fighters climbing to attack them. Outnumbered three to one, both pilots dived to make a head-on attack, passing directly through the enemy's formation. The Fulmar flown by Tillard with his observer Mark Somerville went into a steep dive and was last seen trying to level out at 500 feet. Lt Hay, in the second Fulmar, started to follow him down but was attacked during the dive by two CR42 fighters; to evade them he turned into clouds and then dived down towards the fleet, where he was fired on by the destroyer in the anti-submarine screen. Fortunately, it scored no hits.

A section of three more Fulmars, which had taken off from the *Ark Royal* when the enemy formation was identified, also saw a group of six CR42 fighters coming up to attack them, and they dived into a head-on attack. A confusing mêlée ensued during which Lt Taylour shot off the wing tip of one Italian fighter but was himself shot up by an attacker closing in behind him. His Fulmar was hit, and his observer, Petty Officer Howard, was badly wounded. The other two Fulmars, flown by Petty Officer Dubber and Lt Guthrie, were both badly damaged in the dogfight, but Guthrie, after pulling out of a steep spin at a very low altitude, found one of the Italian 579s in his sights and attacked it twice before his guns failed.

These four shot-up Fulmars – Tillard's plane had disappeared – now circled the *Ark*, waiting to land, which they managed at 1437 hours. The torpedo attack and the battle in the air had lasted just one hour. The guns were now silent, the ready-use lockers in the 4.5-inch gun turrets and the magazines of the rapid-firing cannons restocked and ready for the next attack. The excitement and the adrenalin rush of action, the chaotic noise of every gun in the fleet hammering away, was gone, to be replaced by a quietness that could barely be heard through the ringing in the ears of the gunners. Everyone was keyed up, waiting for the next attack. In the hangar decks, the warning bells on the lifts were sounding as planes were brought down from the flight deck, the fireproof curtains were raised and the fitters and armourers frantically tried to repair the aircraft. An already pathetically inadequate number of fighters on the *Ark* had just been reduced from twelve to seven, an observer was in the sick bay being operated on, and the commanding officer of 808 Squadron, who had been on the *Ark* since November 1940 with several kills to his credit, was dead, as was his observer, Lt Mark Somerville.

It had been a brutal sixty minutes, and another attack could occur at any minute. The *Ark Royal* worked hard to keep four Fulmars in the air as a permanent combat air patrol, aircraft landing and refuelling every hour to make sure that they would always have enough endurance to take on the enemy.

The next phase in the air battle for Operation Tiger started at 1510 when *Sheffield*'s radar spotted a reconnaissance aircraft circling the fleet. Two Fulmars were directed by radio to intercept and shoot it down. At the same time, these two Fulmars and the other section of two making up the permanent patrol spotted an Italian S79 bomber. They all converged on it, shooting enough bullets into it to break it up in the air. As the Fulmars returned to the fleet one of them had to ditch in the sea, its engine pouring out white fumes. The crew were rescued by a destroyer, but the aircraft sank quickly.

At a few minutes after four that afternoon, *Sheffield*'s radar plotter reported several formations of aircraft approaching from various points of the compass, and two of them appeared to be large. Having seen off two waves of attack, the prospect of another must have filled the crew with dread. Their situation was desperate. Only a handful of fighters were available and every pilot had seen combat at least once already that day. All available aircraft were flown off, instructed to climb to 8,000 feet and circle at 5 miles' distance. Three Fulmars from 808 Squadron were sent to intercept the formations, but one was forced to return to the carrier when the pilot was unable to retract his undercarriage. The other two Fulmars, flown by Lt Kindersley and Lt Hay, in the air for the second time that day, continued with the attack. Hay shot at a CR42 from behind, causing it to turn away, then took on three S79 bombers in a head-on attack, disrupting their formation and causing them to jettison their bombs and seek shelter in cloud. Meanwhile, Lt Kindersley was manoeuvring to attack a group of bombers when he was ambushed by four CR42 fighters; he decided to fly into the fleet's anti-aircraft barrage, where the enemy fighters refused to follow. After this attack was broken up the two Fulmars were then directed by the air control officer on the *Ark* to intercept another aircraft that had appeared on *Sheffield*'s radar. The aircraft was another S79 bomber, and Lt Hay shot it down in flames. The third Fulmar in the air was flown by Petty Officer Johnson, who avoided three Italian fighters attempting to fire on him from the rear and then saw an S79 bomber which he chased and eventually caught, firing all of his remaining ammunition into it. By then he was 30 miles from the fleet and had to be directed home. He landed at almost five o'clock in the afternoon.

While Hay and Johnson were making their attacks, three S79 bombers penetrated the anti-aircraft barrages and headed for the

Ark Royal, coming out of the sun, which was now low in the west, clearly hoping to drop their bombs down the centre line of the ship – the ideal approach for an air attack. The *Ark* manoeuvred rapidly to port and opened up with all of her guns. She had been designed and built with a multi-barrelled pom-pom platform on the port side, but they had been in such short supply that even now, this far into the war, the pom-poms had not been fitted. John McCrow in the engine room heard the crack of the big guns and then the machine-gun fire opening up and knew that the ship was in immediate danger. 'I used to curse the bastards who had not given us that pom-pom when I felt the ship heeling over and everything opening up,' he said. One bomber did not survive the bullets and the high explosive the *Ark*'s gunners blasted up into the sky; it turned away and jettisoned its bombs in a desperate attempt to gain some height, but crashed into the sea. The machine gunners and all the flight deck crew, crouched in the walkways at the edge of the flight deck, saw the two other bombers boring on towards them, turning to follow the *Ark* and releasing their bombs. They exploded close to the bows on the starboard side, just ahead of the ship. The *Ark* had escaped again.

At 1720, four aircraft from 807 Squadron took to the air, flown by Lt Cdr Douglas, Petty Officer Leggett, Lt Gardner and Lt Firth. As they climbed to reach another enemy formation Gardner heard a sudden bang. His port wing dipped, and he realized that the panel covering his four machine guns in the port wing had been ripped off in the slipstream. He requested permission to land on the carrier again, but then saw that the *Ark* was firing at another group of approaching bombers. This was not a good time to try to land on, so he climbed and attacked one of them, getting in several bursts before losing his target in cloud. When Gardner gave up the chase and left the cloud he was fired at by the escort ships, so he too sought the shelter of the clouds and waited for the firing to stop before landing on the *Ark* to have his wing panels replaced. The other three pilots also attacked the Italian bombers, firing at and chasing them for some distance, constantly hampered in their pursuit by the low speed of their Fulmar fighters. They too eventually lost their prey in the clouds. They continued to maintain a patrol, occasionally being fired on by their own ships.

Throughout the day, Force H and the transports carrying the tanks and Hurricanes for Egypt had been steaming ever closer to Sicily, and at 1918 hours the radar operators on *Sheffield* picked up echoes that they interpreted as large formations of aircraft approaching from Sicily, 42 miles away. The information was immediately passed to the *Ark Royal*. It was yet another massive incoming attack, and this time it could easily be the Luftwaffe from its airfields in Sicily. The news was received with trepidation, for the reason why some of the Sea Lords in the Admiralty, and Somerville and Cunningham, had argued against trying to pass a convoy of vital reinforcements through the Mediterranean was now materializing. It was the Luftwaffe, whose deadly dive bombers had crippled *Illustrious* and were now sinking British warships rescuing the British Army from Greece.

The Commander Air on the *Ark*, Commander Henry Traill, and the captain rapidly assessed the situation. There were three Fulmars in the air, which would need refuelling in another forty-five minutes, and they had already been in combat so had used up a lot of their ammunition. There were a further four Fulmars on the *Ark Royal* that could make it into the air again, making a grand total of seven aircraft with which to defend the fleet and the convoy on which, according to Churchill, the fate of the British Army in North Africa depended. It was a daunting task. I once asked Val Bailey, who had flown a Fulmar in 808 Squadron on the *Ark Royal*, whether he had ever been frightened. 'We were young and we were fighter pilots,' he replied. 'We had the invincible belief of the young in our own immortality. And anyway, you just had to get on with it. You certainly weren't going to hang about and wait to get bombed – the bloody gunnery people couldn't hit anything. No, you got worried, because there were a lot of things to worry about and go wrong, and because you had so much to do, but you didn't get frightened. Although there was every reason to do so.'

The pilots still in the air on that evening of 8 May were joined by the other four aircraft. Lt Gardner's Fulmar had been repaired and he took off again for his fourth fighter patrol. Petty Officer Dubber, Lt Taylour and Sub Lt Walker followed him off the *Ark Royal*'s flight deck, their Merlin engines hauling the heavy aircraft slowly into the air. Those seven pilots with their observers in the rear cockpits were all that now stood between the *Ark Royal*, Force H and the approaching German dive bombers. They went into the fight extremely aggressively, despite the overwhelming numbers of enemy aircraft that confronted them.

The German aircraft had split up into different sections, and the fighter direction officer on the *Ark* thought they were preparing to make a concerted attack from three directions so that the *Ark* would always be presenting a perfect target to at least one section of dive bombers. The three fighters already on patrol at 8,000 feet were directed by the *Ark* to fly to the north of the fleet, where the radar operators on *Sheffield* had identified a number of aircraft circling above some stratus cloud. As they approached they saw that they were a group of fifteen Stuka dive bombers under the protection of six Messerschmitt Me110s, twin-engined long-range fighters. Lt Commander Douglas turned into the Me110s and fired at two in turn, seeing the second one he had hit go down into cloud. The rear gunners of both Messerschmitts returned fire, and Douglas's Fulmar was hit in the leading edge of both wings, and his hydraulic system was damaged. Petty Officer Leggett, Douglas's wingman, dived straight on to the circling Stukas, but one of the German fighters attempted to intercept him. Leggett turned inside the Messerschmitt and fired a burst of machine-gun fire into the cockpit, putting the rear gunner out of action; the German aircraft seemed to stall and turn, and it dived into cloud with a trail of white smoke behind it. Lt Firth was met by two of the German fighters climbing towards him and he made a head-on approach, firing into the leading aircraft. This one also turned away and dived into cloud with smoke pouring from one engine. The second Messerschmitt was also fired on by Leggett, and this too manoeuvred away from the attack into cloud.

These three pilots had, in an incredibly brave and aggressive approach, driven off six Messerschmitt fighters, probably damaging at least three. The three Fulmar pilots continued to search for them under the cloud but could not locate them. They were soon running short of fuel and ammunition and had to return to the *Ark*.

The four pilots who had taken off from the *Ark Royal* had now climbed to 9,000 feet and saw that as well as the six escorting Messerschmitts there was a group of sixteen Stukas and another group of twelve. Lt Taylour dived into the latter to break it up, carrying out several attacks and pursuing the Stukas into cloud for about 30 miles. His plane was hit and the starboard under-carriage leg dropped down, forcing him to return to the *Ark*.

Petty Officer Dubber, who was Lt Taylour's wingman, made a head-on attack, then turned and started firing from the rear quarter. One of the escorting fighters then attempted to protect the dive bombers and made a stern attack on Dubber's Fulmar, which he evaded by diving into cloud.

Lt Gardner had split off from Lt Taylour's section and aggressively attacked the other section of sixteen Stukas, pouring a burst of gunfire into the nearest one which turned over and dived into the sea. He then hurtled his plane through the formation of Stukas, firing at close range at several others. His own aircraft was hit, bullets smashing the windscreen and punching holes in the engine's radiator, but he managed to break up the formation and several of the Stukas started to jettison their bombs. Gardner's aircraft was badly damaged and he had to return to the *Ark*, but his number two, Lt Firth, continued to attack a formation of three Messerschmitt 110s, which scattered into cloud. Searching for more targets, Firth then flew on and attacked a formation of Stukas before becoming embroiled in a dogfight with an Me110 which broke off the action. Firth again launched his fighter at the Stukas, pursuing a straggler into cloud with smoke pouring from it. Firth's air gunner, Leading Airman Shave, saw at least one Stuka go down in flames.

By 2139, all of the Fulmars had landed back on the *Ark Royal*. Not one Stuka had succeeded in making an attack on the fleet, despite their overwhelming superiority. Yet the day wasn't over. A separate attack had started at half past eight that night. Having sneaked in under the radar while everyone was focused on the attack from the German dive bombers, three low-level torpedo bombers flew at the *Renown* and the *Ark Royal*. One broke away after anti-aircraft fire started to hit it, and bits of its fuselage were seen flying off, but the other two launched their torpedoes. *Ark*

Royal for the second time that day made a sharp turn to port and the torpedoes passed 50 metres away on the starboard side.

This was the final attack of a day that had seen the *Ark Royal* and Force H facing an onslaught of over fifty aircraft in total, defended by a maximum of twelve serviceable Fulmars out of two squadrons on board. The Fulmar, it should be remembered, had been an aircraft accepted into service by the Navy as a stop-gap. It was heavy, barely faster than the bombers its pilots were attempting to shoot down, and less manoeuvrable than both Italian and German fighters. There was a sense of puzzlement on board the *Ark Royal* that the German dive bombers hadn't pursued their attack with more determination. There was a theory that the German pilots had mistaken the Fulmars for the more effective Hurricane fighters. Yet they had faced Fulmar aircraft when they successfully dive-bombed *Illustrious*, so this seems unlikely. The German attack was made late in the day, as it was growing dark, and the vigour and aggression of the Fulmar pilots might have proved a nasty surprise. Several of the Stuka formations were broken up, so the German pilots might have become unhappy about continuing their attack, which was clearly going to be aggressively opposed, in the dwindling light. Whatever the reason, the actions of the pilots, air gunners and observers of 807 and 808 Squadrons had saved an extremely vital convoy.

Several days later Admiral Somerville was told that Winston Churchill had been extremely nervous about Operation Tiger and was very pleased that it had got through. The events of 8 May make it clear that he was quite right to be anxious. The report of Captain Maund stated, 'The immunity of the convoy and fleet from damage due to air attack on this day is largely attributable to the work of this small force of fighters, made possible only by the exceptional efforts of the personnel of the flight deck and hangars.' The fighter direction had been extremely efficient in directing what few aircraft were in the air to their targets. It was just a pity that the fleet's anti-aircraft guns were not so well directed: many of the *Ark*'s pilots found themselves avoiding friendly fire. The only tragedy of the day had been the loss of Lt Commander Tillard and Lt Somerville, Admiral Somerville's nephew. They never returned to the *Ark* and their plane was never found.

Two days later, the group of destroyers that had escorted the transport ships through the Skerki Channel to Malta were returning west when they were attacked by four bombers flying low and using broken cloud as cover. None of the ships had radar or any air defence. Four sticks of bombs were dropped, and the *Faulkner* was severely damaged by a cluster of four or five near-misses very close to the stern. Her speed was cut in half, but she managed to limp back to meet Force H, and eventually reached Gibraltar. It was a salutary reminder that the threat from the air never went away.

The success of Operation Tiger was an enormous boost to morale. The *Ark Royal* and Force H had shown that the presence of the combined air forces of Italy and Germany did not mean that the Mediterranean was a no-go area, though it had been an extremely close-run thing. The *Ark* had become a highly efficient warship, and in combination with the *Sheffield* she was now adept at maximizing the limited air resources available to her.

The *Ark Royal* and its aircraft had succeeded in doing something that it was never intended to do, and which pre-war naval strategists had not thought possible. It had contested control of a sea that ought to have been dominated by the superior land-based aircraft of the enemy.

Shortly after returning to Gibraltar the *Ark* was steaming east again, this time in company with the carrier HMS *Furious* carrying a deck cargo of Hurricane aircraft that were to be flown off to reinforce Malta. It was just another reminder of how important the *Ark* was to Britain's war effort in the Mediterranean.

Later that month she would also prove her value in the war in the Atlantic, becoming the nemesis of a German admiral whose path had crossed the *Ark*'s several times before.

10

THE *BISMARCK* INCIDENT

On 21 May 1941, the *Ark Royal* was steaming into the wind near Cape Bon, on the coast of Tunisia, the western point of the Sicilian channel. It was first light, and the air still had a night-time chill to it. Flight deck crews were busily readying two Fulmar aircraft for take-off. Behind them, clustered at the rear of the flight deck, were twenty-one Hurricane aircraft fitted with long-range fuel tanks. Their pilots were making final checks on their course and working out their fuel consumption before walking out to their planes, eager to take off and get to Malta without being seen by an Italian or German reconnaissance aircraft. There was a sense of urgency in the air, for the *Ark Royal* and *Furious* were close to Sicily. With the Hurricane aircraft on the flight deck they could not launch Swordfish for anti-submarine patrols, and they were defenceless if they were attacked from the air.

The two Fulmars took off, followed by the Hurricanes, but the pilot of one of the Fulmars could not retract its undercarriage so he circled back towards the *Ark Royal*. The Hurricane pilots didn't understand what was happening and, following orders to the letter, stuck to him like glue. Communication was impossible because of radio silence, so the crew of the Fulmar, aware that the Hurricanes were eating into their fuel while they circled the carrier, headed for Malta. They knew that the excessive drag from their undercarriage, dangling in the slipstream, would shorten their range, making it impossible for them to reach their destination, but they decided that their first priority was to lead the Hurricanes to Malta, whatever their own fate. It was an act of extraordinary courage. They took the Hurricanes within easy reach of the island before ditching in the sea. Five other Fulmars and forty-seven Hurricanes arrived successfully in Malta. The mission was a success due largely to their sacrifice. Two days later, the *Ark Royal* was back in Gibraltar.

Far to the north, while the engines of the Fulmars and Hurricanes were running up on the flight deck of the *Ark*, two German warships steamed through the waters of the Skagerrak between Denmark and Norway, heading north. The *Bismarck* and the *Prinz Eugen* were beginning Operation Rhine, the latest sally into the North Atlantic as part of Admiral Raeder's strategy against the Royal Navy. Yet there was a significant difference in the threat posed by this operation. The *Bismarck*, a ship launched in August 1939, was one of the most modern battleships afloat, and one of the most powerful.

She had been laid down in the shipyard of Blohm and Voss in Hamburg in 1936. She was named after the great Prussian general and the first Chancellor of Germany, the creator of the modern state of Germany. That his name should be chosen was an indicator of the national pride that had been invested in this great modern warship. The launching ceremony drew deliberately on this tradition: the ship was launched by Bismarck's granddaughter, and the guest of honour was Hitler himself, whose ambition far exceeded the wildest dreams of the Prussian generals.

There was no other ship at sea that could match the *Bismarck*. Her main armament was eight large guns that could fire shells 38cm in diameter, each weighing almost 800kg. These giant shells could be hurled through the air over a distance of 36 kilometres. In addition, the *Bismarck* carried twelve smaller 15cm-calibre guns that were equal in firepower to a British cruiser. There were also a large number of anti-aircraft guns of different calibres. She was the largest ship afloat because she was so heavily armoured. Of her maximum weight of over 50,000 tons fully loaded, over a third comprised armour protection. At her water line there was almost 39cm of plating, and her designers were confident that she could resist any projectile fired at her from any distance. Even with this enormous weight, the *Bismarck* was almost as fast as any of the modern battleships in the Royal Navy. And it wasn't just the size and armament of the *Bismarck* that made her such a formidable ship. The Kriegsmarine had developed two systems of firing control that were extremely accurate, as the conflict between the *Exeter* and the *Graf Spee* in 1939 had demonstrated. The primary method and the most modern was Seetakt, a form of radar that could locate targets in poor visibility and provide accurate ranges and bearings for the gun directors. There was also a visual rangefinding mechanism that was precise and very easy to use, which was important amid the chaos and confusion of a battle.

When they sailed through the waters between Denmark and

Norway, the *Bismarck* and the *Prinz Eugen* were the most modern and most powerful naval task force afloat. The Royal Navy had never had to face *Bismarck*'s like before. Under the command of Admiral Lutjens, the hero of the Norwegian invasion in 1940 and the latest successful convoy raiding operation by the *Scharnhorst* earlier that year, they were about to continue a strategy that had so far proved extremely successful in the war against Britain.

The fact that one or two warships could absorb the efforts of a large part of the Royal Navy was, of course, an important part of Raeder's strategy. It was his view that any naval operation had to be seen in relation to its effect on other theatres of the war. Against an enemy that was overstretched, a battleship putting to sea could tie down a significant portion of the enemy's fleet. Raeder calculated that the presence of these two battleships in the Atlantic – the *Bismarck* capable of defeating any other warship that might be escorting a merchant convoy, leaving the *Prinz Eugen* free to sink the civilian ships without any hindrance – would have the maximum impact on Britain's war effort at a time when Germany was putting more and more resources into the Mediterranean war. The situation for Britain was growing increasingly difficult, and the Royal Navy's grip on the Mediterranean was becoming weaker.

The Afrika Korps under the command of General Rommel had overwhelmed the British Eighth Army in the Western Desert and advanced to the borders of Egypt. The Royal Navy had had to evacuate some fifty thousand troops from Greece, twenty thousand of whom had been landed in Crete, joining an existing force of another ten thousand. Churchill insisted that Crete must remain in British hands, although General Wavell in Cairo and the New Zealander General Freyberg on the island itself were sceptical that the forces on Crete, mostly disorganized evacuees from Greece, would be able to withstand a German invasion should it come. Admiral Cunningham, the Commander in Chief of the Mediterranean Fleet, had already protested to Churchill about the increasing number of vital tasks his dwindling number of ships had to carry out. His constant complaint was his inability to do anything in the face of overwhelming German air superiority. Churchill had written to Cunningham at the end of April, barely able to disguise his exasperation, though he had at least a little good news: the two battleships *Nelson* and *Rodney* were being taken away from the Home Fleet in the Atlantic and sent to reinforce Cunningham's ships in the Mediterranean.

In your last para you wonder how I could have suggested that *Nelson* and *Rodney* should be spared from the Atlantic to join the Mediterranean Fleet. I thought they were especially suitable because of their deck armour and the apprehension entertained of dive-bomber attack. Whether or not they could be spared depended on the situation in the Atlantic. About this I will now inform you. I have been for a long time in correspondence with President Roosevelt. He has now begun to take over a great part of the patrolling west of the 26th meridian West . . . The easement and advantage of it to the Admiralty is enormous and of course it may easily produce even more decisive events; therefore you do not need at this moment to be unduly concerned about the Atlantic, and can devote your resources to cutting off enemy communication with Africa . . .

Then, on 20 May, Germany launched an airborne assault on the island of Crete. Thousands of paratroopers dropped from the skies, their transport planes protected by squadrons of fighters and dive bombers. At the same time German troop ships landed reinforcements on the north of the island, who captured the airfield. It was while the British Army and Navy were engaged in a desperate and bloody battle for the control of Crete that the *Bismarck* weighed anchor and slid out of the fjord at Bergen. The next few days were to become some of the blackest moments of Britain's war against Germany.

Admiral Lutjens wanted to take advantage of fog and low cloud to make his break-out into the Atlantic undetected. The Admiralty had, however, become aware that the *Bismarck* was on the move. A reconnaissance Spitfire had photographed her at anchor in the fjord near Bergen; a second reconnaissance flight revealed that she had departed, and it was now a question for the Admiralty of guessing which route into the Atlantic Lutjens had chosen. The task of intercepting the German warships was given to Admiral Sir John Tovey, Commander in Chief of the Home Fleet, who considered that Lutjens had two options open to him.

The first was an attempted pass either to the south or to the north of the Faeroe Islands. The southerly route was not ideal for the German ships because it was within range of RAF aircraft in northern Scotland, so the northerly route, between the Faeroes and Iceland, seemed the most logical. It was the widest gap between Greenland and Britain, and it was the most difficult to cover with reconnaissance aircraft. Tovey stationed three light cruisers in this area, and they were supported by *King George V*, a modern, recently commissioned battleship, and the aircraft carrier *Victorious*. In company with these ships was *Repulse*, an old battlecruiser that had been on her way to shipyards in Boston for a refit before being dragooned back into the Home Fleet as reinforcement. Lutjens could also choose a route between Iceland and Greenland. The presence of pack ice made these waters quite narrow, but Lutjens may well have calculated that there was a better chance of poor visibility, giving him extra cover. This was the route he had used successfully when commanding *Scharnhorst* and *Gneisenau* earlier in the year, and Tovey calculated, quite correctly as it turned out, that Lutjens would rely on it again. It was here that he intended to set his trap. Tovey ordered two cruisers, *Suffolk* and *Norfolk*, to patrol these narrow straits, with the *Hood* and the *Prince of Wales*, Britain's most modern battleship, in a position further south. The *Prince of Wales* had only recently been handed over to the Royal Navy by Cammell Laird; dockyard workers were still on board and the ship's crew were still learning how to handle the ship. None of these ships was a match for the *Bismarck*, but Tovey positioned his two forces so that they could quickly reinforce each other once the German battleship had been spotted.

Admiral Lutjens steered for the Denmark Strait, and he was lucky: the weather conditions were overcast, with rain, and there was moderate to poor visibility, as low at times as 200 metres. As the *Bismarck* headed south-west, close to the edge of the pack ice fringing the coast of Greenland, she entered a patch of clear weather. The two British cruisers *Norfolk* and *Suffolk* were patrolling this area, but were still enveloped in a belt of fog clinging to the coast of Iceland and extending some way out into the channel. *Suffolk*, moving slowly ahead, suddenly emerged out of the fog bank into bright sunshine, and barely 6 miles away were the two German warships. Captain Ellis immediately ordered his ship back into the fog and sent a message that she was in contact with *Bismarck*. The message was not received by the Admiralty or by Admiral Tovey, but it was received by Admiral Somerville in Gibraltar, and he put Force H on orders to be prepared to put to sea in two hours. *Suffolk* was equipped with radar, so she continued to track the course of the *Bismarck* while remaining hidden in the fog.

Bismarck had not seen the *Suffolk* and was not aware that she had been sighted, but an hour later the second cruiser *Norfolk* left the fog bank and found herself very close to the German battleship. This time the lookouts saw the British cruiser and the *Bismarck* opened fire with her main armament, using them for the first time in anger. Huge gouts of water burst all around the *Norfolk* as she headed back at full speed into the fog, and a second signal was sent to the Admiralty. This time the message was picked up by both the *Hood*, which with the *Prince of Wales* was 300 miles to the south, and the *King George V*, covering the Iceland–Faeroes gap 600 miles away. Both groups of warships headed at full speed towards the enemy. The fight between the British Home Fleet and the most powerful ship of the German Navy had begun.

In the Denmark Strait, Admiral Lutjens was still steaming in a south-westerly direction, aware that he must have been reported by the cruiser that he had fired on but unaware that Admiral Holland's force, the *Hood* and the *Prince of Wales*, was approaching on a course to intercept him. At a quarter past five in the morning of Saturday, 24 May, a hydrophone operator in the *Prinz Eugen* heard what he thought were the propeller noises of ships approaching from the south-east. Half an hour later, lookouts on the *Prince of Wales* sighted the German warships. Admiral Holland knew that he was heading towards the *Bismarck* and the *Prinz Eugen*, but Lutjens was unclear about the type of ships that were clearly steaming towards him. He was under orders not to engage in battle with British warships unless it was an unavoidable consequence of an attack on a merchant convoy. But it was clear that he was being pursued, and he knew he might not have any choice in the matter. The *Prinz Eugen* signalled, mistakenly, that the two approaching British warships were cruisers, so Lutjens assumed that they were reinforcements for the cruisers that were already shadowing them. Anyway, there was little Lutjens could do in the circumstances. His choice of route to the Atlantic, along the southern edge of the Greenland pack ice, limited his ability to manoeuvre, so he continued his course towards the approaching *Hood* and *Prince of Wales*.

At seven minutes to six Lutjens realized that he was confronted with much more serious opposition when the *Hood* and the *Prince of Wales* opened fire with their main guns. They were two of the most powerful ships in the Royal Navy and their combined firepower might well have been enough to overwhelm the *Bismarck*, but the effect of their initial onslaught was weakened by poor identification and lack of communication. Holland, on the *Hood*, had given the order to open fire at the leading German ship believing it to be the *Bismarck*, but it was in fact the *Prinz Eugen*. The gunnery officer on the *Prince of Wales* had correctly identified both ships but no message was sent to correct the *Hood*'s mistake. Consequently the British gunnery was not focused, the *Prince of Wales* alone firing at the *Bismarck* while the *Hood* continued to direct her fire at the *Prinz Eugen*.

There was confusion on the German ships as well. Admiral Lutjens remained in some doubt about what to do. His orders were not to engage in battle with superior forces and he was not at first inclined to return the fire. But Captain Ernst Lindemann of the *Bismarck* argued that the situation they now found themselves in must counter any other orders. He was not prepared to stand idly by while his ship was shot from under him. The order was given to open fire, and both ships concentrated on the *Hood*. The German gunnery was accurate, and Admiral

Holland's flagship received some direct hits. The shellfire from the *Prince of Wales* was also starting to find its target, and the *Bismarck* received a direct hit of its own from one of the huge 14-inch shells. It entered on the starboard bow above the water line and ruptured an oil tank.

Meanwhile, a fire had broken out on the *Hood*, caused by a direct hit from the *Bismarck*. Then, at six o'clock, the battle all of seven minutes old, the *Hood* was hit again by a salvo from the *Bismarck*. A mountain of flame and a yellowish white fireball burst up between her masts and she split apart in a massive explosion. White stars, probably molten pieces of metal, shot out from the black smoke that followed the flame, and huge fragments, one of which looked like a main turret, whirled through the air like toys. Wreckage of every description littered the water around the *Hood*, one especially conspicuous piece remaining on fire for a long time and giving off clouds of dense black smoke. The *Hood*, the pride of the Royal Navy, a 48,000-ton warship, had disappeared in seconds in a catastrophic explosion.

There are few eye-witness accounts of events on the *Hood* during the battle. So sudden and catastrophic was her demise that out of the total crew of 1,500, only three sailors survived. One of them, Ted Briggs, was on the compass platform, and he described his last sight of Admiral Holland sitting slumped in his chair, staring into space as the forward part of the ship toppled into the ocean. The vast majority of the crew at their action stations, locked in the magazines and engine spaces, had no chance of escape.

The loss of the *Hood* had an impact far greater than the loss of just one ship, tragic though the enormous loss of life was. The Royal Navy could not afford to lose a single battleship of course,

The underwater photograph clearly shows the inverted fairleads and the projecting bracket for the navigating light, also visible in the photograph of the *Ark* being fitted out.

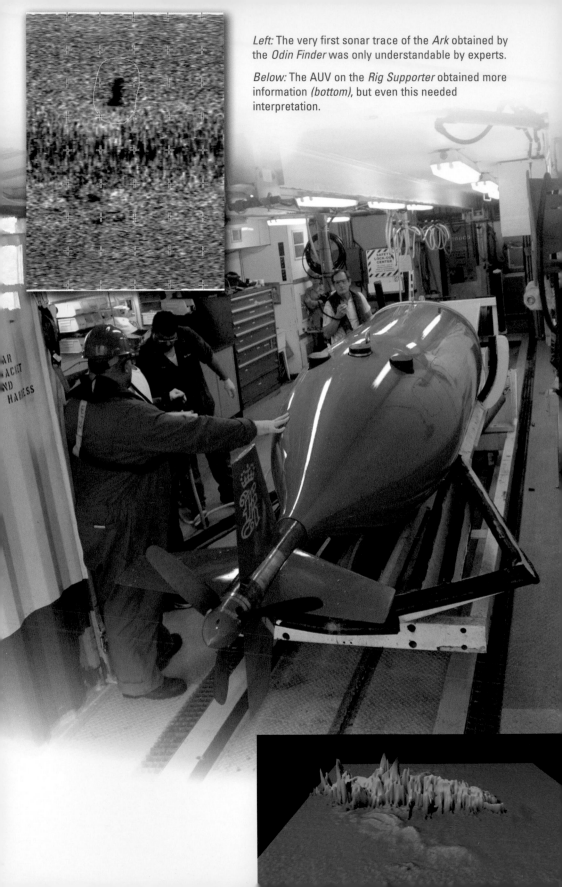

Left: The very first sonar trace of the *Ark* obtained by the *Odin Finder* was only understandable by experts.

Below: The AUV on the *Rig Supporter* obtained more information *(bottom)*, but even this needed interpretation.

Left: The *Octopus*, one of the largest yachts in the world, took the search for the *Ark* to its conclusion.

Right: Val Bailey, Bill Morrison, John Moffat, John Richardson and Ron Skinner look at the *Ark*'s blueprints on board tho *Octopus*.

Below: The Octorov, purpose-built with special lights and cameras, is launched from its hangar on the *Octopus*.

The giant anchors are revealed in the ROV spotlights.

The trail of wreckage contains lockers, with cups and teapots still unbroken, and even small batteries are highlighted by the lights on the ROV *(below)*.

This black and white photograph *(centre)* shows the bows of the *Ark* being painted in Alexandria. The 36-inch searchlight *(top right)* is also revealed, and the depth markings are still there on the hull *(bottom right)*.

OPPOSITE PAGE:
The Fairey Swordfish *(top)* were the workhorses of the *Ark Royal*. Very little remains on the bottom of the sea, but propellers *(middle)* and engines *(bottom)* can still be picked out.

THIS PAGE:
The all-metal Fulmar fighter survives slightly better *(middle)*, but it's impossible to know if this was one flown by Val Bailey *(top)*.

Bill Morrison, Ron Skinner, John Moffat, Val Bailey and John Richardson at the end of their exploration of the wreck *(bottom)*.

The 4.5-inch anti-aircraft guns could elevate almost vertically. Here *(below)*, the rear turret manned by Les Asher is adorned by a Rock Fish, caught in the lights from the ROV.

Above: The camera zooms into the interior of the turret, catching the light reflected from the optical gunsight.

but the *Hood* was far more than just another capital ship. She was no longer the most powerful or most modern battleship in the Royal Navy, but she was certainly the most well known and admired. She had for so many years been seen as the flagship of the Royal Navy. During the 1930s on a world tour, visiting the outposts of empire, showing the flag in the Dominions and in America, at countless Navy Days she had epitomized the power of the Royal Navy and the might of the British Empire. Now she was gone, blown apart after a few minutes of battle. Ron Skinner remarked to me that at the beginning of the war she was considered a very safe posting, and that everyone in his cadet class had been envious of those who had gone to the *Hood*. 'You lucky blighters! When it was announced over the Tannoy on the *Ark*, it was a real shock, a great blow.'

The battle was not yet over, however. With the *Hood* now sunk, both German battleships turned their fire on to the *Prince of Wales*, and within three minutes of the *Hood* exploding the *Prince of Wales* suffered a serious hit on the bridge which killed everybody there except the captain and a signal petty officer. Another shell hit the forward fire control centre, a third shell hit the aircraft crane, and a fourth smashed into the hull below the water line but, with extraordinary luck, failed to explode. The *Prince of Wales* was also suffering some serious mechanical problems, the result of her being pressed into service on the hunt for the *Bismarck* before she had been properly worked up. One of the main turrets could no longer turn properly, and it was impossible for the ship to fire a full salvo. Captain Leach immediately ordered his ship to turn away and escape any more punishing hits under cover of a smokescreen.

It was a remarkable victory for the two German warships. In just a few minutes they had sunk one of the Royal Navy's most famous warships and seen off the challenge of a second. Captain Lindemann knew that he could pursue the *Prince of Wales* and finish her off, compounding the defeat for the Royal Navy, but Lutjens overruled him, arguing that the original mission of the German task force had to take precedence. So the two ships continued on their course into the Atlantic, followed now, at a distance, by the two shadowing cruisers *Norfolk* and *Suffolk*, and a damaged *Prince of Wales*.

This first successful if unplanned action by the *Bismarck* potentially had a far greater strategic impact than the purely tactical advantage foreseen by Raeder. Churchill had been growing increasingly gloomy since the spring of 1940: first Norway and Dunkirk, then the London Blitz, North Africa, Greece and Crete. When news of the loss of the *Hood* reached him at Chequers on the morning of 24 May he was cast into a black depression. It was, in his own words, 'a bitter disappointment and grief to me'. There was no question that the loss of the *Hood* would be a serious blow to public morale; it would also seriously affect opinion in the United States, now seen by Churchill as the only possible source of assistance in a dire situation. His pleas to Roosevelt had become increasingly desperate in recent weeks, emphasizing the serious situation in the Atlantic and urging the United States to enter the war.

Three days earlier Churchill had telegrammed to Roosevelt, 'I hope you will forgive me if I say that there is anxiety here. We are at a climacteric of the war, when enormous crystallizations are in suspense, but imminent . . . You will see from my cancelled message to Wilkie how grievous I feel it that the United States should build 3 to 4 million tons of shipping and watch their equivalent being sunk beforehand.' When Churchill heard that the *Bismarck* was being pursued by the *Hood*, he had sent a further telegram to Roosevelt, saying, 'Should we fail to catch them going out your navy should surely be able to mark them down for us. Give us the news and we will finish the job.' The events of a few hours later proved that that was an empty boast. Ever since the destruction of Oran, Churchill had striven to demonstrate to the world, but more importantly to the United States, that Britain was worth supporting and capable of fighting back. That view would not survive long if there were major defeats in the Atlantic at the hands of the Kriegsmarine.

The *Prince of Wales* and the two cruisers *Norfolk* and *Suffolk* were still shadowing the *Bismarck* but were not prepared to enter into an outright battle with her. The only hope, it seemed, of stopping and sinking the *Bismarck* lay with the other task force of the Home Fleet, which had been guarding the southern route into the Atlantic, the gap between Iceland and the Faeroes. Admiral Tovey, with *King George V*, *Repulse* and *Victorious*, was 600 miles away when news of the first contact with the *Bismarck* had been received, and he doubted he would be able to successfully intercept her before she avoided pursuit and disappeared into the Atlantic. He had to slow her down, so he ordered *Victorious* to mount a torpedo strike on the *Bismarck* with her squadron of Swordfish aircraft.

The *Victorious* had originally been on her way to Gibraltar to help the *Ark Royal* and Force H deliver a consignment of Hurricanes to Malta. She was then going to make a high-speed dash through the narrow channel between North Africa and Sicily and head for Alexandria to reinforce Admiral Cunningham's Mediterranean Fleet. Now, diverted at the start of her journey into the effort to stop the *Bismarck*, she carried only one Swordfish squadron, whose leader, Lt Commander Eugene Esmonde, was an experienced Fleet Air Arm pilot, a survivor of the sinking of HMS *Courageous* in 1939. The rest of the pilots on board, however, were very inexperienced, many of them having made their first landing on the deck of a carrier just a few days before.

They took off in a heavy sea and bad weather with low cloud and poor visibility. After a flight of almost two hours they finally caught sight of the German warship. They made their attack from the east, with the *Bismarck* silhouetted against the setting sun, except for one pilot, Lt Percy Gick, who decided to attack from the west. Coming unobtrusively out of the sun while the anti-aircraft fire of the *Bismarck* was directed against the main group of Swordfish, Lt Gick managed to get close enough to score a hit, causing a massive column of black smoke to rise from the side of the battleship. The warhead exploded against the thick side armour of the *Bismarck*, the concussion killing a crew member. It exacerbated the damage done by the shells of the *Prince of Wales*, but it was not serious enough to slow her down sufficiently for Admiral Tovey to gain on her.

The situation, for the British forces, then worsened consider-ably. The *Prinz Eugen* had already managed to separate from the *Bismarck* under cover of a sudden foray against the *Prince of Wales* by Lutjens' flagship, but the two cruisers *Suffolk* and *Norfolk* had managed to continue shadowing the *Bismarck* by radar ever since their first contact off Greenland. Then, while the two British cruisers were on one path of their zigzag anti-submarine course, the *Bismarck* made a sudden turn to the west and continued in a large circle on to an easterly course, passing behind them. They lost radar contact, and the *Bismarck* was now heading for St Nazaire, clear of any pursuit. Confusion spread through the Admiralty and the ships under Admiral

Tovey's command. It seemed that the Royal Navy had totally failed.

As dawn broke on the morning of 25 May, not only had contact with the enemy been lost, but there was little possibility of finding her again. Visibility was worsening and there was a gale blowing. Aircraft from *Victorious* were flown off to search for the German battleship but found nothing.

Just before dusk on the 25th, Admiral Lutjens, not realizing that he had thrown off his pursuers, sent a lengthy signal to his HQ in Berlin detailing his plans. This signal was picked up by tracking stations in the UK, and it was possible to work out a rough location for the battleship, and for the Admiralty to confirm that the *Bismarck* was in fact heading for the French coast. Admiral Tovey's forces, however, had been directed north by the Admiralty who believed that the German ships were heading back to Norway; he was now too far away to intercept the *Bismarck* before she could reach the protection of Luftwaffe bombers based in France. Moreover, Tovey's flagship, the *King George V*, was running low on fuel and unless the enemy's speed was reduced he would have to abandon the chase at midnight and leave *Rodney*, a First World War battlecruiser, as the sole British warship in pursuit of the mighty *Bismarck*. The situation for the British was bleak. There was now only one hope left: aircraft from the *Ark Royal* must attack the *Bismarck* and slow her down.

At eleven o'clock Force H received orders to assume that the enemy had turned towards the French harbour of Brest, and to head north to mount an aerial search for the *Bismarck*. Somerville made plans with Captain Maund on the *Ark Royal* to be ready to fly off a reconnaissance patrol by seven o'clock the next morning, to search an area of 140 miles by about 90.

Even if *Bismarck* was located, the chances of a successful

strike against her were not good, as the aircraft from *Victorious* had proved: despite a successful hit, the *Bismarck* was unharmed. And the *Ark*'s air crew did not have an impressive record when it came to torpedo attacks against ships at sea. Somerville had instigated a rigorous programme of training in Force H, but certainly the senior officers would still remember the poor showing six months earlier when Italian warships had escaped unscathed from a Swordfish attack at Spartivento. Somerville had nearly been court-martialled as a result of that failure. In addition, the weather was worsening all the time. During the night the headwinds became so bad that it looked as though the *Ark Royal* in company with Somerville's flagship *Renown* would not be able to reach the search area until nine in the morning. The *Bismarck* appeared to be slipping out of the grasp of the Royal Navy.

The crew of the *Ark Royal* had been kept informed of the unfolding events of the past few days. As they headed into the Atlantic, John Moffat recalls, there was an announcement by Captain Maund over the Tannoy: 'We are heading north and we are trying to intercept the battleship *Bismarck*, which has come out from Norway and is now in the Atlantic. We are trying to find her, because at the moment her position is unknown.'

There had been a certain rivalry between the air crew of the *Ark* and the *Illustrious* after the attack on the Italian fleet at Taranto, and the Swordfish pilots of the *Ark* now thought they could redress the balance: 'It was a chance to show what we could do.'

At dawn the *Ark Royal* was struggling through mountainous seas, and the flight deck was see-sawing up and down by over 16 metres. No aircraft had ever been flown from the deck of a carrier in such weather. When the first Swordfish were brought up on the lift to the flight deck for the first patrol extra men were needed to hold them down. The flight deck was 63 feet (19 metres) above sea level, but waves were breaking over the forward edge. The whole ship was covered in spray. Ron Skinner remembers the scene: 'The first reconnaissance aircraft took off at around eight o'clock. The first one missed a wave by inches as it broke over the flight deck. The water coming over the bows reached back to the bridge. It was a sight that none of us would forget.' Ten aircraft in total were launched in the search for the *Bismarck*. They were brought to the centre line, their engines roaring at full power, and as the deck officer's flag dropped they would roll forward, either struggling uphill or heading downhill directly at the sea, depending on the attitude of the ship at the time. As the aircraft passed the bridge the observer read the latest instructions about windspeed and direction scribbled on a blackboard, and it was then off into the storm, heading for the search area.

With her aircraft successfully launched, the *Ark* was herself off on a new course, 50 miles to the north, where the Swordfish that had just taken off would have to try and find the German battleship. About two hours later a signal was intercepted in the *Ark* from a Coastal Command Catalina saying that the *Bismarck* had been spotted, close to the area that was being searched by the aircraft. Within twenty minutes the nearest Swordfish had also located the *Bismarck*, and the signal was sent to the *Ark Royal*: '*Bismarck* in sight'. Ten minutes later another Swordfish in the search pattern had moved to the position given by the first aircraft. Both had visual contact. With two aircraft from the *Ark Royal* now shadowing the *Bismarck*, Tovey's hopes rose from the depths of despair, but it was absolutely vital contact was not lost again. Two other Swordfish fitted with long-range petrol tanks were launched, to relieve the first shadowers.

When he arrived on the scene, Midshipman Ian MacWilliam, an observer in one of those Swordfish, was not certain whether he had spotted the *Bismarck* or the *Prinz Eugen*. The anti-aircraft fire was accurate and it was hard for the trailing Swordfish to stay in one place and make sure of its target. As MacWilliam's aircraft approached from the rear of the ship to take a photo he saw the flash of a broadside, and his pilot turned steeply away and zigzagged; the shells burst 50 yards behind them, and more ack-ack followed, at four salvos a minute. The bursts were well bunched, MacWilliam observed coolly. Captain Maund and his senior officers on the *Ark* were, however, convinced that they had found the *Bismarck*.

When the searching Swordfish came in to land, the stern of the ship was rising and falling through 19 metres. The *Ark* was so unstable that the flight deck officer, Commander Stringer, had to be secured with a lifeline so that he could remain upright. He waved the aircraft away as many as three times before he thought it was safe for them to attempt a landing, although one aircraft was lost when the stern rose suddenly and hit the Swordfish from underneath as she touched down. With the other Swordfish in a circuit all waiting to land before they ran out of fuel, the crashed aircraft was dragged to the stern and heaved overboard.

Admiral Tovey's Home Fleet ships were still over 130 miles away, and at her current speed the *Bismarck*, shadowed or not, would outrun them. She had to be stopped or slowed down enough for the fleet to reach her, and the only weapons available to accomplish that were the Swordfish's torpedoes. In the hangar decks the aircraft were overhauled and refuelled by the riggers and mechanics, and torpedoes in their trolleys were moved forward to the lifts. They would be loaded onto the aircraft once they were lined up on the flight deck. By two o'clock in the afternoon fourteen aircraft were ready to launch an attack, ranged at the rear of the flight deck. At 1445 the first plane took off. They formed up in their attack groups and headed for the position of the *Bismarck*.

Unknown to anybody on the *Ark Royal*, the cruiser *Sheffield*, the *Ark*'s constant companion in Force H, had been sent by Somerville to shadow the *Bismarck*, to make certain that this time the battleship did not escape. The cruiser was in a direct line between the *Bismarck* and the *Ark Royal*, and unfortunately she was the first ship the air crew in the Swordfish came upon. In low cloud and driving rain they turned to attack the *Sheffield*. Eleven of the fourteen aircraft dropped their torpedoes before they realized their mistake. The torpedoes had been fitted with Duplex fuses, designed to make the warhead explode not only on direct impact but also under the influence of a ship's magnetic field. In theory this meant that the torpedo could be set to run deep and explode directly under the hull of a ship, avoiding the belt of armour plating along the water line. In practice, the fuses were extremely unreliable, and they either exploded on impact with the water or failed to detonate at all. It was only this plus the drastic manoeuvres of the *Sheffield* that avoided a catastrophe. It was an inauspicious start to a mission on which so much depended.

The Swordfish returned to the *Ark Royal*. The leader of the attack, Lt Commander Coode, insisted that impact fuses be fitted on the next batch of warheads, and these were set to run at a shallow setting of 10 feet. Fifteen aircraft were armed and refuelled – all the serviceable Swordfish on the *Ark*. It was going to be a massed attack, with flights of three aircraft attacking simultaneously from all quarters, which would make it impossible for the *Bismarck* to manoeuvre and comb the torpedo tracks. It was hoped it would also confuse and break up the anti-aircraft fire.

The weather got worse as the day wore on, and there was cloud as low as 600 feet with banks of driving rain. The sea remained as rough as ever, and the pilots again had to deal with a flight deck pitching through 50 feet. 'We took off in the gloom of the evening,' John Moffat recalled, 'in poor visibility, and the motion of the flight deck got worse as the ship headed into gale-force winds.' He climbed to 6,000 feet but didn't notice the cold because the adrenalin was pumping through him. 'We were leading with the CO, Lt Cdr Coode, who was an impressive figure, a man we looked up to. We were shown the direction to the *Bismarck* by the *Sheffield* and then we entered cloud and started to ice up. The Swordfish got very unstable.'

As they flew away in line astern from the *Sheffield*, which had signalled by Aldis lamp the distance (12 miles) and bearing to the *Bismarck*, they must all have been aware of what they were about to face. Everyone knew that the *Bismarck* bristled with guns. There had been plenty of information at the briefing about her twelve 15mm-calibre guns on twin mountings, sixteen 105mm guns on twin high-angle mountings and fifty 37mm and 20mm rapid-firing guns that were mounted all around the ship. The pilots returning from shadowing the battleship had already spoken of the preparedness and accuracy of the *Bismarck*'s anti-aircraft fire. A remarkable performance would be required from pilots who had already spent several hours in the air in extremely arduous flying conditions.

As they neared the *Bismarck* they flew into a massive cloud whose base was 700 feet above the ocean and which towered to a height of 10,000 feet. As the force climbed through it, ice forming on the wings, they became separated. The leader of the first flight, Coode, descended at a point where he calculated they would be able to attack downwind from astern of the ship, but on breaking the cloud cover they discovered the *Bismarck* was 4 miles away. The ship immediately opened fire, and the barrage was intense. Coode said it began five seconds after they had emerged from the cloud and started their dive. Large bursts came up very close, including one very near-miss underneath his plane, and Coode had the strong impression that each gun mounting had its own radar control. He described the ack-ack as reddish-coloured tracer going past at about one shell a second. John Moffat in Swordfish 5C, the third aircraft in the first flight, thought it was like flying into hail. In the open cockpit of the Swordfish the noise and blast of exploding shells could be directly felt by the pilots and the observers. The smell of cordite was strong. Some bursts, Moffat and his observer Sub Lt 'Dusty' Miller reported, occurred behind them but they were always close. At one point two shells burst together 30 metres to starboard and below, the blasts of which battered the plane and turned it off its course.

After they had dived below 1,000 feet the heavy shellfire seemed to abate. A series of double flashes were seen from amidships but the rate of fire appeared to be slower and the flashes were vivid orange with little smoke. Moffat dived as low as he could, and when he was 2,000 yards from the target the rapid-firing guns started up, orange tracer coming up at him in a dead straight line. Another pilot reported that the gun flashes from the ship appeared vivid yellow tinged with green, with cordite smoke brownish and small in quantity. Then, as the planes got closer, smaller red tracer appeared. Lt Beale, the pilot of a Swordfish in the second flight who was an experienced veteran of many of the *Ark*'s operations, said that the fire was more intense than anything he had experienced before, including the attack on Oran, the Sardinian engagement and the attack on the Tirso Dam.

Moffat got his first glimpse of the *Bismarck* as he turned in to the attack on the port quarter. 'With the CO on the left we headed in at 50 feet. I liked to stay as low as possible because I thought I was more difficult to hit that way. As we came in my observer, "Dusty" Miller, kept saying, "Not yet, not yet." I thought, "My Christ, what is he talking about?" I turned around and there he was, leant right out of the cockpit holding the voice pipe, judging when to drop the torpedo. You can't guarantee that it will drop or run, and in heavy seas you have to drop into the trough of a wave or it will porpoise on the crest and run wild. I thought, "For God's sake get a move on or we'll be right on it." Then he said, "Let her go." And then, "We've got a runner." After dropping we made a flat turn to get away, flat so as not to expose the underside of the aircraft and present a bigger target, and boy did I want to get away from there.'

The intention was that the attacks by the various flights from all sides should take place almost simultaneously, but the weather conditions and the problems of icing when flying through the cloud meant that inevitably the fifteen aircraft couldn't stay in close contact. As it was, four Swordfish initially attacked from the port side, another two attacked from the starboard side, five more attacked from the port side, and finally, another four aircraft – two of which were slightly isolated and were the focus of a great deal of concentrated anti-aircraft fire – attacked again from the starboard side. Remarkably, only one Swordfish was seriously damaged during the attack, both the pilot and telegraphist air gunner sustaining wounds. The aircraft was hit 175 times, and one of its struts supporting the upper and lower wing was severed. Nevertheless the pilot, Sub Lt Swanton, managed to fly it back to the *Ark* and make a successful landing.

On the *Bismarck*, the impact of the attack was profound. A gunnery officer on the ship thought that the Swordfish pilots had been ordered, 'Get hits or don't come back!' 'The heeling of the ship first one way and then another told me that we were trying to evade torpedoes,' he recalled. 'The rudder indicator never came to rest and the speed indicator revealed a significant loss of speed. The men in the control platforms in the engine rooms had to keep their wits about them. "All ahead full!" "All stop!" "All back full!" were the ever-changing orders with which Lindemann sought to escape the torpedoes. We had been under attack for perhaps fifteen minutes when I heard that sickening sound. Two torpedoes exploded in quick succession, but somewhere forward of where I was. Good fortune in misfortune, I thought . . . The attack must have been almost over when it came, an explosion aft. My heart sank. I glanced at the rudder indicator. It showed "left 12 degrees". It did not change.'

The *Bismarck* had been hit in the port steering compartment. Only three hits were observed by the attacking Swordfish and none was expected to have caused any damage, but this effort by forty-three young airmen who had somehow managed to find the courage to attack this heavily armoured ship, and in some cases loiter in the vicinity for some time to make an assessment of the attack, had actually succeeded in damaging the *Bismarck* to the extent that she was reduced to being the helpless prey of the pursuing fleet of battleships.

The *Bismarck* had turned to port – it isn't known whether or not this was done in an attempt to avoid the torpedo that caused the deadly damage – and a torpedo had hit the most vulnerable part of the ship. The long stern had been designed to reduce the drag of the ship through the water, and it was not sufficiently strengthened like the rest of the hull. The explosion had weakened the welded seams and the hull had collapsed on the rudders, jamming them forever in their turn to port. The *Bismarck* was now disabled, unable to steer, and was starting to head back into the Atlantic, towards Admiral Tovey. Ironically, Admiral Lutjens, who had avoided contact with the *Ark Royal* throughout the war, first as the successful leader of the German task force in Norway then in command of the *Scharnhorst* and the *Gneisenau* throughout their successful raiding in the Atlantic, had finally been brought down by its Swordfish aircraft.

The returning Swordfish crews, landing on a wildly pitching deck, did not report any serious damage to the *Bismarck*. It was the *Sheffield*, still trailing the battleship, and a circling Swordfish that noticed her moving in a circle, no longer heading south-east towards the French coast. The course of the *Bismarck* was erratic as Captain Lindemann tried to steer the ship using alternate power on the propellers, but with the rudders jammed permanently, forcing the ship's bows to port, nothing could be done. The crew of the *Bismarck* were doomed, and they had hours to contemplate their end, like men in a condemned cell. At 2140 hours Admiral Lutjens radioed to the Kriegsmarine Group West in Paris. 'Ship unable to manoeuvre. We will fight to the end. Long live the Führer.'

On the *Ark Royal* the next morning, the crews of the remaining twelve Swordfish prepared for another strike. The wind was now so fast, over 50 knots, that the Swordfish were armed with torpedoes and their engines started while the ship steamed away from the wind. Extra men were ordered onto the flight deck to hold the aircraft steady. When all the aircraft were ready with their engines running, the *Ark* prepared to make a turn into the wind. 'Going on to full speed we put the rudder hard over,' Captain Maund recalled. 'The old ship, always a delight to handle at speed, swung round like a top, but even so she took several heavy rolls before she got round and two of the aircraft slipped as much as 8 feet sideways. It was an exciting moment with the crews holding on and the propellers heaving round. But once round speed had to be reduced to 6 knots and the Swordfish with their torpedoes took off one after the other in rapid succession.'

In the meantime, the battleships *King George V* and *Rodney* had at last come within range of the *Bismarck*. Their first salvo was fired at 0842 hours. The shells from their big guns caused serious damage to the front of the *Bismarck* and her two forward main turrets. She was travelling at slow speed in an attempt to maintain some sort of course, but she was essentially unmanoeuvrable. Shortly after receiving these first hits from the British guns, the *Bismarck* could no longer reply to the fire and she became a floating butcher's block. Heavy shell after heavy shell landed on her, causing total mayhem inside the hull. The bodies of the dead and dying lay piled up in every space, and the living scrambled through blood and smoke searching for non-existent shelter. The British ships continued to fire on the battleship for almost half an hour after her guns had been silenced, but eventually Admiral Tovey, with his flagship *King George V* low on fuel, realized that shells would not sink the *Bismarck* and ordered the *Dorsetshire*, a cruiser that had joined the ships from the Home Fleet, to torpedo her. The final act of the crew members still alive on the *Bismarck* was to set scuttling charges, and they and the *Dorsetshire*'s torpedoes finally sent what had now become a giant metal coffin to the bottom of the Atlantic.

The Swordfish from the *Ark Royal* had arrived while the shelling was still continuing, and they stayed to the end, until the last survivors of the 2,400 men who had been on the *Bismarck* were struggling in the water. Admiral Tovey did not respond to the pilots' signals requesting instructions, and they finally returned to the *Ark Royal*. Before they landed on, a German four-engined Focke Wulf bomber appeared in the sky and dropped a stick of bombs that landed in the sea to the starboard side. The battle had moved inside the range of the Luftwaffe based in France, so the *Bismarck* had been hit and crippled at the very last possible moment.

At a meeting of the War Cabinet in London on the morning of 27 May, while shells were still exploding on the *Bismarck*, Churchill told his colleagues that all chances of winning the battle in Crete had disappeared and that Britain should face the prospect that most of its forces would be lost. It was almost impossibly bad news to announce; Churchill had wanted to tell the House of Commons that afternoon that hard fighting was still continuing. Parliament met that day in Church House, opposite Westminster Abbey, because the Houses of Parliament had been bombed earlier in the year. It was an extraordinarily tense session, but during it Churchill was handed a note, and he was able to announce to the House that the *Bismarck* had been sunk. The news broke the sombre spell and prompted wild cheering.

But John Moffat does not remember the flights he made over the *Bismarck* with any sense of elation. Speaking to me in his comfortable home in the peaceful rolling hills of Dunkeld in Scotland, he said, 'The worst part of the war, the thing that always crosses my mind when it shouldn't, is my second trip over the *Bismarck*. She was smoking like fury, and just as I approached, the ship turned on its side. I flew across and there were all these bods in the water, hundreds of them; there were heads in the water. It was a terrible thing, a terrible sight really. That haunts me, the hopelessness of life. When we all got back we had a drink, and nobody said great or anything. That was why we had a drink, because we all thought, "There but for the grace of God." '

11

THE *RIG SUPPORTER*

In October 2002 I was squeezed into a Gibraltar taxi, its windows misting up and the heating full on, with Rick Davey from C&C Technologies, cameraman Richard Rankin and a sound recordist. The rain was lashing down and the streetlights were still on, although at five o'clock in the morning the sky was beginning to lighten through the low scudding clouds. We had left our hotel, driven past the old offices where the *Gibraltar Times* printed the first news of Nelson's victory at Trafalgar, and were heading for the harbour.

When we arrived at the dockside we loaded our bags and aluminium equipment boxes onto the oily deck of a harbour tender. The pilot, unshaven and with a cigarette dangling from his mouth, untied the ropes holding us to the jetty and gunned the motor. We were heading out to board the *Rig Supporter*, the boat that carried C&C's unique surveying tool – the autonomous underwater vehicle. It was the opportunity to use the AUV in the search for the *Ark Royal* that had first made me contact Rick. Now, finally, it was waiting for me and I could discover precisely what had been located on the sea bed by the *Odin Finder* five months earlier.

As we cleared the outer mole the sea got rougher, and further out it was covered in white caps whipped up by a strong westerly wind. Our boat started pitching and rolling as we made a wide sweeping circle around a big grey and white vessel that was slowly moving through the water.

'That's the *Rig Supporter*,' said Rick.

It was a big ship, about three times the size of the *Odin Finder*, with a high prow, capable of crossing the Atlantic or dealing with a storm in the North Sea. Above the stern was a helicopter landing pad.

'How are we going to get on board?' I asked.

'I'm not sure,' Rick replied.

The *Rig Supporter* had been working in the Mediterranean for weeks, and the survey crew and the technicians who ran the AUV were very keen to get home, which for most of them was back in Louisiana. They wanted to spend as little time as possible on this extra job that they had not bargained for. Furthermore, the fee I had negotiated would barely cover their fuel costs, so the project manager on board had been unwilling to spend time and money on entering harbour. I thought that transferring passengers and gear in this way was taking a risk, but short of abandoning the trip there was little I could do.

As we approached the ship it towered above us. I had half expected a companionway or a set of stairs to be lowered, but all I could see was a rope ladder hanging down the swaying side of the ship. Our boat matched the *Rig Supporter*'s speed and pulled alongside. A rope was lowered to winch up the equipment boxes, but we would have to grab the ladder and climb up to the deck above. Our boat was pitching to a height of 5 or 6 feet; if anyone missed their footing they would be crushed between the *Rig Supporter* and our boat. The sound recordist had gone extremely pale. He turned to me and said, 'Mike, I can't swim.' Being able to swim would not prevent anyone from getting killed in that dangerous gap, but I knew that now was not the time to point this out. I should not have put him in this situation at all; legally speaking I should have aborted the whole thing. But I had gone too far now to turn back. What he needed was some reassurance, some action on my part that showed he was being considered, otherwise I would never persuade him to make a leap for the rope ladder. Any hesitation on his part out of fear would be fatal.

'Rick,' I shouted, 'we need some life vests. Can they throw some down to us?'

Rick knew that what we were doing was silly, so he shouted up to the deckhands. Within a few minutes I was helping put one on the sound recordist. As the deck of our boat rose up he grasped the rope ladder and his feet found the bottom rung. He pulled himself up and was hauled by his lifejacket harness onto the deck of the *Rig Supporter*. We all followed safely, and within a few minutes the *Rig Supporter* had picked up speed and was heading to the wreck site, buffeted by crosswinds and an angry sea.

Once on board the ship I could appreciate why the *Rig Supporter* was so large. The survey room, or lab, was extremely spacious, with an array of screens that emphasized the enormous computer capacity the ship carried. She was designed to be self-sufficient, accommodating the AUV and its support staff as well as a large surveying party anywhere in the world.

The sonar survey from the *Odin Finder* had provided very little information about the size or condition of the target, so Rick had asked me to bring along as much background material about the *Ark* as I could. I had full-size reproductions of the large-scale blueprints of the *Ark Royal* from the Maritime Museum. I also had some enlarged black and white photos of the *Ark* on the slipway at Birkenhead, and a variety of views of the ship to help us identify anything we might capture an image of. As I spread these out on the chart table I was joined by Zak Rivers, the surveying party chief, and Phil Devall, the chief technician for the AUV. Zak was young and stocky with a goatee beard, while Phil was thin with a slightly startled air about him. Gradually the other computer programmers and the technicians gathered around.

They knew very little of what I was proposing to do. As I described the brief history of the *Ark Royal* and passed around photos of the ship almost hidden by gouts of water thrown into the air by exploding bombs, I could hear muttered comments and the odd 'wow'. I explained how I had gone back to the Board of Inquiry records and drawn up the search area, and finally how we had located this target outside it. Before I had finished talking a couple of the technicians had left the small group and were examining the blueprints, taking measurements and looking at the black and white image produced by the sonar on board the *Odin Finder*. Their curiosity had been fired. They too were becoming engrossed in the challenge of finding this wreck.

There were a few things I didn't dwell on in detail. One was that in the months since the discovery of what could be the wreck of the *Ark* by the *Odin Finder* it had proved almost impossible to get offers of co-production money for a series on the history of the Royal Navy. It was too British. This to me was a reason why the British Broadcasting Corporation, which was after all financed by British licence payers, should make it, but in every conversation I had with senior management at the BBC I could tell my arguments were falling on deaf ears. Originally I had proposed a search for the *Ark Royal* because I thought that the discovery and footage of such a historic ship could form the centrepiece of a series about the Royal Navy, and give the programmes a much higher profile when they were broadcast. Now it was beginning to look as though there was not enough money to produce the series I wanted to make, certainly nowhere near enough to film the *Ark Royal*, if that is what we had found.

I was lucky in one respect, however: I was being allowed to use the AUV and the *Rig Supporter* for almost nothing, so whatever the fate of the series I could take a few more steps in the right direction and hopefully determine whether or not I had found the *Ark Royal*. There was a distinct possibility I hadn't.

When I'd returned to London I'd had very little to show for my four-day trip and the thousands of dollars paid to the *Odin Finder* except an accurate position for what I was assured was a substantial metallic object that roughly fitted the known dimensions of the *Ark*. On paper they looked like two dark squares about 1cm by 1cm on a background of black and white dots like the interference on an old TV screen. When Rick Davey and I worked out how we were going to search for the wreck, we assumed we might have several targets that would require investigation. However, I was very conscious of a lack of time and money and it was convenient to assume that what I had found was indeed what I was searching for. It was the closest target to my original search area. But then, if the *Ark* had drifted from the point where it had capsized, as the captain of the *Odin Finder* had suggested, it could have drifted quite a way, and what we had found might be the wreck of a totally different ship.

One way of calculating the probability of locating a different wreck in that area was to give the Wrecks Section of the UK Hydrographic Office a set of co-ordinates and ask them to check if they had any relevant information. I did this, and after a few days their reply arrived. To my utter dismay I saw that in the early 1960s a bulk carrier registered in Liberia had been reported missing not far from the position of the target I had located. Had I found the wreck of a cargo ship? This possibility was too awful to contemplate. To have wasted so much time and effort, not to say money . . . There was, of course, only one way to find out, and that was what we were about to do.

Rick had told me a great deal about the AUV, but I had never set eyes on it. It was housed in a container that everybody on board referred to as 'the van', set onto the rear deck of the ship, underneath the helicopter landing pad. As I walked into the container I caught my first sight of the AUV. Under the harsh neon lights was an object like a fat torpedo, coloured bright orange, with a multi-bladed propeller and four fins at the rear, which was the narrowest part of it. It looked about 2 metres in length and over a metre in diameter. Panels on its side were being opened, and technicians wearing goggles and masks were plunging their hands inside it, as though they were operating on some strange animal. It was a remarkable piece of machinery, and was, according to Rick, the very first one of its type to be working commercially. The key to its success was its batteries which used a fuel based on aluminium and oxygen. These could drive it at a speed of over 3 knots for up to fifty hours. While it was doing this a variety of sonar sensors would be probing the sea floor and sending information back to the ship with its massive computers. There were also computers on board the AUV that could steer it on a predetermined course to an accuracy of 1 metre.

The company that owned the AUV, C&C Technologies, was owned by two brothers, Thomas and Jimmy Chance, whose father had made a lot of money from an oilfield services company in the 1960s. The Chance brothers had decided that new technology could transform the oil industry. The AUV was the result. The development costs had been very high, explained Rick, and although it was proving to be very successful it was still a long way from making a profit. Knowing how little I was paying for the privilege of using the AUV, I reflected that trying to hunt down the *Ark Royal* was not going to transform their finances in the slightest.

Back in the lab, Zak and his team had already drawn up a tentative search pattern around the target. The best way to visualize the AUV and the way it works is to think of a radio-controlled model aeroplane, except that the AUV would be flying through water, not air, and would be controlled by high-frequency sound waves, not radio signals. The AUV had cost $10 million to build so nobody wanted to be reckless with it. To avoid dangers such as a collision with a loose piece of wreckage, or getting tangled up in some old fishing nets that had fouled the wreck, Zak worked out a complicated pattern for surveying the wreck. The AUV was going to pass over the wreck at a height above the sea bed that would give the AUV about 20 metres' clearance. These distances were based on the assumption that it was the *Ark* down there, measured from the sets of blueprints I had brought on board. After two or three high-level passes the AUV would fly a star-shaped pattern over the wreck at a variety of heights and distances from it. In all we would be covering an area of about 1 square nautical mile. The end result would be that we would have a variety of different images which the computers on board would be able to combine into a three-dimensional image.

The process of preparing the computer program started. Once the loading of the information from the mother ship's computers to the AUV's was finished, the delicate and dangerous job of fuelling the AUV was started. Within a few hours of the *Rig Supporter* arriving above the wreck site the AUV was ready to launch.

The rear doors of the van opened very slowly, framing the sea and reflecting golden highlights from the late evening sun – a surreal contrast with the harsh industrial lighting of the AUV's container. The whole ship vibrated as the bow and stern thrusters fought against the wind and the current to keep the ship on a precise position. The AUV slowly slid out of its cradle then dropped into the sea. Bobbing on the choppy waves, its strobe light flashing, it looked suddenly small and fragile. Then it was gone. It would take about an hour to descend to depth, and for the technicians to test that everything was working before starting its mission.

I waited in the lab for the first signals to come back. There was a considerable amount of uncertainty and anxiety among the people gathered there. Most equipment used underwater is purpose-built, and is extremely complicated. The AUV was a unique machine and had travelled many thousands of kilometres underwater, but it was still in a sense experimental. Its very sophisticated electronics and computers were expected to work at extreme pressures immersed in salt water, and then to communicate an enormous amount of information via sound signals through water whose nature, in terms of temperature and salinity, was changing all the time. In these circumstances there is a lot that can go wrong, and the possibility of a breakdown or other form of failure is always present in the technicians' minds.

Naturally it was present in mine too, but I did not bear the responsibility for the effectiveness of the AUV. I was much more worried about what we were going to discover when the AUV reached its working depth. What would we see on our computer screens when the first signals were sent back from the object over 1,000 metres below us? Far more experienced people than I had set out to find wrecks and failed, and in a few hours I could be in for a horrible shock. The *Odin Finder* had found two targets separated by almost a kilometre and neither of them exactly matched the dimensions of the *Ark Royal*. Many famous wrecks have been found in pieces, of course. The *Titanic* lies in two large pieces, but the ship was subjected to considerable stress at the time because the rear part of the hull was raised high above the water when she was sinking. HMS *Hood* also lies in pieces, but she suffered an enormous explosion, and the *Bismarck* was not only the recipient of an enormous bombardment, she also fell several hundred metres down the side of a trench before hitting the sea bed. Many other ships have suffered severe damage to their hulls but remain intact in their final resting place. The eye-witness evidence I had read suggested that the *Ark* had simply turned over and slipped beneath the waves in one piece. There was in fact considerable room for error about what exactly we were sending the AUV down to investigate.

However, Rick Davey, who had directed me to the *Odin Finder* and had put the *Rig Supporter* more or less at my disposal, knew about most of these uncertainties and remained perfectly calm. As far as he was concerned what we were doing was the logical next step in our search.

The lab had filled with people. At each of the screens someone was monitoring the progress of the AUV on its pre-planned route, or checking the sonar imaging systems it was carrying; others just waited to see the first image appear on the screen. Slowly we followed the path of the AUV as it approached the first leg of the search pattern. Small objects were being picked up by the sonar, but it was impossible at this height and angle to tell what they were. As the AUV approached the precise position where we were expecting to find something, there was a perceptible stillness in the lab. All eyes were on the screens. It was a very tense moment. A thousand metres below us a small machine was blindly propelling itself through a pitch-black ocean and, I hoped, slowly approaching an object a thousand times its own size that had remained hidden for over sixty years.

On a large flat screen in the lab a shape appeared. There were murmurs from people crowded behind me. Zak said, 'We have a target.' It looked nothing like the *Ark Royal* or an aircraft carrier, but as the images cascaded down the screen, Zak added, 'This is big.' There was a perceptible sense of relief, and people started jostling to get a better view. But to my eyes it was hard to see what we had found. It was very high off the sea bed, about 20 metres, and had disappeared again fairly quickly. There was nothing else to see.

'Oh, hey, look at this,' Zak said suddenly.

There were excited sounds from other people in the room. On the screen was something that filled the whole edge of the swathe of sound the AUV was sending out into the darkness; clearly it was echoing back from something very big. It continued as the AUV travelled on its course, and then disappeared again.

'What is it?' I asked.

'There's no doubt it's a very big vessel,' said Rick. 'We'll wait for the AUV to come back on its return course, and then we'll start to get a bigger picture.'

On the next run Zak was the first to read out the dimensions. 'It's nearly 200 metres long, and it's looking about 18 metres high at this point.' He looked very pleased, and very certain that we had found what we were looking for.

Over the next few hours the AUV passed back and forth over the wreck and gradually a black and white image was created, looking like an X-ray, with dark shadows and greyer tones. It was hard to read the images sometimes, but Rick and the other people in the lab had a clearer understanding of what they were looking at. Looking at a sonar image is like looking at a black and white negative, the dark shapes not real but rather the shadows of shapes. Although in the world of sonar signals and computer-generated images it is sometimes better to have a very loose concept of what is real, with the aid of the computers on board, it was possible to obtain very accurate measurements of the objects that were being detected. There was a strange pyramid-shaped object on the sea bed that was over 20 metres in height. Then, almost 700 metres away, was a large shape that was clearly a long square object, which the AUV had travelled parallel to on its first run. It was this object that was going to be the *Ark Royal*, if that is what we had found.

As the AUV passed over the wreck at different heights and directions, people gazed for a long time at the screens then moved over to the long table at the back of the lab to look at the large photos of the ship and pore over the blueprints in the hope that some shape, some silhouette would trigger a moment of recognition. Again I was reminded of how remote this whole process was, how we were attempting to visualize an object over a thousand metres away, in pitch dark, in a place where we could never go, using not light but sound, to be transformed into images. It was frustrating, but also intriguing, because these images demanded so much more from our imagination.

Zak pointed to one part of the screen. 'What's that?' he said.

I looked. There were two short parallel lines sticking out of the side of the wreck, and then another pair.

'Are they guns?' he asked.

He measured the distance between them and I laid a ruler over the blueprints. Yes, they were two anti-aircraft gun turrets. The distance between them exactly matched the blueprints. At last, here was some proof! Twenty minutes later we spotted the faint square image of the safety netting that was also clearly visible in a photograph of the *Ark*. It was outlined around what was now clearly the huge overhang of the flight deck at the stern of the ship.

I was overjoyed. For the moment I was not concerned with the strange object to the south. I knew that we had found the *Ark Royal*, and it was in one piece! But it was hard to see whether the wreck was lying on its keel or was upside down. Two strong reflections ran the length of the wreck and they were impossible to identify. Zak suggested they were the bilge keels, strips of metal that run the length of the hull on a round-bottomed ship to help with stability, but on measuring them they seemed too long. Then a shape was identified that looked as though it was one of the propellers. This did seem to be in the right place, tucked some way under the stern of the flight deck. Were we looking at an upturned ship? It was hard to say.

Then Phil Devall said something that really startled me: 'This is the *Ark Royal*, for sure. Look, Mike, that's an aeroplane. It's one of the planes on the deck when she was hit.'

I looked closely at the image on the screen. It was tiny, but the cross shape was extremely suggestive of an aeroplane.

'But how can it be an aeroplane?' I said. 'She capsized a long way from here. The planes on her flight deck would have fallen off soon after she was hit.'

I went back to the photos on the table. One of them was of the *Ark* taken from the destroyer *Legion* as she approached the carrier to evacuate the crew. A flight of Swordfish had been landing on when she was torpedoed, and six aircraft were parked up on the forward section of the flight deck ready to be taken down on the forward deck lift. One of them, presumably the last plane to have landed on before the torpedo hit, still had its wings extended. But I was sure Phil was mistaken, and thought nothing more of it. I was still convinced that the *Ark Royal* had capsized more or less in the position I had worked out from all the evidence from the Board of Inquiry and that it had drifted some way as it slowly sank. Any aircraft on the flight deck would have slid off where the *Ark* capsized.

The AUV completed its predetermined course and was brought back to the surface. I went up to the stern to watch it being recovered. In the middle of the night I saw its small strobe light blinking on and off. It had done a very good job in a very short space of time, and it had a great deal more information stored in its computers to be downloaded once it was back on board. Searchlights on the bridge lit up the sea around it, and the surface of the water boiled as shoals of fish flocked to the light. A grapnel gun was fired, and the AUV was hauled back on a cable and hoisted up onto its cradle in the van.

Mission accomplished, we headed back to Gibraltar. Everybody had agreed that we were not going to get off the boat in the same way we had got on it, and we steamed slowly past the mole into the harbour. Nearly sixty-one years earlier the two tugs *Thames* and *St Day* had headed out past this same mole, accompanied by several motor launches, to come to the aid of the crippled *Ark*. Now at last we knew where she had finally come to rest. I felt an enormous wave of relief that the initial contact made by the *Odin Finder* had proved to be the *Ark*. As I stood on the dockside and looked at the *Rig Supporter*, I also felt amazed that I had been able to get this far. I owed a great deal to the goodwill of people like Rick Davey, Elisabetta Faenza and the Chance brothers, but I was also proud that I had pulled it off through my own determination and persuasion. It was the sort of moment when I felt like punching the air and shouting 'Yes!' at the top of my voice. But I didn't.

In the lab of the *Rig Supporter* the combined sonar images had been printed onto long strips of very fine photographic paper, reproducing in a single line all the different passes that had been made over the wreck by the AUV. In some places the image was severely distorted by the height of the AUV, but in others the image was instantly recognizable. They showed in remarkable detail the railing around the flight deck, the gun mountings and other identifiable pieces of equipment. It was without doubt the *Ark Royal*. I pressed Rick on camera to say as much, but he was wise and cautious enough to avoid an absolutely categorical statement. Like Andrea Pupa, the captain of the *Odin Finder*, he knew that nothing was certain under the sea. We would only know for sure that it was the *Ark Royal* when we had pictures of the name on the side of the hull.

Rick and I and the camera crew went to our hotel, and then went into Gibraltar. In a small, densely flowered cemetery we looked at the memorial to the dead of Trafalgar, the words from Lord Collingwood's dispatch chiselled into the stone, still legible under the moss and lichen: 'The ever to be lamented death of Vice-Admiral Lord Viscount Nelson, Duke of Bronte, the

Commander in Chief, who fell in the action of the 21st, in the arms of Victory . . .' This memorial had been here when the *Ark Royal*, a ship Nelson would never have recognized, sailed out to bomb Italy, or to hunt down the *Bismarck*; when Swordfish flew past to land on the temporary landing strip at the old racecourse. The tradition was continued when a memorial to Admiral Cunningham, the man who had directed the naval conflict in the Mediterranean, was placed next to Nelson's in Trafalgar Square.

The cemetery was a sunlit, tranquil refuge after the dry, air-conditioned atmosphere and harsh industrial lighting of the *Rig Supporter*. There is nowhere quiet on a ship, especially a warship – the noise of machinery, the ceaseless thud of the waves as a ship travels across the ocean – and I wondered whether men from the *Ark Royal* and Force H ever sought some peace here. More likely the constant violence and threat of death would drive you into the noisiest bar you could find.

Later that night Rick and I looked over the printout of the sonar images with a magnifying glass. There was a shape that did look as though it could be an aeroplane. Close to it, lying flat on the sea bed, was a square piece of debris with a regular square pattern on it. But I was still unwilling to admit that we had found an aircraft. I believed the sequence of events was that the *Ark* had been torpedoed and had started to list to starboard. At some point in the night when she was being towed the list got worse and the aircraft on her flight deck slid off into the water. Later, after fire broke out in the boiler room, the tow was abandoned, the *Ark* settled even further in the water, and eventually she capsized and disappeared from view. However, she didn't sink immediately, but slowly drifted below the surface before hitting the bottom. Our initial assessment of the sonar images was that the ship was intact and that any aircraft on board would still be in her hangar decks. There was therefore no reason to find aircraft, particularly any with extended wings, on the sea bed around the main hull.

The prospect of finding an old Swordfish was exciting, though. There are very few of these old biplanes left. Perhaps the only one still flying is housed on the Fleet Air Arm base at Yeovilton. Rick and I decided that we would ask C&C Technologies in Louisiana to produce some computer enhancements of various sections of the wreck and the debris field, including the aeroplane-like shape.

A few days later, after I had returned to London, Rick emailed an image to me of this piece of the debris trail, enormously enlarged by C&C's computers. As soon as I opened it, it was clear that I was looking at a Swordfish aircraft, its wings extended. The aeroplane was lying upside down with its undercarriage in the air. It looked as though it was still in perfect condition. The square object we had spotted close to it had been labelled by Rick 'unknown debris'. I looked at it for some time, and then it struck me. I printed off the picture, and unrolled the blueprints. I measured the wing span of the Swordfish. Then I measured the sides of the square object. They were both about 10 metres. I looked again at the blueprints. The square object was the exact shape and dimensions of a deck lift from the *Ark Royal*, and the regular square pattern was the bracing on the underside.

If my interpretation of these images was correct then I had to completely abandon my previous explanation of why the *Ark Royal* was so far from the position where I believed I would find her. There was only one explanation for a Swordfish and a deck lift to be so close together in the wreckage trail of the *Ark Royal*: everything had happened in roughly the same place. The *Ark* had sunk in the spot where she had started to list and where she had also capsized. What naturally followed from that conclusion was that the story told to the Board of Inquiry about the *Ark* sinking and the efforts to salvage the vessel was inaccurate. That was the reason why all my investigations for the search we had conducted on the *Odin Finder* had not produced a result.

At that point I decided that once again I would go back to the files in the National Archives and see if there was anything in them I had missed or failed to interpret properly. However, that was for another day. For now, I had absolute proof that we had found the wreck of HMS *Ark Royal*, and I had an absolutely stunning and uniquely accurate sonar survey of the whole of the wreck site and the debris field. Moreover, in front of me was an image that was absolutely fascinating: the last Swordfish to land on the flight deck of the *Ark Royal*. Now, surely, there would be no problem in raising the money to get cameras down to film the wreck. We would at last be able to see that enormous shape once more. Those giant bows that towered over the dockyard workers at Cammell Laird were there, waiting to become part of our life again.

But there was still a mystery. In all of its passes around the wreck, the AUV had failed to get a coherent image of the massive shape 700 metres to the south of the main hull. It might be part of the main wreck, or perhaps the wreck of another ship altogether. At every step in this search I had remained unsatisfied. Every stage of the investigation seemed to raise new questions I was desperate to answer.

There was only one way to lay the speculation to rest, and that was to mount another expedition. So I had yet another search in front of me, this time for a survey ship and a remote vehicle that could descend a kilometre into the ocean with a set of lights and a camera so that I could finally film the *Ark Royal*. Once again I had absolutely no idea how difficult that task was going to be.

12

TARGET *ARK*

When in the early summer of 1941 the *Ark Royal* entered Gibraltar harbour she was fêted as the hero of the hour, the ship that had saved the reputation of the Navy and the fortunes of Britain. It was particularly good news because at the time there was very little for Britain to celebrate in the Mediterranean. At the start of the war recommendations had been put to the War Cabinet that the Mediterranean should be abandoned because it would be militarily impossible to maintain a naval presence there. The Cabinet, in particular Winston Churchill, had roundly rejected that advice, but it now looked as though Britain was powerless to prevent total defeat in that theatre.

The German Army had stormed through Greece and captured the island of Crete. The Mediterranean Fleet based in Alexandria had lost a vast number of ships to the Luftwaffe: three cruisers, six destroyers and forty-four transports and fleet auxiliaries were lost, and two battleships, an aircraft carrier, six cruisers and seven destroyers were badly damaged. Rommel, Commander in Chief of the Afrika Korps, was gearing up to make a further advance towards Alexandria, the main base of the British Army in North Africa, whose very existence was now under serious threat. The one remaining stronghold in the Mediterranean was Malta. Everything rested on protecting the island. The ability of the submarines and bombers based there to cut the central Mediterranean supply route to Rommel's army was crucial to British plans. But Malta itself was under siege, savagely bombed on a daily basis and facing the threat of invasion. The island's survival hung on the ability of Force H and the *Ark Royal* to keep her supplied with food and weapons.

Admiral Somerville summed up the situation in his preamble to orders to the ships for Operation Substance on 20 July: 'For over a year Malta has held out most gallantly against all assaults of the enemy. Until Crete fell we were able to supply Malta from both ends of the Mediterranean, but since the evacuation of Crete the situation has changed. For the present Malta can only be supplied from the west and this is the task with which we have been entrusted.' Then he ended his message with this uncharacteristic exhortation: 'The convoy must go through!'

Operation Substance was another attempt to escort cargo ships through the Mediterranean, not this time to Alexandria at the eastern end, but to Malta itself. Before this operation started the *Ark* had carried out a number of single missions to transport Hurricane aircraft far enough down the Mediterranean so that they could fly off to Malta. The Hurricanes were transported from the UK, usually in crates by one or other of the aircraft carriers *Furious* and *Argus*. They would be assembled en route, and on reaching Gibraltar two or three squadrons of completed Hurricanes would be taken on board the *Ark* and stored on the flight deck. Then a high-speed run by the *Ark* in company with the other carrier would see both ships and their escort of destroyers within 300 miles of Malta while dawn was breaking. With the Hurricanes on the flight deck it was impossible to launch any other aircraft, so the two carriers were particularly vulnerable. There would be an anxious hour or so while the Hurricanes took off and an extremely nervous lookout was kept for Italian reconnaissance aircraft. The Hurricane pilots had a long distance to fly over the sea before coming into range of Malta, and they had to fly a course that would take them as close as possible to North Africa to avoid the Luftwaffe on Sicily. Sometimes two Fulmars guided the Hurricanes, but in later operations a pair of Blenheim bombers would fly from Gibraltar and rendezvous with the carriers at their flying-off point; they would then steer a course for Malta, the Hurricane pilots obediently following. In this way, in the month of June alone 145 Hurricanes were delivered to the beleaguered island. Operation Substance followed this up with seven merchantmen carrying 5,500 men and nearly 50,000 tons of stores. Somerville was optimistic that there was a 'fair chance' of a proportion of the convoy actually reaching its destination, though he knew it would be a dangerous voyage.

On 21 July the *Ark Royal* left Gibraltar, but by nine o'clock that morning the troopship *Leinster* had run aground. Somerville pressed on, and as expected, on the third day of the convoy the first onslaught from the Italian Air Force took place. The Italians had refined their technique over the months of war in the Mediterranean and had become increasingly effective. Attacks from high-level bombers and low-level torpedo bombers were now synchronized, making it harder for the anti-aircraft barrages to be co-ordinated. This tactic also stretched the air defence capabilities of the Fulmar fighters the *Ark Royal* could put into the air. The Fulmars had never been particularly well suited to their job. They were slow, and took ages to climb to a height where they could take on high-level bombers. They were not very manoeuverable either, and Fulmar pilots didn't want to become engaged in a fight with the bombers' fighter escorts. There would be a permanent fighter CAP, or combat air patrol, of a section of three Fulmars from day three of an operation, when an attack could be expected. As soon as enemy aircraft were picked up by radar as many Fulmars as were available would be sent into the air by the *Ark* and directed to meet the bombers, and an attempt would be made to shoot down and break up the formation to force the enemy to abandon their attack before they were above the fleet. The torpedo bombers, however, would make a low-level approach, staying below the radar, hoping to come upon the fleet unseen until the last minute.

At 0910 on 23 July, six torpedo planes and eight high-level bombers attacked the convoy and its escorts. They were extremely successful: torpedoes hit the destroyer *Fearless* and the cruiser *Manchester*. Thirty-five members of the crew of *Fearless* were killed, fires were started on board, and both engines were put out of action. Somerville ordered the ship to be sunk after the remainder of the crew had been taken on board another destroyer, the *Forester*. The *Manchester* was less critically damaged, but she had 750 troops on board so Somerville ordered her to return to Gibraltar immediately.

Later that day, in the afternoon, another attack group of torpedo bombers was picked up on the radar at a distance of 43 miles coming in from the north-west. They were five torpedo bombers, and they were sighted fifteen minutes later on the port quarter, but a section of Fulmars pounced on them and two of the bombers were shot down; the remaining three gave up and turned away. Nonetheless, the determination of the Italian attack was becoming apparent.

As the convoy approached the Sicilian channel, Force H turned west, leaving the merchantmen to make the dangerous voyage through the narrows to Malta with an escort of destroyers and the cruisers *Hermione* and *Edinburgh*. Aircraft from Malta also arrived to escort the convoy, but they failed to prevent a high-level bombing attack which damaged the destroyer *Firedrake*. The convoy was attacked for a fourth time at three o'clock in the morning by a squadron of fast torpedo boats that had set out from the island of Pantelleria, but only one ship, the *Sydney Star*, was damaged and that was by friendly fire from one of the destroyers. The convoy and its escort finally arrived in Valletta harbour on the afternoon of 24 July. The supplies had got through, but at considerable cost.

Force H continued to suffer attacks from the air as it tried to escort the damaged *Manchester* back to Gibraltar. They also had to wait to escort the cruisers and destroyers tasked with bringing empty merchant ships from Malta to Gibraltar on 24 and 25 July. On the 25th in particular a large group of Italian bombers tried to attack the fleet, but they were beaten off by Fulmars from the *Ark*. In Somerville's words, the Fulmars 'attacked with great dash and bombs could be seen being jettisoned far away. Three high-level bombers were shot down for certain.' But the *Ark* lost six Fulmars, and the crew of only four of them were recovered.

Sub Lt Alan Goodfellow, a Fulmar pilot, was on the *Ark* during Operation Substance. He had been in the air when the second wave of torpedo bombers attacked the fleet on 23 July, and had shot down one bomber and its seaplane guide, a Cant 506B, a large three-engined floatplane. Goodfellow now lives in a small village in Norfolk and clearly remembers the fighting he took part in over the Mediterranean in the summer of 1941. It was a constant struggle to keep aircraft and pilots in the air. 'We were so short of oxygen that our instructions were not to use it at all except when we were in combat,' he said. 'And we were patrolling at 18,000 feet. Two hours at 18,000 without oxygen was pushing it a bit. And we certainly lost one crew that I know of through lack of oxygen. We were desperately short of ammunition. You know, everything was in short supply in that time. Their tactics, generally speaking, they came in with one wave at somewhere around 12,000, something like that, with bombs, and they would try to co-ordinate that with another wave coming in at low level with torpedoes. So you caught them up at about 12,000, and those that had been scrambled from deck would catch up with anything coming in lower down.' As well as the nervous strain on the pilots, there was enormous stress on their physical endurance as well. 'I did six patrols from the 23rd to the 25th, so in three days six patrols at two hours plus each patrol.'

There had been a newsreel crew on board the *Ark Royal* during Operation Substance, and over the next few months in cinemas throughout Britain audiences learned that 'the convoy did get through'. It certainly did, but the Italian torpedo bombers had shown that they were now a force to be reckoned with, as Goodfellow confirmed. 'As far as I recall we must have been patrolling up at 18,000 or thereabouts and were vectored on to these 79s coming in. We finished up literally at sea level. The Italians were very hot on their low-level flying. In fact, these

SM79s with three engines, they flew so low that you could actually see three slipstreams on the water, rippling the water underneath. They were literally down at sea level. And of course to attack them it was more difficult. I think the Fulmar had a 50-knot advantage in speed, that's all.'

Another relief convoy to Malta was planned for September, and the importance of this convoy succeeding meant that a considerable amount of preparation went into it. There were no illusions about the necessity of getting it through: Rommel's supply line was being hit, badly, and it was holding up his advance on Egypt and the British headquarters in Alexandria. But neither were there any illusions about the difficulty of doing so: the Luftwaffe controlled the skies over Malta, and the sea around it, and they were trying to squeeze the island to death. If the Germans succeeded in cutting Malta's lifeline from Gibraltar, Britain would lose the war in North Africa and the Middle East, and perhaps the war in Europe. Somerville asked for a big effort from the RAF in the Mediterranean, calling on them to keep up attacks on Italian airbases prior to the convoy entering the Mediterranean. Force H itself was heavily reinforced with the addition of two battleships, *Prince of Wales* and *Rodney*, and four cruisers. Submarines from Alexandria and Malta were stationed off Sardinia, Sicily and southern Italy to intercept the Italian fleet if it should put to sea. However, the main threat to the convoy, the Italian and German air forces, would have to be dealt with, as always, by the Fulmars from the *Ark Royal*.

On 24 September, the convoy of nine merchant ships laden with food, ammunition and 2,500 troops passed through the Straits of Gibraltar to meet up with the *Ark Royal* and the rest of Force H on the morning of the next day. Their journey was uneventful until day three of the operation, 27 September, when as expected the convoy came under air attack. Somerville knew that the enemy would try their hardest to stop this convoy. There was such a high level of anxiety that on the 26th the Swordfish aircraft in the hangars had had their tanks drained as a precaution against fire. By midday on the 27th there were sixteen Fulmars in the air awaiting an attack from the Italian Air Force. Almost an hour later, three Fulmars were directed to the north of the fleet, where they encountered twelve torpedo bombers; another nine Fulmars were sent to assist them. The dogfight spiralled down until both the bombers and the Fulmars were fighting at sea level. The Fulmars were able to shoot down one of the bombers, which crashed into the sea, and to damage another three of the bombers, forcing them to abandon their attack, but six torpedoes were dropped, although the fleet managed to avoid all of them. One Fulmar was shot down by friendly fire from the *Rodney*, and the crew were lost.

A second attack developed at 1327 hours with a group of BR20 three-engine torpedo bombers carrying two torpedoes each making an attack from the west. The Fulmars again dived on them and one was shot down, but they pressed on, and in the mêlée of low-flying aircraft and the *Ark* and the battleships taking avoiding action, a torpedo hit the *Nelson*, Somerville's flagship, in the bows. The battleship slowed and turned to leave the convoy, but soon after that a signal was received from an RAF reconnaissance patrol that the Italian fleet had put to sea and was heading south to intercept the convoy, so the *Nelson* turned and rejoined Force H. Two Swordfish were sent off from the *Ark* to locate and follow the Italian fleet, and twelve more were loaded with torpedoes. Because there were still Fulmars in the air that needed to land, the reconnaissance Swordfish were not launched until 1448. One of them was attacked by some CR42 fighters on its way to search for the enemy fleet and had to return to the *Ark*, but the other continued to the last known position. Despite spending over five hours in the air it failed to locate any of the Italian warships, because unknown to the Swordfish crew the Italian fleet had reversed its course.

Alan Goodfellow was one of the Fulmar pilots in the air; he had shot down the BR20, after a long chase. He had to wait for the Swordfish to take off before he could land back on the *Ark*, despite being very low on fuel. 'We were flying for two hours twenty-five, which is a lot, and a lot of that was at full throttle,' he recalled. 'The other two of the section landed on with literally a gallon of petrol left in the tank, but I didn't make it. No. I was on the approach with flaps down at about 150 feet and the engine cut dead. And within a very short space of time I was in the water. I managed it all right, and was picked up by the *Priun*, a Polish destroyer. When you are in the water and the bows of a destroyer are approaching she looks absolutely huge. She came by at about 3 knots and we scrambled up the nets she had let down the side. Then they put us in the ward room with a bottle of Haig, on water for a few hours '

After the attack the *Nelson* managed to steam to Gibraltar, but she was too badly damaged to be repaired in the dockyard there and had to return to the UK. It was another victory for the Italian torpedo bombers, but the Fulmars from the *Ark* had shot down five Italian aircraft, and another three had been destroyed by anti-aircraft fire. Moreover, the most important objective had been achieved: the convoy of food and ammunition succeeded in reaching the grand harbour in Malta.

The island was an incessant thorn in the side of Rommel. His supplies, particularly of petrol, were being reduced by as much as a third because of the constant attacks on his supply convoys from Italy by submarines and bombers based on Malta. His planned assault on the British Army in Egypt had been postponed twice, and could not be delayed much longer. Hitler made a decision to send a flotilla of U-boats into the Mediterranean, much against Admiral Raeder's wishes.

On 13 November, *U-81*, captained by Friedrich Guggenberger, was cruising off the coast of Spain, waiting. The day before he had received an intelligence report over the radio that Force H was expected to return to Gibraltar after delivering yet another convoy to Malta. It was not entirely correct: the *Ark*'s latest mission had not been to escort a convoy; instead she had made a high-speed dash to deliver more Hurricane fighters to Malta. The journey to the point where the Hurricanes could take off and reach Malta had to be carried out at high speed under the cover of darkness, but bad weather had intervened, delaying the aircraft that were meant to meet the *Ark* and guide the Hurricanes to the small island 300 miles away. Cruising at high speed on a zigzag course to evade submarines, everyone on board the *Ark*, permanently at their action stations, spent anxious hours waiting for enemy bombers to strike. When the last Hurricane finally flew off, Force H thankfully headed for home. Two days later, they were nearing Gibraltar.

Admiral Somerville had been warned some days earlier that German U-boats had been sighted south of Malaga. Force H normally approached Gibraltar to the north of the Spanish island of Alboran where it had long been assumed that German spies reported details of their course. This information would be immediately passed to the U-boats which threatened the safety of Somerville's ships, so he tried to fool the spies by steering to the south of Alboran, then ordering a rapid change of course to the north at the last minute. At half past eight on the morning of

13 November he sent a message to all the ships in the fleet warning them of the danger of enemy submarines. Swordfish aircraft from the *Ark* began flying at first light, two patrolling a wide arc about 3 kilometres ahead of the destroyer screen, with another six aircraft on long-range patrol.

Seven hours later, at half past three, the square signal light on the bridge above the flight deck changed from red to green and the last of a squadron of Swordfish aircraft lifted into the air, their single radial engines at full throttle, sending out deep, reverberating bass notes. Shortly after that, with a thud and squeal of tyres on the deck, the first of the six Swordfish that had been circling hooked onto the arrestor wire stretched across the deck. It taxied forward so that the ground crew could fold its wings ready to be taken down to the hangars. In quick succession, the other five Swordfish landed.

The first two pilots to land were Percy Gick and Eugene Esmonde. They went down to the officers' mess where others were reading, playing cards or, like Val Bailey, playing backgammon. Percy Gick's telegraphist air gunner, Les Sayer, went to the ratings' mess, where he got a cup of tea, then, exhausted from the noise and wind of several hours spent in an open cockpit, fell asleep. The *Ark* was nearing Gibraltar, and the crews were no longer at action stations, so for the ordinary seamen on board like engine room artificer John McCrow and marine Cyril Asher it was time for a change of watch. They too went to their various messes for tea. All over the ship that afternoon, a third of the crew were being served bread and jam and a mug of tea or cocoa.

It had been a long time since the crew had had any home leave. They needed a rest, and the *Ark* needed a refit. The ship's sides were showing the streaked and damaged paintwork from countless near-misses and the blast of the anti-aircraft guns. Throughout the mess decks cockroaches were becoming unbearable, and rats were beginning to nest in any crevice they could find. In an hour or so the crew would be in Gibraltar and the rumour was that home leave and a major refit in an American port was on the cards, although many crew members recalled the last time they'd heard 'it's home for Christmas'. Instead they had put to sea from Gibraltar, on Christmas Day no less, in a fruitless search for the German battleship *Admiral Hipper*.

At twenty minutes to four, the sonar operator of HMS *Legion*, one of Force H's escort destroyers, reported hearing something on the anti-submarine sonar, but he could not identify the noise. They were close to another destroyer and the officer of the watch thought they were hearing the sound of its propeller. One minute later, at 1541 hours, the 230kg warhead of a German torpedo exploded against the hull of the *Ark Royal*. The position was reported as 36.03° North and 04.40° West. On the *Ark* there had been no warning of an impending attack. The ship was lifted violently by the explosion, and the aircraft on the deck were thrown several feet into the air. In the mess decks below, crockery went flying.

Seaman John Elias was on the lower deck of the *Argus*, watching the *Ark*. 'I saw this fountain of water shoot up from the side of the *Ark*,' he said, 'a huge amount of spray was thrown up on the starboard side, and it seemed to me that there were two explosions. She took on a list almost immediately – within thirty seconds I would say.' Captain Maund, on the flight deck when the explosion happened, saw brown smoke billowing out of the hatch of the bomb lift, which brought bombs from the magazine deep inside the hull up to the flight deck. He rushed to the bridge to find that the telegraph system to the engine rooms was not working. When the ship was finally brought to a stop it had already shipped a lot of water and was listing heavily. The torpedo had struck the middle of the ship, tearing a hole in the starboard side and opening up the boiler rooms to the sea.

There was pandemonium on the *Ark*. Marine Cyril Asher recalled, 'There was a huge crash and the lights went out. The klaxon went off and we rushed back to the guns for action stations. There was a heavy list to starboard, and we found we were looking down at the sea from the turret.' The unthinkable had happened. 'In convoy at night you would see ships being attacked and on fire. The first thing you would be aware of would be either a flash or an explosion, and you rush to action stations. You were always afraid of it happening to you, and you would think, "Thank God it wasn't me."'

Those closest to the explosion, in the engine spaces below the water line, were the most vulnerable. Senior stoker Pocock was on duty in the starboard boiler room, on the side of the ship that had been hit by the torpedo. 'The lights went out and the place filled with fumes,' he said. 'We were thrown off our balance, and water came up a few seconds after the explosion. We evacuated straight away. We went back with a light after two or three minutes and the place was half full of oil and water. Then there was a signal to abandon ship so we went up to the lower hangar deck. By the time we left the water was 10 feet above the floor plates.' Able Seaman Peter Downing, nineteen at the time, was monitoring the power supply in the main switchboard room, which directed electrical power throughout the ship. After the explosion fuel oil started to fill the compartment, and he escaped up a ladder. Next to the switchboard room was the ship's main telephone exchange where another nineteen-year-old, Able Seaman Tarbet, was on watch. 'I felt a big explosion underneath me,' he said. 'The lights went out and I heard the sound of glass breaking. Fumes filled the space, and on evacuating oil poured into the space from the door. The fumes seemed to be burning our lungs and I felt sure that we could not last very much longer with it. I thought our last days had come.'

The last days had certainly come for one man. Able Seaman Mitchell was a sailor who had already seen active service during the First World War. He was one of the oldest ratings on the *Ark*, a fatherly figure to many of the younger ratings, and respected by his senior officers. He had just entered the lower steering room compartment when the torpedo struck. Lieutenant Baker later reported that he saw 'oil and water gushing out of the lower steering room compartment. I considered that nothing could be done but close the watertight hatch.' Able Seaman Mitchell was never seen again.

The torpedo had hit between the bomb store and the fuel bunkers, almost directly under the bridge. Compartments on either side of the explosion started to flood with seawater immediately, but the torrent of fuel and fumes that hit the electricity switch room and the telephone exchange was just as damaging. Electrical power failed in the rear half of the ship, and it was impossible for the captain and senior officers on the bridge to communicate with the engine room or other parts of the vessel. The order 'action stations' was given on the public address system but was never heard; instructions had to be passed around the ship verbally, by runners using bosun's whistles. The *Ark Royal*, one of Britain's most modern ships, had been knocked back to the age of sail.

John McCrow recalled the confusion. 'I was having tea in the artificers' mess when the explosion happened. I mean, we were used to them, but there had been no call to action stations. Then the ship heeled over, and we expected it to come back up, but it didn't, and someone shouted, "Good God, we've been torpedoed!" Then the Tannoy gave a sort of rattle. I heard someone say "Abandon ship!" Then, "No, it's action stations!"' John struggled up the steeply sloping decks through closed-down hatches and ladders to his action stations on the flight deck.

Captain Maund and his senior officers had set up a temporary command centre at the base of the superstructure. By the time John reached them the *Ark* had heeled over even more. On everyone's mind, including that of the captain, was the fate of *Courageous* and *Glorious*, the other carriers that had sunk earlier in the war, taking half their crews to their deaths. Captain Maund turned to John McCrow and said, 'ERA, there's nothing you can do here. It's abandon ship!'

Messengers piped the order throughout the ship, and the crew assembled on the port side of the lower hangar deck and the flight deck. Ropes were flung down the side, and a destroyer, HMS *Legion*, slowly approached. Crowds of sailors lined the open galleries on the lower decks while others clambered over the edge of the flight deck that was now steeply inclined to starboard. Steam was pouring out of the boiler room ventilation shafts as men went hand over hand down the ropes onto the deck of the *Legion*.

Two of the remaining pilots in the wardroom, Percy Gick and Val Bailey, who thought they were in a slightly different league from ordinary sailors, came up with their own very individual solution, as Bailey explained. 'Percy said to me, "If we're sinking, we should lower a boat." So we went along to the port side to where the lifeboats were. There was no panic. We stopped in the stores to get some caps and waterproofs, and tried to lower a boat. But of course there was no electricity, and everything on the *Ark* was driven by electricity. So we got some hacksaws and managed after a while to swing the davits out and then lowered the boat by hand. We were just about to cast off when the captain shouted down to us and said, "What are you doing?" "As you can see, sir, we've lowered a boat." "Don't be so bloody stupid. Get back on board." So we climbed back.'

By now, thirty minutes after the torpedo had hit, Captain Maund and chief engineer Tony Oliver had received some preliminary damage reports. The *Ark*, although listing badly, had apparently stabilized in the water. The watertight bulkheads were holding, and Gibraltar was close. Admiral Somerville, Captain Maund and the senior officers knew what was at stake. The German Navy would achieve a major propaganda coup by destroying the ship that had triumphed over the *Bismarck*. But the loss of the *Ark* would be far more serious than that. Without her, Force H was finished, leaving Malta exposed and the whole of Britain's war in the Mediterranean theatre in peril. Leaving the destroyers to defend the *Ark* against further attack, Somerville steamed at full speed in his flagship HMS *Malaya* to Gibraltar. There he immediately ordered a massive salvage operation to rescue the *Ark*. Tugs and a small fleet of other vessels put to sea to tow the *Ark* back to Gibraltar for repairs. The *Ark* must be saved!

But a serious flaw in the design of the *Ark* now became apparent to the damage control party left on board. There was no emergency source of electricity. All of the ship's power was provided by the main turbines, driven by steam from the boilers. Now the boilers were shut down, and most of the engineering staff had abandoned ship. John McCrow, now on the deck of the *Legion*, heard a loudspeaker announcement ordering all engine room personnel back on board. He made the difficult climb back up one of the ropes to the deck of the *Ark*, and almost immediately became aware of the scale of the task. 'We had very large 125-ton pumps in the hull that could shift enormous quantities of water,' he said, 'but these were useless without power. The starboard boiler room was flooded, and so was the centre one, but the two boilers in the port boiler room had escaped flooding and could be used. But we needed electricity to pump water into them, because the feed tank had been allowed to empty.'

At 1730, less than half an hour later, another escort destroyer, HMS *Laforey*, came alongside to supply water to the boilers, and to run a cable onto the *Ark Royal* so that power could be supplied to some portable pumps. Water was by this time seeping into the Marines' mess deck and the starboard engine room. Val Bailey was pressed into action. 'The ship could do nothing without electricity; we needed electricity to start our own boilers. Then a chap came on board from a destroyer with two great electric cables, but our torpedo officer [on every ship electrical power was the responsibility of the torpedo officer] was still on the *Legion*, so we stumbled about trying to work out where to connect it. We spent some time desperately struggling to get some portable pumps from the *Laforey* down into the lower decks of the *Ark* but it was hellish difficult with the lack of light and the steep angle to the doors and so on. Then I was detailed to go down to investigate the depth of water. I got a torch. It was pitch black and very eerie going below; the ship was heeling over, and it was totally quiet. The odd creak and so on. It was pretty alarming, and then after a few decks I just stepped into the water. So I went back and made my report.'

Swordfish from Gibraltar had by this time flown out to the *Ark* to supplement the anti-submarine patrols of the destroyers. They circled the *Ark*, and the photographs they took show a thick black slick of oil stretching out from the starboard side and five Swordfish still clinging perilously to the sloping flight deck, with one of the deck lifts halted in its ascent. The *Ark Royal* that had only recently sailed at nearly 35 miles an hour across the South Atlantic and the Arctic Ocean and driven its bows deep into massive waves in pursuit of the *Bismarck* was now lifeless in the Mediterranean's currents like so much driftwood.

At eight o'clock in the evening the *Thames*, one of the tugs from Gibraltar, reached the *Ark* and managed to secure a tow rope. But the big emergency pumps in the bilges were needed to reverse the list, and without power from the engines that was impossible. It was all very well to attempt a tow, but the men in the engine room were the only people who could save the ship.

John McCrow, Tony Oliver and their fellow engineers were struggling to restore some order. All they had were torches and battery-powered emergency lighting as they squeezed through watertight hatches and clambered down narrow ladders to reach the port boiler room. There was no ventilation in the engine and boiler rooms, and there was the constant threat that the ship would suddenly capsize, taking them to their deaths. The emergency supply from the *Laforey* was enough to power a pump to fill the boiler with water and fire up the oil burners. With two burners running it would take about forty minutes to raise enough steam to power a generator, and by nine o'clock they had enough steam pressure to provide power for the portable pumps. The engine control room had been flooded as well, and John and the other engineers struggled to rig alternative controls for the port boilers and the engine room. Two hours later they had one of the large pumps in the rear part of the ship working, the lights were restored, and the big ventilation fans to the boiler room were slowly rotating.

The second tug to arrive failed to get a tow rope onto the bows of the ship and then disappeared into the darkness – an unbelievable piece of incompetence at such a time. But all on board now believed that the situation had been completely reversed, and that they were proceeding at about 3 miles an hour towards Gibraltar. Admiral Somerville received a signal from the captain of the *Laforey* saying that the *Ark* 'has her own steam and power, flooding is apparently under control and no more tugs are required until off harbour'. As Somerville later remarked in a letter to his wife, 'they were too optimistic'.

Val Bailey had by this time been ordered to go forward to join the tow rope party in the bows. 'And so we sat there. Every so often you could hear these horrible noises of things crashing about inside the ship – not very pleasant at all. It seemed to me that the list was slowly getting worse.' John McCrow was still working in the port engine room, and he too knew that the fight to save the *Ark* was far from over. 'We were not making enough impact on the flooding,' he said. 'The water pressure in the flooded central boiler room was buckling the port boiler room bulkhead, and some of the watertight doors were leaking. Then a decision was made to try to raise enough steam to drive the port propeller, and that proved our undoing. For the short time that the port shaft was turning it was instrumental in creating additional stresses on the already stressed bulkheads of the ship. Compartments hitherto untouched were beginning to flood as the lower joints were leaking under the pressure of water.'

There is a very strong current in the Straits of Gibraltar at night, and the single tug that had managed to get a tow rope onto the *Ark* couldn't make any headway against it. Despite the optimistic signals that were being sent to Gibraltar, the captain and the chief engineer realized that without more power the *Ark* would never make it back to port. She was drifting helplessly in the fast current. To raise sufficient steam to power the port propeller meant that more oil burners in the boilers had to be lit. But, as Val Bailey suspected, the water level had gradually been rising inside the ship and it had flooded the vents from the boilers, blocking the exhaust of the hot gases. At two o'clock in the morning John McCrow noticed that the trunking that fed all the exhaust gases into the funnel was glowing cherry red, and that the boiler was on fire.

Smoke started to fill the boiler room and engine spaces. The fumes became overpowering. Moving about the ship, which was leaning heavily in the water, was taxing the strength of the crew; opening air lock doors was getting more difficult because the ship was listing so much. It could take almost ten minutes to go from the engine room to the boiler room. The only means of escape on the port side was a small hatch leading into the auxiliary hydraulic room. Two engineers collapsed in the heat, and another needed artificial respiration. They had struggled for hours to save the ship, but now they realized that she was lost. 'My last recollection before leaving the boiler room,' John told me, 'was the arrival of senior engineer Clark. His boiler suit no longer white, sweat pouring down his smoke-blackened face, staring up at the pressure gauge on number two boiler, he told me to return to the machinery control room as the boilers could no longer be steamed. I clambered up the ladders in the air intake duct to get out, and all the lights went out again. The ship was heeling over as we clambered frantically up and along the steeply sloping hangar deck. It was dark when I got my turn to slide down the rope into one of the launches.'

By four o'clock in the morning the *Ark* was listing at thirty-five degrees, and ropes attached to the *Laforey* began to snap as the ship heeled over even more. The order to abandon ship was given again. Val Bailey and the rest of the crew in the bows never heard the order, and stayed in their places until the *Ark*'s flight deck was almost vertical. 'A motor launch came past with someone shouting, "*Ark Royal* ahoy! Anyone on the *Ark Royal*?" We then just walked down the side of the ship into the water, and we swam off a little way and were finally picked up by a motor launch. I think I was the last one off the *Ark Royal*.'

A gunner, Christian Herring, was the only person who clearly described the *Ark* as she sank. He had been thrown into the water as he tried to remove a tow rope from HMS *Laforey*. He swam for half an hour before he was picked up by a motor launch. After that he heard the noise of explosions as bulkheads collapsed and gave way. 'She first rolled right over on her beam ends so that half the flight deck was visible. She appeared to pause there for perhaps three minutes. She then rolled right over, and it appeared to me that a third of her length had been torn out. There was a great deal of noise and escaping air, and then I thought she had broken in two, and the two pieces were torn away from each other. The after part sank first, followed by the visible piece of the stem, and she went down from that position in two minutes.'

Since the Nazis had first claimed to have sunk the *Ark Royal*, she had steamed a distance equivalent to almost six times around the Earth, and her crew had lost count of the torpedoes and bombs they had narrowly avoided. She was a lucky ship, and for most of the crew a happy one. Under her various captains, and particularly under the direction of Admiral Somerville, the *Ark* had confounded those who had said she was a waste of money.

In just five days in May 1941 she reinforced Britain's vital out-post in the Mediterranean and then destroyed Germany's biggest threat in the Atlantic. Ultimately her luck ran out under an increasingly determined and powerful onslaught by the German armed forces, but in two years of war the *Ark Royal* had played a crucial role, buoying up Britain at a time when defeat seemed inevitable. Only the *Ark* could have done it; now there was nothing to replace her.

The crew members who had abandoned ship shortly after the torpedo hit were taken straight to Gibraltar by HMS *Legion*. When they woke up the next morning they fully expected to see the *Ark* berthed at the mole in Gibraltar harbour. They were to be utterly disappointed. Both they and Britain had lost a famous ship; but they had lost a home as well.

On 19 January 1942 an application for trial by court martial of Captain Maund was heard. The charges were that he had failed to take proper steps to ensure the safety of His Majesty's Ship *Ark Royal* after that ship had been damaged by explosions, and that he had failed to ensure that His Majesty's Ship *Ark Royal* was in a sufficient state of readiness to deal with possible damage while engaged in operations of war in dangerous waters. The thrust of the indictment was that the engine and boiler room crews and repair parties had been brought up prematurely from below. It was this that had led to the loss of all steam and electrical power in the crucial hours after the torpedo hit. This was undoubtedly true, but Admiral Somerville, in a letter to his wife written shortly after the Board of Inquiry was held in Gibraltar, understood the harshness of this judgement and why Maund had ordered that the ship be evacuated: 'When you see that enormous great flying deck canted over at an angle of 20 degrees, you certainly get the impression that the ship must be going right over, and with over 1,700 people on board and the difficulty getting on deck in a carrier, I for one don't blame him for this decision.'

It seems to have been assumed without question by the court that the *Ark* could have been saved. But one important piece of evidence was never mentioned in the court martial's summing up. Lieutenant St John Hewitt Heather, the captain of Motor Launch 137 which had rescued Val Bailey and Gunner Herring, claimed that as the *Ark* capsized he saw the hole in her side. It stretched from the funnel casing to the stern for about 130 feet, and was about 30 feet wide between the centre line of the ship and the starboard bilge keel – a hole so large that it was remarkable the *Ark* stayed afloat for as long as she did. Equally remarkable were the casualty figures, as Ron Skinner reminded me sixty-three years later when we saw the wreck for the first time. 'Seventeen hundred men were saved and only one man died,' he said. 'I think the *Ark* was a lucky ship to the end.'

13

THE JOURNEY BACK

By the start of 2004 my quest to film the *Ark Royal* had hit a complete dead end. A year earlier the *Sun*, the *Daily Mail* and others had published stories about the discovery of the wreck of the *Ark Royal*. The *Mail on Sunday* had devoted two whole pages to it, and others had published pictures of some of the sonar images we had obtained from the *Rig Supporter*. I was surprised by the interest that these mainstream papers had shown, but since this flurry of publicity the year had ground on frustratingly, with meeting after meeting during which I tried to hammer out a plan and, more importantly, find the money to get cameras down to the wreck.

Underwater filming is now a commonplace event, but it still requires complicated and special equipment to do it properly. I needed to hire a ship big enough to house crew, technicians and a large, remotely controlled underwater vehicle, a robot commonly called an ROV, with its supporting cables on the rear deck. The ship would need to be able to launch and control the ROV in a choppy sea, and to be fitted with equipment so that it could keep an accurate position above the wreck, despite winds and currents. Most likely the ship would need to travel to the wreck site from a port in the North Sea, a journey of several days, before any videoing of the *Ark* could even start. Although I had become so obsessed with this project that it had assumed an importance way above the documentary I wanted to make, I still wanted the images of the wreck we might eventually capture to be broadcast on television. This meant I needed the ROV to carry the best possible cameras, and lights that could penetrate the darkness with a brightness and intensity that could approximate to daylight. Commercially available ROVs are not normally fitted with such high-powered lights and high-definition cameras. They were available, but scarce and very expensive to hire; moreover, an expert would be needed to fit them to the ROV. They were also prone to failure.

Suitable ships with such equipment earn their bread and butter by carrying out essential maintenance work on offshore oil rigs and pipelines, or by helping to build new ones. The owners of those ships need to keep them working, or at least free, for their big customers, the oil companies. I looked at various ships and talked to various companies. I had a couple of meetings with James Cameron, the director of *Titanic*, who was extremely interested, motivated like me by the fascination of what might lie thousands of metres below the sea as much as by a personal interest in any film or documentary he might be able to make about the *Ark Royal*. Finally I managed to organize a meeting in a conference room in White City with a group of managers from

Thales, a large engineering multinational, and some executives and accountants from the BBC.

One of Thales' operating divisions specialized in underwater engineering and surveying, and I had approached them to see if they would be prepared to hire out one of their ships to the BBC. After several telephone conversations I realized that some of Thales' senior managers were excited by the prospect of being the first to film the *Ark Royal* and had decided to subsidize their side of the operation, to a certain extent at least. By this time the BBC was thinking about broadcasting the first filming of the wreck as a live event. It meant that more money might be available, but of course it also raised the costs and would force Thales to commit to a specific date to make their ship available.

The meeting went ahead, but before it was over I knew that our demands would make the venture impossible not only for Thales but for any company with the equipment and expertise we needed. As one of Thales' representatives said to me later, 'We would be happy to do it, but we have to be able to choose the time. If a big oil company suddenly wants us to go and investigate a problem with a pipeline or an oil rig, we just couldn't refuse on the grounds that we were doing something for television. We would be the laughing stock of the industry.' And without the live broadcast there would be less money from the BBC. However we cut it, even with the considerable assistance from Thales, there was always a funding gap. It was never going to work. I waited a few days to see if Thales would increase the amount of money they were prepared to spend, but I knew they wouldn't. I was the only person in the BBC aware of the difficulties of what we wanted to do, of how expensive delays caused by bad weather and equipment failure can be. Thales, however, understood such things only too well and knew exactly where to draw the line.

Defeat has an intensely corrosive effect on one's morale, so corrosive in fact that it is hard to judge how deeply one has been affected. It had certainly affected me very deeply, to the extent that a year later on an Airbus on the final approach to the airport at Nice I was almost certain that my trip was going to be a waste of time. I was on my way to a meeting on one of the largest private yachts in the world. It was my last throw of the dice.

About six weeks earlier I had received a very brief and, on the face of it, absurd email. It stated baldly that the sender was the captain of a yacht in the Mediterranean equipped with an underwater camera; could he be of any help with the *Ark Royal*? My instant response was to assume that the sender was a well-meaning eccentric, but he was well meaning at least, and he deserved a reply. I pointed out that the *Ark* was at a depth of 1,000 metres and it would need a very sophisticated underwater camera to take pictures of it. I thought I would hear nothing further, but the answer I received to that email made me think again. It was clear that the captain of the yacht was well aware of the problems associated with underwater exploration and did have the ability to send an ROV to depths of 1,000 metres or more. That still wasn't something I immediately associated with a yacht. The emails and then phone conversations continued.

I was met at the gate in Nice airport by the captain of the yacht, the man I had first thought of as a well-meaning eccentric. Despite his forty-odd years, Richard Bridge did everything with what I have always assumed to be a quintessentially English middle-class, boyish enthusiasm. His energy and humour were a tonic after the long months of frustration I had had to put up with at the BBC. I learned later that he had once been a senior officer on the *QE2*, and had then captained an old sailing ship taking handicapped children on recreational cruises. It was his present job, however, that was the reason for our meeting. He was the captain of the *Octopus*, a yacht that had been built for Paul Allen, one of the richest men in the world who owed his fortune to his one-time partnership with Bill Gates of Microsoft. Allen had subsequently diversified into a variety of other industries.

I had very briefly met Paul Allen before. He owned a football team in Seattle, the Seattle Seahawks, and had wanted to demolish their giant domed stadium, the Kingdome, and replace it with something more modern. I made a documentary about the demolition, which was going to be done quickly and dramatically with explosives. Just before the tense countdown started, Allen quietly paid a visit to the explosives engineers and shook everybody's hand. It seemed a nice, personal touch. He had arrived at the demolition site, I recalled, in an anonymous people carrier, but there was nothing anonymous about his yacht, which I saw as soon as we entered the port in Antibes.

The *Octopus* was at that time the largest private yacht in the world. As I walked along the dockside it looked bigger than the *Rig Supporter*. And its size wasn't the most impressive thing about the *Octopus*. The most remarkable thing about this motor yacht was the elegance of her hull and the deep gloss of her paintwork. Everything was clean and sparkling; anchors and hawse pipes gleamed in stainless steel or chrome. This impression was reinforced as I walked onto the mahogany decks, as pristine-looking as virgin snow. Richard Bridge showed me round, and it was beautiful. Passageways and staterooms were lit with concealed, atmospheric lighting, and everywhere there were thick carpets and furniture decorated in subtle hues of aquamarine and taupe. In some parts of the ship, in the cinema for example, where each seat was furnished with its own cashmere throw, it was impossible to believe that we were afloat.

I was not there to admire the work of the interior designers, however, and Richard was keen to show me the hangar from which the ROV would be launched, and its control room. Outside the guest areas the ship was just as spick and span, fresh from the showroom, but it had been built with equipment similar to a commercial survey vessel. The remote vehicle was not in the hangar that day: it was back with the manufacturers being modified and equipped with high-definition cameras and a battery of high-intensity lights all of which would be able to function a kilometre below the water line. The *Octopus* had also been built with the ability to manoeuvre so that it could maintain station above the sea bed to an accuracy of a few metres, even when the winds and sea were running fairly roughly. I had no doubt that the *Octopus* could do the job; the question for me was whether I wanted them to do it.

Richard and I went for a meal in Antibes, and then we returned to the yacht, where we were scheduled to have a conference telephone call with some representatives of one of Paul Allen's companies in Seattle. Since my first contact with Richard the project had grown. As well as filming the wreck I was going to arrange for several veterans from the *Ark Royal* to come on the cruise; a cameraman and sound recordist would accompany us to shoot footage of their reactions when they saw the wreck. The budget was expanding, and more and more people in Seattle were having a say in the management of the expedition. I jokingly said during the telephone conversation that despite the enormous information gathered during the survey with the AUV it was possible to misread sonar images; I might have located the wreckage of a Liberian-registered bulk carrier instead. When one of them then raised the question of whether the wreck really existed in the place where I claimed it was, I lost my temper and threatened to withdraw from the project immediately. In an embarrassed silence I left the captain's office and went to my cabin.

Like the rest of the guest quarters on the *Octopus* it was discreetly luxurious. I felt ashamed, for I knew what had really caused me to lose my temper. My obsession with the *Ark Royal* had grown as the difficulties of finding the wreck and raising the money to film it had multiplied. The harder it had become, so my sense of ownership had strengthened; I now found myself reluctant to concede control to anyone else. The logic of my position was, however, inescapable: if I wanted to realize my dream of seeing the wreck of the *Ark Royal*, I would have to share my knowledge of the wreck's location plus all the survey data that I had accumulated with the people who worked for Paul Allen. If I left the next day, and flew back to London without agreeing to work with the owner of the *Octopus* and his company I might never have another opportunity to view the *Ark Royal*. There was really no choice for me, though emotionally I knew I would always feel angry about any loss of control.

The next morning I reassured Richard that I was not going to take my bat away, and we tentatively set a date for the expedition to start in the middle of September. The ROV for the *Octopus* was still being modified by its manufacturers. Richard and the person who was directly responsible for it, Mark Quenneville, wanted it to be fitted with some moveable arms that could change the angle of the lights during its voyage underwater. Everything had to be designed and manufactured from scratch, and it was unlikely that it would all be tested by September. On the other hand, the weather in the Mediterranean could be severe in the late autumn and winter. It is an enclosed sea, and winter storms can create very choppy seas; conditions in, say, November might be too rough to launch the ROV. Nobody wanted to delay now that we had agreed to go ahead, and I soon realized I was not dealing any more with a defensive bureaucracy but the first-rate crew of a well-equipped ship with a well-heeled owner. They wanted things to happen, and to happen now.

On 23 September 2004, the *Octopus* slowly moved away from the dock at Gibraltar. Richard was on one wing of the bridge, looking down at the quayside as he slowly moved a small throttle lever that fed power to the bow thrusters. I still could not get used to the sight of seeing these big vessels being manoeuvred with little joysticks, as though the officer of the watch were playing a computer game. The *Octopus* slid smoothly out of the harbour and we headed for the position of the wreck of HMS *Ark Royal*. The ROV, with Mark Quenneville and Jackie Sullivan, had arrived from Seattle and was installed in its garage on the lower deck. We had two days to do a test dive and make sure that the ROV was working properly. The *Octopus* had also taken on board four ROV pilots with a great deal of experience, and we would be able to keep the ROV underwater and working round the clock if we needed to.

The weather threatened to become windy during the night, but we hoped that by the next morning it would ease off and we would be able to launch. The *Octopus* had one disadvantage that a commercial vessel didn't suffer from: the ROV was launched from a garage low down on the water line at the side of the vessel, so if the sea was too rough the ROV garage could flood, and the ROV itself would be driven against the sides of the ship. I imagined that for the designers of the world's biggest luxury yacht, building an A frame and a winch at the stern had been a step too far.

The next day the *Octopus* was about 500 metres from the centre of the wreck site, and at very slow speed, with the ship's echo sounder switched on, we headed towards it. With the sea floor a thousand metres below us the echo sounder was unlikely to show anything, but there was just a chance. The one piece of equipment that was lacking on the *Octopus* was something called HiPap, which stood for high precision acoustic positioning, a system that would have enabled the *Octopus* to locate the ROV in relation to her own position and steer it very accurately to the wreck using the survey data from the *Rig Supporter*. Instead we were going to have to steer the ROV towards the wreck using the ROV's very short-range sonar and some dead reckoning.

First, however, we had to get the ROV launched. Mark Quenneville had arrived on the *Octopus* with the ROV just two days earlier, and the complicated electronics and hydraulics that would enable us to guide and control it a thousand metres below the sea were proving more complicated than anybody had expected. The *Octopus* loitered off Gibraltar while Mark and the chief engineer toiled in the ROV hangar to make sure that the swinging arm, the array of lights and the various controls for the camera were all working properly. Our expected launch time of 10.30 a.m. was moved, then moved again, until twelve hours later the ROV was finally hoisted out of the hangar and lowered carefully into the sea. This is a delicate operation. An ROV pilot stands in the hangar with a mobile control console hanging from his neck, ready to instantly power the ROV away from the ship's side as soon as it is in the sea. Any delay or hesitation will increase the chances of a collision between the ship and the ROV causing who knows what damage to the robot and its electronics. Thankfully, the manoeuvre was completed successfully. The ROV descended to 500 metres and everything seemed to be working. At last we were in good shape, and the next day, at eight a.m., we would be back on site ready to make the dive.

The following morning the wind had picked up again; there was a heavy swell with white caps on the waves. Moreover, in the ROV hangar two of the six HMI lights had failed and would take time to fix. We waited once more for the technicians to solve the problem. When they were finished the wind was still blowing at 25 knots, and it continued into the night.

At midnight it eased off, and we quickly decided to try and dive to the wreck. The ROV pilots gathered in the huge guest dining room that I had had converted into a control room. The captain had put a large screen at one end and we could talk directly to the ROV pilots three decks down in the ROV garage. To help us identify any pieces of the wreck we might find and guide the ROV around them, I had placed large photographs of the *Ark Royal* on the walls, and spread out on the enormous dining-room tables were copies of the engineering drawings of the *Ark* with the data from the survey we had carried out on the *Rig Supporter*.

The sonar survey became the focus of urgent attention. We gathered around the printed charts and I was anxious to point out to the ROV pilots the questions I wanted to find answers to. What position was the ship lying in? Would we be able to identify anything of the superstructure, or was the ship lying upside down? Was the massive shape 700 metres to the south of the main hull another ship? Would we be able to identify the torpedo damage on the bottom of the *Ark*'s hull? Could we find and film an intact Swordfish? The ROV pilots weren't so interested in these questions, which would all be answered eventually; they wanted to work out what pieces of wreckage might snag the ROV and its umbilical cable, trapping hundreds of thousands of pounds' worth of equipment on the sea floor before the expedition had even started.

At just a few minutes before one o'clock in the morning the garage door in the side of the *Octopus*'s hull opened once more and the ROV was lowered into the sea. Almost immediately it was snatched by a current that was speeding past, and slammed into the side of the ship. It was the same current I had seen at night in the *Odin Finder* – water funnelling through the Straits of Gibraltar into the Mediterranean. The motors of the ROV were not powerful enough to fight it, and it would be fatal to launch the ROV in these conditions. It was quickly recovered and once more checked for any damage. We had been at sea for two days and still we hadn't managed to get anywhere near the wreck. I went back to my cabin exhausted and dispirited.

The next day at nine a.m. the ROV went seamlessly into the water. The sea was a flat calm, a hazy mist hovering over it that was rapidly being burned off by the morning sun. It was a perfect day, and as the ROV descended deep into the sea the pilots reported that everything was working perfectly. At last things seemed to be moving in our direction.

The *Octopus* was stationed 500 metres from the southerly point of the main target, and to the west; the ROV, once it was a few metres above the sea floor, would move forward slowly until the wreck came into view. It inched forward excruciatingly. A tense atmosphere developed on the bridge for we were now so close to our target, but the forward-looking sonar on the ROV revealed nothing. By midday we were barely a hundred metres away from where the wreck of the *Ark* should be. The *Octopus*'s first officer looked at me and said, 'We should be seeing something soon, whatever it is.' Then, making a reference to my earlier joke about a Liberian bulk carrier, he added, 'Even if it's only the word Monrovia.' It was an attempt to break the tension, but I found it in extremely poor taste. I was sure that we were heading towards the wreck of the *Ark Royal*, though I still retained a germ of doubt. Like Rick Davey, I knew that you could only be absolutely certain you had found a ship when you could see the name on the side.

Slowly the ROV advanced. All we could see in front of it was the empty sea bed, and of course the deep waters of the Mediterranean, which became impenetrable a few metres in front of the beam of light from our HMIs. Then something grey and angular appeared, at the same time as the ROV pilot said, 'Something big on the sonar.'

We had arrived. Slowly moving across the television screens suspended from the ceiling of the bridge was the edge of a deck and what looked like a broken headlight. Looking at objects far below the surface of the sea is disorienting. The direction of the light from the ROV can produce strange shadows, and sediment over the years falls like drifting snow, covering and obscuring familiar features. There is also a disconcerting loss of perspective that makes it hard to judge the size of objects caught in the glare of the lights. As the ROV slowly approached I stared, puzzled for some time as to what we were looking at. It hit me suddenly that we had come stern on to the wreck and we were looking at the rear end of the flight deck, the giant overhang that was one of the *Ark*'s most prominent features. We were looking from not very far away at the safety net around the flight deck, the stern light and the Admiral's light, all of which were mounted on the stern. It was the *Ark Royal*. Definitely. There was absolutely no question about it. At last, after a search of two and a half years, I was looking at her wreck. I told Richard that we were looking at the broken stern light of the *Ark Royal*. There was no whoop of joy, no cheering or high fives, but throughout the ship there was an absolutely palpable collective sigh as the suppressed tension of the last two days was released.

I left the bridge and went down to the control centre we had set up in the dining room. On the way there I looked in on the cinema, where the large screen was showing the images from the ROV. A few people were sitting there wrapped up in throws, and one of them murmured to me, 'Awesome.' Projected onto a big screen in the darkness of a cinema it did look truly impressive. It was the best place on the *Octopus* to appreciate the scale of the wreck, but I wanted to follow the course of the ROV, and made my way to the room where Richard was poring over the plans.

The ROV was moving slowly along the starboard side of the *Ark Royal* at a level just below the flight deck. The big 4.5-inch anti-aircraft guns in their twin turrets were appearing, bathed in the light of the HMIs, and the camera operator on the ROV was slowly zooming into an optical sight above the barrel. Then we saw the water depth marks painted on the side of the hull, which enabled us to fix our position on the wreck. The rear section had hit the sea bed stern first and had sunk in the mud to a considerable depth. The rudder and three bronze propellers, 16 feet in diameter, were hidden from view, and so was the ship's name on the side of the hull. But as we moved forward the height increased until the sea bed was almost at the level of the original water line. This part of the wreck was on an even keel, so I thought it would be interesting to find out why the AUV survey we had conducted from the *Rig Supporter* had led us to believe – although Rick Davey later modified this view – that the flight deck had separated from the hull. For the moment, though, I was just happy to watch the pictures of the *Ark Royal* as the ROV was piloted gingerly along her starboard side.

Forward of the hull, where the funnel and the bridge used to be, there was a complete break in the structure, with nothing recognizable beyond torn plating and twisted and buckled decks. There was no obvious sign of any hole caused by the torpedo explosion: it was either below the level of the mud, or had been ripped away as the forward part of the hull had disintegrated. The evidence from the captain of the motor launch, who had submitted a drawing of an enormous hole to the Board of Inquiry, would remain uncorroborated.

It was now almost two in the morning, and I was extremely tired, even though I felt quietly euphoric, more relaxed now than I had been for a long time. I don't think I have ever worked for so long, and sometimes with such lack of hope, to fulfil such a focused ambition. But I was now looking at the wreck of the *Ark Royal*. At last I had got there. I had succeeded when everyone else had been prepared to write the idea off because I had refused to abandon a project that had seemed doomed to failure. One of the stewardesses on the *Octopus* brought me a huge coffee, what she called a 'cuppacino', and a cognac. Yes, I was, for the first time in months, happy.

The next day, after the dive had lasted for almost six hours, we pulled the ROV out of the water and returned to Gibraltar to pick up four of the *Ark* veterans who were flying out to board the *Octopus*. The weather at Gibraltar was bad, and their flight was diverted to Malaga. Late that night, 26 September, we tied up at

Malaga and finally four men, all in their eighties, arrived on the *Octopus*: John Moffat, the Swordfish pilot who had taken part in the attack on the *Bismarck*, who had travelled all the way from Dunkeld in Scotland; Ron Skinner, Leading Writer for the Commander (Air), who had journeyed from a small village in the Cotswolds; and Bill Morrison (able seaman) and John Richardson (stoker), who had travelled from Nottingham and Newcastle respectively. All were extremely tired, but not too tired to be amazed by their surroundings as they bedded down for the night on the largest luxury yacht in the world, guests of Paul Allen.

The weather was sunny and the sea calm as everybody gathered in the dining room the next day. We had the rest of the wreck site to explore, but while the ROV was again being prepared we replayed the previous day's voyage along the starboard side of the hull to the former members of the *Ark*'s crew. Bill Morrison was eloquent about the effort required to load the clips of 2lb cartridges into the pom-pom anti-aircraft guns, and everybody recalled that it was the noise of these guns opening up that heralded a close attack on the *Ark*. But by and large they were still tired and content to watch the hypnotic images from the bottom of the sea flow across the screen.

For the second dive we planned to head south from the stern to investigate the enormous structure 700 metres away, and the large number of pieces of wreckage that lay in between. I wanted to search for the Swordfish aircraft, the image of which we had enhanced from the AUV's sonar survey. It was fairly isolated but close to what I had identified from the sonar picture as an upturned flight deck lift, and in order to navigate to it we would need to take a fix from the large section to the south. I must say I regarded this Swordfish as the ultimate target of our search.

Those antiquated-looking biplanes had proved to be Admiral Lutjens' and the *Bismarck*'s nemesis, snatching victory for Britain from the jaws of a humiliating defeat. It was these aircraft that had underpinned the *Ark Royal*'s legendary status. First, however, we had to find the large section to the south, which I was now fairly convinced was the bow section. At one time, on the *Rig Supporter*, we had guessed that the large object might be the stern, but we had seen just twenty-four hours ago that the stern was still firmly attached to the main hull.

Over lunch, Ron Skinner reminded us of the time when the 'silly little admiral', in his words, sent a flight of fifteen Skuas to bomb the *Scharnhorst* in Trondheim Fjord, and only seven had come back. 'It was my job to write their names on the board when they took off, and write them down when they had landed,' he said. 'Sixteen names were missing.'

By late afternoon the ROV was poised above the sea, ready for another dive. The weather was still fine, the sea calm, and the ROV descended to the main body of the wreck before heading south. An hour later it was travelling just above the sea bed at a fast walking pace. Pieces of debris and machinery would appear in the lights, but they were hard to identify. Even the former crew members of the *Ark* were puzzled by some of them. Then, a few hundred yards from the bow section, the ROV's sonar began to detect a substantial set of targets. Before long its lights were reflecting off gleaming metal. Lying in front of the ROV were the shapes of several aircraft, the shiny aluminium of their bodies showing through the corroded and flaking paintwork. 'They're Fulmars,' said John Moffat. 'Look, there's the tail wheel, and that's a folded wing section.'

He was right. We were looking at pieces of the slow, under-powered RAF reject that had flown through the sky over the

Mediterranean sixty years ago, whose pilots, despite being hugely outnumbered, had broken up attack after attack by Italian bombers and German Stukas. These Fulmars had not been on the flight deck on the day the *Ark* was torpedoed, they were in the hangar; they had their undercarriages down and their wings folded back. I remembered Val Bailey, a former Fulmar pilot who was due to helicopter onto the *Octopus* in two days' time, telling me that as he sat in the bows of the sinking *Ark* tending the tow ropes and drinking wine he had liberated from the mess, he heard rumblings and crashing noises from aircraft in the hangar decks breaking free and plunging down the deck. The Fairey Fulmars, all of them in pieces with parts of wings missing and tail sections snapped off, must have tumbled out of the *Ark* as the ship split in two. At the court martial of Captain Maund, one of the witnesses, Gunner Herring, had described seeing the lifts jammed with aircraft as the ship capsized.

The ROV continued slowly into the wreckage, the camera lens zooming in to look at the gun ports on the wing and manoeuvring gently to peer into the cockpit, the remains of the control column and instruments still visible. It was a remarkable sight, and as the ROV slowly pirouetted around the aircraft the banter between the ROV pilots, the camera operator, Richard and me in the control room ceased. We were observing something quite unique and unexpected. The wreckage of these aircraft from the hangars of the *Ark Royal* spoke eloquently of the massive destruction that had occurred in the ship in her last minutes, as this 800-foot-long, 22,000-ton carrier had rolled over and broken open. Any remarks from us seemed completely unnecessary.

Continuing the journey south, we approached the massive target we believed marked the southern end of the wreckage area. It was so high that the sidescan sonar on the AUV had not been able to obtain a clear image. Our first contact with it was a strange piece of debris that took some time to identify; it was the huge curved forward edge of the flight deck that had become separated. A few metres further on we saw the grey plates of the ship's side. The ROV slowly rose in the water, first 10, then 20 metres, and there, etched sharply against the darkness in our bank of lights, was the ship's keel, stretching into the gloom, with a massive kink and fracture 12 metres from the stem. The whole of the bow section was lying upside down, the giant anchors still suspended from the hawse pipes, the tow ropes that had proved useless still tied around the bollards on the gallery deck.

That evening over dinner Ron Skinner reminded everybody that John Moffat was one of the pilots who had attacked the *Bismarck*, and that according to a recent analysis of the squadron's records it was his torpedo that might have crippled the battleship. John quickly took up the story, pointing out that the classic way to avoid a torpedo was to turn the ship's head into the direction of the attack, but that the *Bismarck* had turned the wrong way, probably to avoid a separate flight of Swordfish. His description of the way the *Ark*'s flight deck pitched up and down in the storm was graphically illustrated with a twisting dinner plate; he said that no other plane would have been able to carry out that mission in those conditions. Ron believed that the *Bismarck* had to be sunk, but John was adamant: the sight of the doomed German sailors struggling hopelessly in the water was indelibly etched in his mind, and pity overrode any other emotions.

For the next dive we planned to investigate the port side of the main wreck, and it was during the briefing in the morning with the ROV pilots to plan a route round the site that Dougie, one of the pilots, suggested that now would be a good time to give John the controls. Later that day John went down to the hangar to get a good look at the ROV and to see it launched. Then he went off to the control room, from where he deftly manoeuvred the ROV onto the *Ark*'s flight deck. It was an emotional moment for him.

We did not have unlimited time, however, and both Richard and I wanted to capture as much footage of the wreck as we could. Whenever the ROV was launched we would keep it submerged for as long as it was working, but there were always adjustments and minor repairs to be made, particularly to the lights and the moving arm that carried the directional spotlight. Richard and I would sit in the control room until four a.m., kept awake by cups of strong coffee from one or other of the hostesses on the boat.

The opportunity to investigate the main hull and the bow section was absolutely incredible and I would have been happy to spend days looking at every inch, but there was one target out of all of those revealed by the sonar survey from the AUV that intrigued me: the image of what I was sure was a Swordfish aeroplane lying upside down on the sea floor, its wings spread. It certainly appeared to have the same wingspan as a Swordfish, and the clinching detail, for me, was what appeared to be the sonar reflection of the landing gear with its triangular struts. There were five Swordfish on the flight deck when the *Ark Royal* was torpedoed, and it appeared from the photographs taken at the time that four of these had had their wings folded back. The fifth, which had just landed, still had extended wings. I believed that we had a sonar image of this very same aircraft, and I thought that this was convincing evidence that the *Ark Royal* had not drifted for miles after it had capsized, as we had first thought on the *Odin Finder*, but had capsized and sunk more or less where we had found the wreck. Of course the wings and fuselage of a Swordfish, a biplane designed in the 1930s, were covered in fabric. The only metal parts of the airframe were the struts between the two wings, the ribs and framework of the fuselage and wings, and the area of the fuselage surrounding the single radial engine. It seemed unlikely that after six decades at the bottom of the sea a canvas-covered aeroplane would be in good enough shape to produce such a clearly defined sonar image, but that is what we had. If by some astonishing chance of chemistry the canvas covering of the Swordfish had been preserved, it would be a remarkable discovery – an almost intact Swordfish from the flight deck of the *Ark Royal* lying a kilometre beneath the sea.

The Swordfish, if that was what it was, lay close to the bow section, so after another survey of this section of the *Ark Royal*, for the benefit of Val Bailey who had recently arrived on board, the ROV headed on a north-easterly course to locate this mysterious object. As it moved slowly forwards there was no indication on the sonar that anything lay in front of it. We saw nothing but sea bed. Then, caught in the spot light, the deck lift appeared, lying, as I'd suspected, upside down. We had gone past the Swordfish. The ROV turned and slowly headed back at a slight angle, and there, sticking up, was the wheel strut of a Swordfish. We had found it! But it was not what I had expected. It was a ghost of a Swordfish, upside down to be sure, but the undercarriage was tilted at a drunken angle. Both wings had collapsed onto each other and were lying, denuded of canvas covering, extended out from the fuselage which had itself collapsed in a pile of fragments. It seemed as fragile as paper after it has been consumed by fire. An object lesson in the interpretation of sonar images – or perhaps in the interpretation of dreams. John Moffat gazed at the images, astounded.

Over the next three days and nights we covered everything that had been identified in the sonar survey by the AUV on the *Rig Supporter*. By examining the wreck and every piece of debris we could find, and constantly referring to the copies of the original blueprints, we believed we had a good idea of the layout of the wreck site.

The wreck of the *Ark Royal* was in two main parts. The bow section, the large object to the south of the main wreck, was lying upside down and had broken off cleanly from the main hull about 20 metres back from the stem. To the north of this was a very large piece of twisted and tangled wreckage approximately 30 metres long and 10 metres high. This was the funnel and the bridge, with sections of the flight deck and side plating attached to it. Then there was the 'Fulmar field', as we called it, a surreal area of aircraft wreckage that reflected our light whenever we approached. This part of the debris field can only have been created when the ship broke apart. To the north of that lay the main hull. There was a severe tear in the side of the hull, level with the rear pom-pom on the starboard side, clearly indicating where the funnel and bridge had separated. The port side of this piece of the wreck was intact for a greater length, but the guns and their sponsons were far more damaged than the ones on the starboard side. It seemed likely that it was the port side that had first hit the sea bed.

What we found appeared to confirm the evidence of Gunner Herring. This young rating had been pulled overboard by a tow rope at four in the morning on 14 November, the day the *Ark Royal* sank. Fortunately he was picked up by a motor launch, and he observed the ship sinking two hours later. His account clearly states that the *Ark* stayed motionless on her beam ends then slowly capsized, and as she turned completely upside down she appeared to break in two; the stern sank first, followed by the bow. The *Ark* had capsized and sunk almost exactly where we had found the wreck, swept a short way to the east by the strong diurnal current streaming through the Straits of Gibraltar.

As we headed back to Gibraltar, I spoke with the former crew members of the *Ark Royal*, eager to hear their feelings. Naturally everybody said that they felt privileged to be on board and to be a part of such an experience, though John Moffat said that he had thought hard about it. Had many of the men on the *Ark* died that day he would have refused to take part; as it was, he was glad he was there. He went on to say that looking at the wreck had solved something that had been nagging him for years, and that was the question of whether the *Ark Royal* could have been saved. I had heard a variation on this view from others, notably George Baldwin, the pilot from 803 Squadron who flew Skuas from the *Ark* during operations over Norway. He said that the general view of the loss of the *Ark* in some squadrons was that it was another screw-up by the fishheads – the somewhat derogatory term used to refer to sailors in the Fleet Air Arm. John now said that as far as he was concerned the *Ark* could never have been saved; the doubt had been removed from his mind. For everyone, despite the war, despite the fear that they experienced, seeing the ship again had reminded them of friendship and solidarity. It was a happy ship, and a lucky one.

Ron Skinner was the most profoundly affected. After pointing out to me that the *Ark* had sunk with the loss of just one life, Able Seaman Mitchell's, and that 1,600 had survived – proof that the *Ark*'s luck held even after the attack by the U-boat – he was moved to tears. 'I'm just a silly old man,' he said, 'but the *Ark* was my home for three years, and those years were an important part of my life. Looking at the wreck brings it all back.'

That evening we held a party for everybody on the *Octopus*. Ron had written a poem, and it was read out.

> Was it a dream or did I see
> A vision here beneath the sea?
> A scattered frame, a shattered shell,
> The detritus from dates in hell,
> A war-torn body, sorely pressed,
> In silent grandeur, now at rest.

There was a silence in the room for some time afterwards.

14

The *Ark* Lives On

The *Ark Royal*'s story continued both in public and behind closed doors long after she disappeared beneath the sea on the morning of 14 November 1941.

The Board of Inquiry that was hurriedly called to investigate why the *Ark Royal* was lost found enough evidence to charge her commanding officer, Captain Maund, with negligence. The court martial, the trial that followed from this, was held in England in February 1942. The prosecution was aggressive, challenging young ratings about their actions when they abandoned compartments flooding with water and fuel oil, and questioning the reliability of eye witnesses who described the final movements of the *Ark* as she sank. The court martial heard evidence that the explosion of the torpedo had destroyed the communication system on board the *Ark*. Many witnesses described confusing orders being passed along verbally or by bosun's whistle, as we have seen. Captain Maund was found guilty on two counts: first, he was held to be negligent for failing to ensure that properly constituted damage control parties had remained on board after the rest of the crew had been evacuated; secondly, it was found that the ship was not in a sufficient state of readiness to deal with possible damage.

It was a harsh decision, and the members of the court martial knew it. Almost immediately they started backtracking from their judgement. That February, after the court martial was over, they wrote a memorandum to the Admiralty, explaining their decision. They recognized, the memorandum said, that they were 'expecting a very high standard of conduct of a Captain of one of his majesty's ships . . . there is a very thin boundary line between an error of judgement and negligence'. Furthermore, they stated that in finding Captain Maund guilty the court had considered it necessary 'to discuss whether he was not paying too much attention to the safety of his ship's company rather than to the saving of the ship'.

Captain Maund's career didn't suffer too severely because of the guilty verdict. He was not given command of another aircraft carrier, or any other big warship, but he was given a shore-based job in charge of Fleet Air Arm bases in the Middle East. In reality, after the loss of the *Ark* there were more Fleet Air Arm aircraft on land than at sea in the Mediterranean. Six months later, in the summer of 1942, he became head of the Directorate of Combined Operations in the Middle East. He took part in the preparations for the Allied landings in North Africa and Italy, and was given the acting rank of Rear Admiral.

The Admiralty was well aware that the loss of the *Ark Royal* could not be laid too closely at the door of the captain. They had set up a body called the Bucknill Committee early on in the war to investigate what lessons could be learned from the loss of important ships in wartime. Their report on the *Ark Royal* highlighted one of her major design faults, which was the complete lack of alternative sources of electricity. Once the boilers had shut down there were no emergency generators to provide lighting, power the main pumps, or prime the main boilers again. The committee also recommended improvements to the internal bulkheads, to prevent rapid flooding of the boiler and engine rooms, and modifications to the plans of future carriers to prevent the exhaust uptakes becoming flooded if, like the *Ark*, they took an extreme list.

Over sixty years after Captain Maund was found guilty and the Bucknill Committee reported its findings, had the fact that we on the *Octopus* had found the wreck of the *Ark* and recorded it on hours of high-definition tape clarified any of the events of the night of 13–14 November 1941? It is a legitimate question that can be asked of most underwater investigations, so it is worth asking here. To answer it, it's necessary to reprise a little of what we know.

After completing the filming we were in a position to put together a very detailed map of the entire wreck site. The main part of the hull lies on a north–south axis, its front part broken off and missing, as is the funnel, the island and the whole forward part of the starboard side. The *Ark* is lying right side up, although she is deeply embedded in the mud, particularly at the stern where the heavy propellers and rudder are located (they are not visible). Seven hundred metres to the south of this is the huge bow section, lying upside down, the keel jutting up 25 metres above the sea floor. Just to the north of this lies the upturned deck lift, and the wreckage of a Swordfish aeroplane which must have fallen from the flight deck when the ship heeled over. Then, 60 metres further to the north-west is the cluster of wrecked Fulmar fighter aircraft that could only have spilled from the forward upper hangar, where they were normally kept, when the hull split in two. A hundred metres north of these wrecked aircraft are the remains of the superstructure, the island and the funnel.

This clear separation of the bow section, the main hull and the island structure into three distinct parts fully supports the evidence of Gunner Christian Herring, one of the last people to see the *Ark* sink. 'She first rolled right over on her beam ends so that half the flight deck was visible,' he testified at the court martial. 'She appeared to pause there for perhaps three minutes. She then rolled right over, and it appeared to me that a third of her length had been torn out. There was a great deal of noise and escaping air, and then I thought she had broken in two, and the two pieces were torn away from each other. The after part sank first, followed by the visible piece of the stem [the bow], and she went down from that position in about two minutes.' This description fits so closely with what we mapped on the sea floor that it is safe to say that the site of the wreck is where the *Ark Royal* finally capsized and sank – a position that is a considerable way from where she was first hit by the torpedo from *U-81*.

Add to this knowledge some extra details from the archives (mostly ignored by the court martial) and information from John McCrow, one of the *Ark*'s engineers who risked his life in the engine room as the ship slowly flooded, and it is possible to explain why the *Ark* came to rest so far from the point where she was struck, and why she had moved no closer to Gibraltar, despite enormous efforts over fourteen hours.

The *Ark* had been severely damaged by the torpedo, and the ship started listing very heavily to starboard. Initial attempts to control the flooding were hampered by loss of electricity, and the loss of communication. However, after a few hours the port boiler was relit, electrical power was once more available, the pumps began their work, the list was reduced and the ship was stabilized. On the face of it, the *Ark* had been saved. The only task left was to tow her to safety in Gibraltar.

She was, however, in the grip of a strong current, and would only be able to get to Gibraltar under her own power. The decision to get the port propeller turning again to fight the current sealed the *Ark*'s fate. The propeller turned for twenty minutes, but the increased strain on the hull opened up further leaks. The air pressure in the boiler room wasn't high enough to sustain increased power and the oil burners flashed back into the boiler room, putting it out of action once more. The pumps stopped working and the *Ark* began to list even further to starboard, until slowly she turned completely over and sank.

If this was the course of events that 13–14 November night, and I believe it was, then the *Ark Royal*'s loss seems to be the fault of no one person in particular, certainly not the captain.

The fact that the *Ark Royal* had been sunk did little to reduce her fame. That same month, November, a feature film called *Ships with Wings* was showing in cinemas throughout Britain. The dramatic sequences of Skuas taking off and landing, and mechanics urgently loading torpedoes and handling aircraft in the hangar decks, had been filmed when the *Ark* was on active service in the Mediterranean. Proof that she had gained true celebrity status was provided by the fact that HMS *Ark Royal* received bigger billing than any of the stars of the film. Of course, many people saw the film before they knew that the *Ark Royal* was lost. Val Bailey told me that a relative of his left the cinema after seeing the film, and then saw a newspaper placard saying '*Ark Royal* Sunk'.

The film had been produced by Ealing Studios. It was an unhappy mixture of light comedy and almost documentary realism, and at first there were doubts about whether the film should be aired at all. It was shown to Churchill, who thought it made the Fleet Air Arm look ridiculous, but Pound, the First Sea Lord, disagreed with him, and the film was eventually released. Ron Skinner told me that in his view it was the worst film ever made, but it was very popular at the box office. Because of the initial doubts about the film, Michael Balcon, the proprietor of Ealing Studios, commissioned a survey of audience opinion and the impact it was having on public morale. The report was sent to Balcon, then forwarded to Admiral John Godfrey, the Director of Naval Intelligence. It said that the film was popular and well received, and mentioned that the sentimental appeal of the *Ark Royal* was a particular asset of the film.

This report may have encouraged the Navy to continue the exploitation of the *Ark Royal*'s popular appeal and produce, in the summer of 1942, the pamphlet *Ark Royal: The Admiralty Account of Her Achievement*. It sold remarkably well. It was the first of a short series of pamphlets the Admiralty authorized about the Navy during the war, and the only one about a single warship. Finally, the *Ark*'s illustrious name was given to a new, larger, more modern carrier that was launched in 1947, and with a few breaks there has been a carrier called the *Ark Royal* in the Navy ever since, although whether this will be the case in the future seems unlikely.

She deserved her fame, for she was truly a ship that changed the course of history. The crucial engagements and convoys in which she was involved were executed by ordinary human beings, young men in their teens or early twenties who didn't think at the time of the importance of what they did, or its historical significance. These members of the *Ark Royal*'s crew were underpaid clerks in the City, apprentices, Barnardo's boys or young graduates from Dartmouth. Whatever their position, airmen, gunners or engineers, they all faced enormous danger at a time when the world was in utter chaos.

For me, the enduring aspect of my search for the *Ark Royal* will not be the image of the bow appearing out of the depths, stunning and impressive as it was, but the memories of the former crew members I met and talked to. They lived through the most extraordinary times and experienced the most harrowing events, but they came through it with their humanity intact, and their sense of humour undimmed. They, and the many crew members sadly no longer alive, are what made the *Ark Royal* the most famous ship in the world.

INDEX

Abyssinia, 35–6, 89, 133, 159
Acasta, HMS, 84
Achilles, HMS, 56, 58–60
Active, HMS, 95
Admiral Hipper, German cruiser, 70, 161, 176, 252
Admiral Scheer, German pocket battleship, 41
Admiralty: Air Ministry relations, 32, 67–8; aircraft, 67–8; aircraft carrier policy, 42; *Ark Royal* construction, 22–3; *Ark Royal* loss, 288–9; *Bismarck* operation, 210–11; convoy system, 44, 138, 183; French fleet policy, 95; Italian mainland strike, 130; Operation HATS, 137; relationship with Somerville, 154, 176–7; River Plate victory, 62; shipbuilding programme, 21; view of Italian Navy, 156
Africa Shell, MV, 55
Air Ministry, 32, 66–7, 68
aircraft carriers, 21, 25, 28–33, 42, 158
Ajax, HMS, 56, 58–60
Alboran, 250–1
Alessandro, survey technician, 110, 116
Alexandria: German advance, 161; *Illustrious* in, 164; Mediterranean Fleet, 36, 89, 176, 241, 247; RAF, 146; reinforcements for army, 137–8, 183
Allen, Paul, 268, 269, 270, 278
Almeria, 108, 110, 111, 112, 126
Altmark, German depot ship, 55
anti-aircraft artillery, 49–50, 72, 79–80, 134
Ardent, HMS, 84
Arethusa, HMS, 130

Argus, HMS: construction, 30–1; deck landings, 69; design, 31; hunt for *Graf Spee*, 56; Hurricane deliveries, 133, 136, 144 5
Ark Royal, HMS: aircraft on board, 45–6, 140–5, 187; *Bismarck* sinking, 1, 215–23; blueprints, 9, 227, 284; boiler rooms, 56–7; cabins, 27; Christmas Day 1940, 174–6, 252; command, 38, 80, 141, 183 4; construction, 20–1, 22; convoy escort, 161–2; cost, 22–3, 43; crew, 293; damage from Swordfish accident, 181–2; deck lifts, 82, 129, 239; design faults, 289; discovery of wreck, 124–7, 233–6, 264; engines, 23, 25, 256–9; finding the wreck, 124–7, 233–6; fitting out, 25–8; flight deck, 23, 25–7; guns, 24, 52, 79–80, 189, 278; hit by torpedo, 252–6; hull, 23, 25; hunt for *Bismarck*, 211–14; hunt for *Graf Spee*, 55–8, 60–1, 174; launch, 6, 18–20, 25; Malta defence, 133, 165, 209, 242; in Mediterranean with Force H, 130–40, 141–57; mess spaces, 27; Norway campaign, 76–87; Operation Catapult, 93, 97–106; Operation Substance, 243–7; origins, 21–2; photographs, 227, 273; pilots, 76, 100, 142; plans, 22; position of wreck, 6–7, 10–11, 107, 109–10, 115, 121–2, 290; refit in Liverpool, 140–1; refit planned, 164, 251–2; reputation, xiv, 39–40, 46, 52, 62–3, 65, 261–2, 285, 292–3; role in Second World War, 3, 43, 45–6, 50–1, 55, 87, 133, 164–5, 195, 256, 261–2;

salvage operation, 8, 9–10, 256–61; search for wreck, 3–5, 107–27, 225–33; sinking, 7–10, 238–40, 261, 263, 284–5, 287–8, 290–1; sonar surveys, 124–7, 233–6, 238–40, 264, 273, 278, 284; speed, 23–4; Tirso Dam raid, 166–70; torpedoes, 152; trials, 38; view of wreck, xii–xvi, 234–5, 238–40, 275–7, 278–84; wreck site, 284, 289–90

Ark Royal: The Admiralty Account of Her Achievement, 5–6, 292

Arnell, Albert, 167

Asher, Cyril, 251, 252

Asher, John, 56

Asher, Les, 38, 79

Athenia, SS, 44, 45, 53

AUV: appearance and design, 229–30; cost, 12, 228; development, 11–12, 230; role, 12; search for *Ark Royal*, 225, 230–6; search time, 13–14; sonar images of wreck, 234–5, 240, 269, 282, 284; support staff, 226–7

Azores, 156

B-29 bomber, 3

Bailey, 'Val': career, xiii, 35, 140; on film show, 291–2; on Fulmars, 140; on Gibraltar air-raid alarm, 44; on Operation Catapult, 95–6; on pilots, 191; ROV survey, 283; on Royal Navy, 34–5, 37; view of *Ark Royal* sinking, xiii, 251, 255–7, 259–61, 263, 280

Baker, Lt, 254

Balcon, Michael, 292

Baldwin, George, 69, 73, 76–7, 78, 84–5, 285

Ballard, Robert, xiii

Barham, HMS, 65, 141, 143

BBC, 14, 17, 108–9, 228, 266

Beale, Lt, 217–18

Beatty, David, 29, 31

Belfast, HMS, 15

Bergen, 70, 71, 72–4, 202

Berwick, HMS, 141, 146, 147, 176

Bianca, German supply ship, 179

Bismarck, German battleship: air attacks on, xiii, xvi, 209–10, 214–22, 279, 281; *Ark Royal*'s role in hunt for, 1, 3, 211–22; construction, 41, 198–9; damage to *Prince of Wales*, 207–8; encounter with *Hood* and *Prince of Wales*, 204–6; encounter with *Norfolk* and *Suffolk*,

203–4; guns, 199; hit by *Prince of Wales*, 206, 210; hunt for, 209–11; launch, 199; Operation Rhine, 198–200, 202; role, 200; sinking, 1, 221–3, 232; sinking of *Hood*, 1, 206; TV programme, 15; wreck, 2, 14, 232

Blackburns, 67, 68

Blenheim bombers, 243

Blucher, German cruiser, 70, 71

Bluebird, 2, 3

Board of Inquiry into *Ark Royal* sinking: documents, 7, 227; evidence, 9–10, 115, 117, 240, 277; findings, 11, 109, 262, 287; members, 7

Board of Inquiry into Operation Collar, 153–4

Board of Inquiry into Operation White, 153

Boyd, Denis, 159, 162

Breconshire, HMS, 183

Bremse, German cruiser, 70

Bretagne, French battleship, 92, 96, 128

Bridge, Richard, 267–70, 276, 280, 282

Briggs, Ted, 206

British Army, 137–8, 182–3, 190–1

Brokensha, Sub Lt, 99

Bucknill Committee, 288–9

C&C Technologies: AUV development, 11–12, 119, 224–5, 230; computer enhancements, 239; search for *Ark Royal*, 107–8, 112, 115, 121

Cagliari, 132–3, 135–6, 138, 142–3

Cameron, James, 265

Cammell Laird: *Ark Royal* construction, 25, 28, 38, 40, 240; *Ark Royal* contract, 22; *Ark Royal* launch, 6, 18–20; *Ark Royal* plans, 24; *Prince of Wales* construction, 28, 203; shipyard, 20–1, 28, 34, 38

Campbell, Dennis, 47

Campbell, Donald, 2, 3

Canary Islands, 177

Cant seaplanes, 134, 138, 143, 246

Catalina aircraft, 213

Chamberlain, Neville, 44–5, 74, 80–1

Chance, Thomas and Jimmy, 230, 237

Charlier, Sub Lt, 168

Chatfield, Lord, 27, 33, 34

Churchill, Winston: *Ark Royal* visit, 48; *Athenia* incident, 53; Crete policy, 200, 222; First Lord of Admiralty, 44–5; Fleet Air Arm policy, 33; French fleet policy, 94, 95, 105; Italian mainland attack, 130,

173; Mediterranean convoy policy, 137–8, 183, 191, 194; Mediterranean policy, 90, 173, 201, 241; Narvik expedition, 74, 80; Prime Minister, 81, 88; relationship with Roosevelt, 53, 201, 208–9; relationship with Somerville, 105, 137–8, 145, 153; response to *Bismarck* sinking, 222; response to *Hood* sinking, 1, 208; River Plate victory, 62; success stories in press, 65; U-boat strategy, 45, 48; view of *Ships with Wings*, 292

Clan Forbes, transport freighter, 146
Clan Fraser, transport freighter, 146
Clark, Senior Engineer, 260
Clement, SS, 54
Coke, Charles, 77
Collingwood, Lord, 237
Compton, Lt, 103
Condottiere class cruisers, 151
Coode, Trevenen Penrose, 215–17
Cork and Orrery, Earl of, 153
Cornwall, HMS, 56
Courageous, HMS, 32, 45, 48–9, 71, 210, 255
Coventry, HMS, 138
Crete, 200–2, 222, 241
CR42 aircraft, 186, 188, 248–9
Cross, Kenneth, 81–2
Cumberland, HMS, 56, 58, 60
Cunningham, Sir Andrew: attitude to anti-aircraft artillery, 50; Greece evacuation, 184; Italian strategy, 165; on Luftwaffe attacks, 163, 164; Mediterranean reinforcements policy, 137–8, 190; memorial, 238; reinforcements for, 166, 209; relationship with Churchill, 201; Suez Canal strategy, 36; Taranto raid, 158–60
Curlew, HMS, 77

Daily Mail, 264
Darlan, Jean-François, 94
Davey, Rick: on AUV, 229–30; contact with, 11–13; plans for search, 15–16, 107, 110–12, 115, 119, 228; *Rig Supporter* voyage, 224–7, 232–4; view of search area, 13–14, 275, 277; view of sonar images, 237–9
De Gaulle, Charles, 140
Delhi, HMS, 130
Denmark, 69

Despatch, HMS, 36
Deutschland, German pocket battleship, 41
Devall, Phil, 227, 235
Diamond, HMS, 184
Doric Star, SS, 57
Dornier seaplanes, 50
Dorsetshire, HMS, 221
Dougie, ROV pilot, 281–2
Douglas, James Sholto, 189, 192
Downing, Peter, 253
Dubber, Petty Officer, 186, 191, 193
Dunkerque, French battleship, 92, 96, 102–5, 128, 130
Dunning, Edwin Harris, 30

Eagle, HMS, 30–4, 56, 159–60
Ealing Studios, 292
Edinburgh, HMS, 245
Elias, John, 252
Elkington, Robert, 65, 77, 83, 134, 181–2
Ellis, Robert, 203
Elmas airfield, 130, 138–9, 142
Enterprise, HMS, 36
Esmonde, Eugene, 209–10, 251
Exeter, HMS, 56, 58–9, 60, 199

Faenza, Elisabetta: *Odin Finder* owner, 16, 108, 110, 237; *Odin Finder* voyage, 110–11, 118, 126; search area, 16, 111, 122–3
Fanad Head, SS, 45, 47–8
Faulkner, HMS, 130, 195
Fausset, Godfrey, 168
Fearless, HMS, 244
Firedrake, HMS, 245
Firth, Lt, 189, 192, 193
Fisher, Sir William, 36
Fleet Air Arm: aircraft types, 49, 69, 73, 140; *Konigsberg* sinking, 73; Middle East bases, 288; origins, 33, 66; pilots and observers, 109, plans for, 42; relationship with Navy, 33–4, 285
Focke Wolf bombers, 222
Forbes, Sir Charles, 7, 43, 71–2, 75, 80
Force F, 137
Force H: Atlantic patrol, 177–8; Cagliari attacks, 130, 133, 135–7, 140; command, 90–1; forces, 129–30, 141, 157, 247; hunt for *Bismarck*, 203, 211–12, 215; Italian Air Force attacks, 130–5, 140, 143, 151, 162, 245; Italian intelligence, 169–70, 184; Italian mainland raids,

165–9, 170–2; Italy confrontation, 102; Luftwaffe attacks, 191, 194; Malta missions, 133, 136–7, 139–40, 141, 146, 209, 242, 250; Operation Catapult, 91–6, 102, 106, 130; Operation Collar, 145–53, 154; Operation Tiger, 183, 185, 190–5; Operation White, 144; origins, 90; role, 128, 137, 155–6, 164–5

Force K, 55–8, 60–1

Forester, HMS, 95, 244

Foxhound, HMS, 93, 97, 132

France, 88–9, 140

Franco, Francisco, 36, 90, 165, 172

Franconia, transport ship, 146

Free French Forces, 140

French Navy, 89, 91

Freyberg, Bernard, 200

Fulmar aircraft: combat air patrols, 244; design, 68, 244; guns, 140, 144; hunt for *Scharnhorst*, 179, 180–1; Italian Air Force encounters, 142–3, 155, 162, 186–8, 190, 245–9; Luftwaffe encounter, 190–4; Malta missions, 197–8, 243; patrols, 151, 167; pilots, xiii, 191; production, 67–8; squadron on *Illustrious*, 158, 163, 184; squadrons on *Ark Royal*, 140, 184, 280; wreck site, 279–80

Furious, HMS: aircraft landings, 30–1; Home Fleet, 43; hunt for *Graf Spee*, 56; Malta missions, 196, 197; Mediterranean Fleet, 33; Norwegian campaign, 71–2, 81; rebuild, 32; seaplane carrier, 29–30; Tondern raid, 31

Gardner, Lt, 189–90, 191, 193

GAS, 108, 110

Genoa, 165, 166, 169, 171, 172

Gensoul, Marcel, 93, 94–5, 97

German Army, 160–1, 182, 241

German Navy, 29, 40–1, 173–4, 176

Gibraltar: *Ark Royal* sinking, 109; Board of Inquiry, 153; British presence, 36, 89; cemetery, 237–8; convoys, 161; defence, 90, 92, 156; Force H, 92, 102, 133, 141, 144, 250; harbour, 26, 174; hunting for U-boats, 118; Operation HATS, 137–8; Spanish position, 165, 166, 172

Gibraltar Times, 224

Gick, Percy, 210, 251, 255

Giorgio, survey technician, 110, 120

Glasgow, HMS, 141

Glorious, HMS, 32–3, 55, 76, 81–4, 255

Gloucester, HMS, 56, 163–4

Gneisenau, German battlecruiser: attacks on convoys, 177, 220; guns, 40; hunt for, 181–2, 203; Narvik operation, 82; Norway invasion, 70, 71; sinking of destroyers, 84; size, 40

Godfrey, John, 292

Goebbels, Joseph, 52

Goodall, Sir Stanley, 27

Goodfellow, Alan, 245–6, 249

Goodfellow, Peter, 68–9

Graf Spee, German pocket battleship, 41, 54–62, 174, 199

Griffiths, Guy, 47

Guggenberger, Friedrich, 250

Gurkha, HMS, 72

Guthrie, Lt, 186

Haile Selassie, 36

Halifax, Lord, 90

Hall, Signalman, 46

Hamburg Radio, 52–3

Hampden bombers, 72

Hare, Geoffrey, 72

Harwood, Henry, 56, 58, 60, 62

Hatston, 65–6, 72, 75–6

Hay, Lt, 186, 188

Heather, St John Hewitt, 263

Heinkel bombers, 51, 52, 77, 78, 161

Henderson, Reginald, 43, 49

Hermes, HMS, 31–2, 45, 56

Hermione, HMS, 245

Herring, Christian, 261, 263, 280, 284–5, 290

Hitler, Adolf, 22, 41, 74, 94, 199, 250

Hoare, Lady Maud, 18–19

Hoare, Sir Samuel, 18

Holland, Cedric 'Hooky': *Ark Royal* command, 80, 141, 148; career, 80, 92, 183–4; Christmas celebrations, 175; French fleet policy, 92–5, 97; hunt for *Scharnhorst*, 180; Italian Navy contact, 150, 153

Holland, Lancelot, 204–6

Home Fleet: *Ark Royal*'s presence, 43, 76; Force H, 157; hunt for *Bismarck*, 204, 209, 214; size, 35

Hood, HMS: attack on French fleet, 95; attack on *Prinz Eugen*, 205; Force H, 93, 130, 135; at Gibraltar, 89; Home Fleet, 129; hunt for *Bismarck*, 203–4, 209;

Mediterranean Fleet, 36; news of loss, 208; reputation, 39, 207; at Scapa Flow, 137; sinking, 1, 205–6; TV programme, 15; wreck, 2, 232

Howard, Petty Officer, 186

Hurricane aircraft: on *Ark Royal*, 129, 197–8; convoy to Egypt, 183, 190; convoys to Malta, 133, 136–7, 139, 144–5, 153, 161, 196, 198, 209, 242–3; 250; losses, 153; Norwegian campaign, 81–2

Illustrious, HMS: *Ark Royal* rivalry, 212; convoy protection, 162; design, 158; loss, 164–5, 172; Luftwaffe attacks, 162–4, 184, 190; Operation HATS, 137, 138; radar, 138, 162; rebuilt, 164; role, 158; Taranto raid, 146, 159–60

Indomitable, HMS, 164

Institution of Naval Architects, 27

Italian Air Force: attack on *Ark Royal*, 185; attacks on Force H, 130–5, 146, 150, 151, 243–9; bases, 129, 139, 165, 247

Italian Navy: Force H encounters, 130, 132, 144, 146, 147–51, 159, 248–9; forces, 129, 156; in Spanish Civil War, 128; Taranto withdrawal, 161

Jellicoe, John, 29

Johns, Sir Arthur, 21, 22, 23, 24, 25

Johnson, Lt, 188

Johnson, Wendy, 23

Johnstone, Mervyn, 148–9

Jordan, Ron, 79–80, 85–6, 87

Joyce, William, 53

Junker bombers, 78, 161, 163

Jutland, battle of (1916), 29

Kenya, HMS, 179

Kindersley, Lt, 188

King George V, HMS, 202, 204, 209, 211, 221

Kongsberg Simrad, 3–4, 11, 108

Konigsberg, German cruiser, 70, 71, 72–4, 85

Laforey, HMS, 257, 258, 259, 261

Lambert, Andrew, 5, 8

Langsdorff, Hans, 54–5, 58–9, 61–2

Lawrence, Michael, 48

Leach, John, 207

League of Nations, 22, 36, 89, 159

Leggett, Petty Officer, 189, 192

Legion, HMS: *Ark Royal* crew evacuation, 16, 236; sonar operator, 252, 255–7, 262

Leinster, troopship, 243

Lemp, Lt Commander, 47, 48

Lindemann, Ernst, 205, 208, 219, 220

Liverpool, 140–1

Livorno, 170

London Naval Treaty, 24

Luftwaffe: attack on *Ark Royal*, 78; attacks on *Illustrious*, 163–4, 176; base in France, 222; base in Sicily, 161; damage to Mediterranean Fleet, 241–2; *Fliegerkorps X*, 163; over Malta, 247; Mediterranean role, 157, 183–4; Norway invasion, 71, 161

Lutjens, Günther: Atlantic convoy attacks, 177, 200; Atlantic route, 202–3; *Bismarck* command, 200, 202–5; career, 70; end of *Bismarck*, 220, 279, mission of task force, 204, 208; Norway invasion, 70, 71, 200; return to Brest, 182; signal intercepted, 211

Lutzow, German pocket battleship, 70

Lyster, Sir Lumley, 159, 162

McCrow, John: career, 39; on Christmas Day 1940, 174–5; on guns, 189; on reputation of *Ark Royal*, 39–40; on sinking of *Ark Royal*, 251, 254–5, 256–60, 290

McKay, George, 47

McKay, Hugh, 3–5, 11, 12, 16, 108

MacWilliam, Ian, 214

Magagnoli, Massimo, 110–12, 114, 117, 119, 120–6

Mail on Sunday, 264

Malaya, HMS, 56, 166, 171, 177, 178, 256

Malta: air attacks, 176, 247; defence, 90, 133; Force H missions, 133, 136–7, 139–40, 141, 146, 209, 242, 245, 250; guns, 137; harbour entrance, 26; Hurricane deliveries, 133, 139–40, 144–5, 161, 196, 198, 209, 242–3; Hurricane losses, 153; *Illustrious* repairs, 163; Mediterranean Fleet, 36, 89; submarines, 250; supplies for, 161, 165, 247, 249–50

Manchester, HMS, 146, 244, 245

Marschall, Wilhelm, 82–4

Martin aircraft, 145

Maund, Loben: *Ark Royal* command, 184;

career, 288; court martial, 11, 262–3, 280, 287–8, 289; evidence at Board of Inquiry, 7; hunt for *Bismarck*, 211–12, 214, 221; Operation Tiger, 194–5; sinking of *Ark Royal*, 252–3, 255–6, 262–3

Mays, Henry, 149

Mediterranean Fleet, 35–6, 45, 66, 89, 137, 241

Messerschmitt aircraft, 84–5, 129, 161, 184, 192, 193

Miller, 'Dusty', 217, 218

Miller, Rex, 59, 61

Mirs el Kebir, 89, 91, 93, 94–8, 104, 153

Mitchell, Able Seaman, 254, 285

Moffat, John: anti-submarine patrols, 178–9; attack on *San Casimiro*, 180; attacks on *Bismarck*, 217–18, 222, 281; career, xii–xiii; hunt for *Bismarck*, 212, 216; on *Octopus*, 278; ROV control, xii–xiii, xvi, 282; on sinking of *Ark Royal*, 285; Spezia raid, 170; training, 151–2; view of wreck site, 279, 284, 285

Monrovia, 229, 270, 275

Moore, James Stewart, 150

Morrison, Bill, xiii, 278

Mussolini, Benito, 22, 35, 88, 89, 165, 172

Narvik, 70, 74–5, 80–1, 84

Naval Air Fighting Development Unit, 69

Nelson, HMS: damage to, 62, 248, 249; Force H, 93; Mediterranean Fleet, 201; Operation Catapult, 93, 95; submarine escort, 50

Nelson, Lord, 237–8

New Zealand Star, transport freighter, 146

Newson, Captain, 103–4

Norfolk, HMS, 203–4, 208, 209, 210

North, Sir Dudley, 92, 153

Norway: *Ark Royal*'s role in campaign, 76–80, 81–7; British response to German invasion, 71–6, 80–1; German invasion, 69–71, 74

Octopus: elegance, 268–9, 270; ROV launches, 269, 271–3, 274–6; ROV pilots, 271; search for wreck of *Ark Royal*, xii–xvi, 271–6, 289; veterans on, xiv–xv, 277–8, 286

Odin Finder: base, 14; cost of, 14, 116; discovery of *Ark Royal* wreck, 124–7, 232, 237; search for *Ark Royal*, 107–8,

110–24, 228, 274; size, 225; sonar survey, 15–16, 107–8, 227

Official History of the War at Sea, 7, 10

Oliver, Tony, 256, 258

Operation Catapult, 91, 93

Operation Coat, 141

Operation Collar, 153, 154

Operation HATS, 137, 146, 153

Operation Hurry, 133, 146

Operation Picket, 166

Operation Result, 166

Operation Rhine, 198

Operation Substance, 242, 243, 245–6

Operation Tiger, 183, 185, 187, 194, 195

Operation Weserubung, 69

Operation White, 144–5, 153

Oran, 91, 93, 97, 145, 209, 218

Pantelleria, 162, 184

Parry, W. E., 59

Pattison, Ken, 169

Pearl Harbor, xiv, 3

Pearson, Sub Lt, 104–5

Pétain, Henri, 88, 94

Pisa, 170–1

Pocock, Senior Stoker, 253

Polykarp, German supply ship, 179–80

Pound, Sir Dudley, 48, 50, 90, 94, 105, 138

Power, Arthur, 38, 40, 43, 46, 57, 80

Prendergast, Lt, 104

Prince of Wales, HMS, 28, 203–10, 247

Prinz Eugen, German cruiser, 176, 198, 200, 204–5, 210, 214

Priun, Polish destroyer, 249

Provence, French battleship, 96

Pupa, Andrea, 114–16, 118, 121–3, 126, 237

Queen Elizabeth, HMS, 56, 183

Quenneville, Mark, 270, 271, 272

radar: Seetakt, 199; on *Sheffield*, 77, 138, 141–3, 186–8, 190–1; ships equipped with, 138; on *Valiant*, 132, 138

Raeder, Erich, 173–4, 176, 182, 198, 200, 250

Ramillies, HMS, 146, 147, 149

Ramsay, Bertram, 91

Rankin, Richard, 224

Renown, HMS: air attacks on, 193; flagship, 129, 138, 147, 212; Genoa bombardment, 171; hunt for *Bismarck*, 212; hunt for *Graf Spee*, 57–8, 60–1,

174; Force H, 156, 185–6; Force K, 55–8, 63; speed, 149; Tirso Dam raid, 166
Repulse, HMS, 56, 202, 209
Resolution, HMS, 36, 37, 93, 95, 130
Reynaud, Paul, 88
Richardson, John, xiii, 278
Riddler, Petty Officer Airman, 98
Rig Supporter: aboard, 225–6, 238; AUV on, 11–12, 224–5, 231; cost, 228; search for *Ark Royal*, 228–9, 232–7; size, 226; survey data, 237, 264, 272–3, 277, 279
River Plate, 58–63
Rivers, Zak, 227, 230, 233–5
Roc aircraft, 67, 68, 76, 77, 78
Rodney, HMS: in Alexandria, 36; Force H, 247–8; hunt for *Bismarck*, 211, 221; Mediterranean Fleet, 201; submarine escort, 50
Rommel, Erwin, 161, 182, 200, 242, 247, 249–50
Roosevelt, Franklin D., 53, 201, 208–9
ROV, xv–xvi, 265, 267, 271–7
Royal Air Force (RAF), 32, 66, 86, 156, 247
Royal Naval Air Service, 32
Royal Naval Volunteer Reserve (RNVR), 141, 145
Royal Navy: aircraft carriers, 28–32, 42; *Bismarck* issues, 200; budget, 18–19, 28; civilian evacuations, 37; Fleet Air Arm, 33–4, 37, 66–7; forces stretched, 157, 173, 176, 201; Italian Air Force conflict, 130; Luftwaffe onslaught, 164; Mediterranean Fleet, 36, 38, 137, 91; RAF relations, 32–3; speed of fleet, 23–4; Taranto plan, 159; tradition, 34–5
Royal Oak, HMS, 64

St Day, tug, 236
San Casimiro, German supply ship, 179–80
Sardinia, 130, 165–9, 218
Savoia Marchetti aircraft, 142, 162
Sayer, Les, 251
Scapa Flow: *Ark Royal* at, 65–6, 80, 89; *Glorious* at, 82; Home Fleet HQ, 43, 64, 72; *Hood* departure, 137; U-boat attack, 64
Scharnhorst, German battlecruiser: air attacks on, 84–6, 178, 279; attacks on convoys, 177, 200, 220; guns, 40; hunt for, 179, 181–2, 203; Narvik operation, 82; Norwegian invasion, 70, 71; sinking

of destroyers, 84; sinking of *Glorious*, 83; size, 40
Sergio, survey technician, 110, 116, 119
Shave, Leading Airman, 193
Sheffield, HMS: Force H, 141, 215; hunt for *Bismarck*, 215–16, 220; Norwegian campaign, 77; radar, 77, 138, 141–3, 186–8, 190–1; Tirso Dam raid, 166
Ships with Wings, film, 291–2
Simpson, James, 47
Skinner, Ron: on air attacks, 51–2, 172; on *Ark Royal* command, 38, 43–4; on *Ark Royal* sinking, 263, 285–6; career, xiii; on *Hood* loss, 207; on Narvik campaign, 81, 86–7; on *Octopus*, 278, 281
Skua aircraft: attack on *Dunkerque*, 102–5; attack on German seaplanes, 50; attack on *Konigsberg*, 72–4, 76; attack on *Scharnhorst*, 85–6, 178, 279; attack on U-boat, 47; bombs, 178; Cagliari mission, 133, 136; design, 66, 68; development, 66–7; filmed, 291; guns, 144; Hatston defences, 65, 72–3, 75–6; Italian air force encounters, 130–2, 134–5, 138, 143, 151; lack of power, 69, 77, 144; launches, 167; Malta mission, 145; Messerschmitt encounters, 84–5; 129; Operation Catapult, 93, 97, 98–9; reputation, 68–9; role, 66, 68; spin problems, 67, 69, 73, 98; squadron on *Furious*, 71; squadrons on *Ark Royal*, 46, 130, 184; training exercises, 169
Smeeton, Richard, 151
Somerville, Sir James: *Ark Royal* relations, 141–2, 155, 162, 166, 261; *Ark Royal* loss, 256, 259, 262–3; Boards of Inquiry, 7, 153–4; career, 91, 128; character, 91, 153–4; flagship, 129, 138, 147, 212; Force H command, 90–2, 97, 99, 129–32, 134–5, 155–7; Genoa raid, 172; hunt for *Bismarck*, 203, 211–12, 215; on Italian Air Force, 185; Operation Catapult, 93–5, 102–3, 105; Operation Collar, 145–51, 153; Operation HATS, 137–40; Operation Result, 166; Operation Substance, 242–5; Operation Tiger, 194; Operation White, 144–5, 153; RAF relations, 247; relationship with Admiralty, 153–5, 155–7, 176–7, 190; relationship with Churchill, 105, 137–8, 145, 153; on sonar operations, 118; Tirso Dam operation, 169; training exercises,

132, 134, 155; U-boat sightings, 250
Somerville, Mark, 155, 180, 186, 187, 195
Sopwith Camels, 31
Southampton, HMS, 146, 163–4
Spanish Civil War, 36–7, 40, 91, 128
Spartivento, 168, 212
Spearfish, HMS, 50
Spezia, 146, 170
Spitfire aircraft, 202
Spurway, Lt, 138, 143–4
Strasbourg, French battleship, 56, 92, 96, 98–102, 128, 151
Stringer, Pat, 214
Stuka bombers, 163, 184, 191–4, 280
Suffolk, HMS, 75, 203–4, 208, 209, 210
Sullivan, Jackie, 271
Sun, 264
Sunderland flying boats, 145
Swanton, Sub Lt, 219
Sweeney, Leonard, 20, 25, 28
Swordfish aircraft: air crew, 141; anti-submarine patrols, 178–9, 181, 197, 257; attack on *Bismarck*, xiii, 216–22; attack on *Dunkerque*, 102–5; attacks on Italian fleet, 147–52, 160, 248–9; attacks on U-boats, 46, 48; Cagliari missions, 135–6, 139, 142–3; convoy surveillance, 147; design, xii–xiii, 99–100, 279, 283; guns, 144; hunt for *Bismarck*, 212–15; hunt for *Scharnhorst*, 179–81; landings, 251; launch accident, 181–2; launches, 167, 181, 213; Operation Catapult, 93, 97–101, 105; photographs of *Ark Royal*, 258; pilots, 100; raids on Spezia and Livorno, 170–1; squadron on *Glorious*, 83; squadron on *Victorious*, 209; squadrons on *Ark Royal*, 46, 130, 140–1, 177; Tirso Dam raid, 165–70; torpedo dropping, 100, 151–2; training exercises, 169; wreck site, 239–40, 278–9, 282–3, 289–90
Sydney Star, 245

Tacoma, freighter, 62
Tactical School, Portsmouth, 49
Taranto: air attacks on, 146, 160, 163, 212; Italian fleet withdrawal, 160–1, 165; port, 89, 146, 159–60
Tarbet, Able Seaman, 253–4
Taylour, Lt, 186, 191, 192–3
Thales, 266–7
Thames, tug, 236, 258

Thurston, Richard, 47
Tillard, Rupert, 155, 162, 180, 181, 186, 195
Tirpitz, German battleship, 41
Tirso Dam, 165–9, 172, 218
Titanic, SS, 232
torpedoes: Duplex fuses, 152; Italian Air Force attacks, 185, 244–5; Swordfish, 99–100, 105, 214–15, 281; U-boats, 46
Toulon, 100, 128
Tovey, Sir John: Home Fleet command, 202, 124; hunt for *Bismarck*, 209, 210–11, 213, 214, 220–2; hunt for *Scharnhorst*, 202–3
Traill, Henry, 190
Trevanion, MV, 55
Tripoli, 137
Trondheim: British response to German invasion, 75–6, 84; British withdrawal, 78; cemetery, 86; German invasion, 70; hunt for *Scharnhorst*, 84, 178, 279; losses, 85–6, 87

U-boats: attacks on *Ark Royal*, 46–7; *Courageous* sinking, 48–9; fleet, 41; magnetic mines, 62; Norwegian position, 75; sunk, 46, 47–8; threat to merchant shipping, 44–7; threat to Royal Navy, 64, 172, 250
U-30, 47–8
U-39, 46
U-81, 250, 290

Valiant, HMS: Force H, 130; Italian Air Force attacks, 130, 132, 162; Operation Catapult, 93, 95; Operation HATS, 137; radar, 132, 135, 138
Versailles Treaty (1919), 22
Victorious, HMS, 202, 209–11
Volkischer Beobachter, 53

Walker, Sub Lt, 191
Walsh, Vic, 35
Warspite, HMS, 55, 162
Washington Naval Treaty, 24
Wavell, Archibald, 137, 182–3, 200
Welham, John, 34
Wellington bombers, 72
Wells, Lionel, 51, 58, 60, 82, 141
Wrecks Section, UK Hydrographic Office, 6, 13, 229
Wryneck, HMS, 184

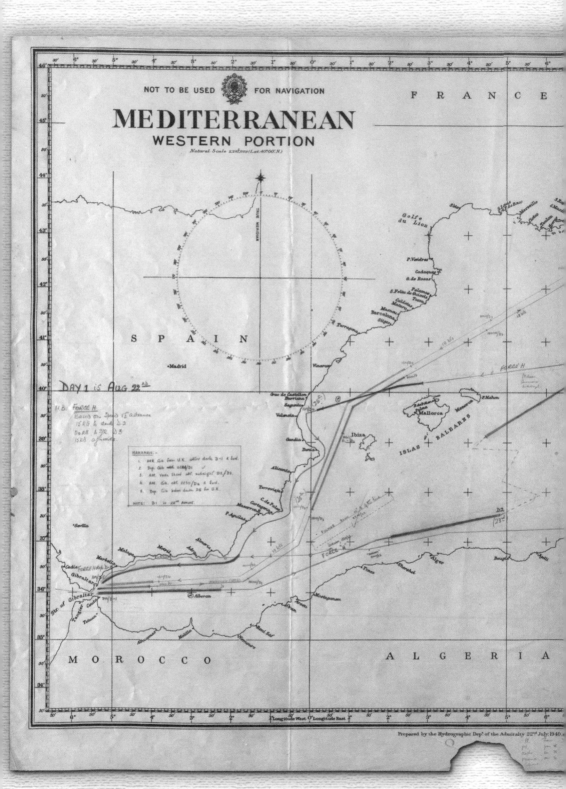